Thurlestone
At War

1914 - 1918

by Robin Macdonald

Published in the UK in 2018
by South West Books UK

ISBN 978-1-9996930-0-8

Price £7.50

All proceeds from the sale of this book will be donated to the
Friends of Thurlestone Church

Front Cover Photograph - Thurlestone War Memorial on Remembrance Day.
Back Cover Photograph shows the Brunskill family at "The Bungalow" circa 1913.

Table of Contents

Introduction

This project began at Christmas 2013 with the approach of the centenary of the start of the Great War 1914-1918, and the realisation that, while there are names recorded on the War Memorial on our village green, little or nothing had been recorded about who they were, where they came from, or how they came to serve their country and lose their lives.

I gathered a small team of volunteer researchers and we began collecting details which were subsequently included in an exhibition Thurlestone At War, in the Parish Hall from 23-25 August 2014. My report in the October 2014 issue of Village Voice provided a detailed account of the event.

One of the sources of information about WW1 in Thurlestone was the second edition (1920) of the Rev Frank Egerton Coope's "little red book", Thurlestone Church and Parish, which included the names of all those parishioners who had served in the war, as well as those who did not survive it. They too deserve to be remembered in a little more detail.

Coope also records that from 1428 "the manor of Thurlestone was held by the Courtenays until the Earl of Devon sold it to the trustees of Stephen Brunskill in 1869". This rather prompted the questions "Who was Stephen Brunskill? And what happened to the manor of Thurlestone after 1869?"

The centenary of the Armistice on 11 November 2018 provides an opportunity to find out a little more information about Stephen Brunskill's legacy and its impact on the social structure of the parish, as well as to carry out some further research into the lives and war service of those parishioners who also joined the armed forces in 1914-1918 - but who fortunately came back alive.

Robin Macdonald

Acknowledgements

First on my list must be Rev Frank Egerton Coope, whose book Thurlestone Church and Parish (2nd Edition, 1920) provides the (almost) definitive list of the people of his Parish who served in the Great War.

Second come the descendants or relatives of many of the families included here, who were able to prevent me pursuing the wrong families of the same name in several instances, and also to provide additional family information and pictures.

Next, to the Internet. The digitization of records of all kinds, and their accessibility on-line (though not always free), has made family history research so much easier, quicker, and rewarding. A plethora of websites, from Ancestry to Wikipedia, has enabled the most obscure of records to be tracked down. Much of this information is in the public domain, and if I have inadvertently included any items which did not receive an appropriate attribution, my apologies are due to the authors and owners concerned.

The National Archives at Kew, and the Devon Archives at Exeter, provided useful information on servicemen's records and the Brunskill Estate.

Finally, grateful thanks to my dear wife, who put up with my long hours at the computer without demur, and who kindly proof-read much of the text of this book.

Chapter 1

Before the War

The Brunskill Legacy

Before the War - The Brunskill Legacy

The manor of Thurlestone had been held by the Courtenay family, Earls of Devon, from 1428. With their seat at Powderham Castle, they were not in close contact with everyday events in the parish of Thurlestone, and their impact on the lives of its parishioners was probably fairly low. Thurlestone remained a typically structured rural English community until the latter half of the nineteenth century. The Lord of the Manor owned most of the land in the parish, though in this instance he did not live in it. The church provided the oldest building, and a community hub for the three villages of Bantham, Buckland, and Thurlestone, with the Rector a central figure in community life.

Thurlestone had been fortunate to have as its incumbents two outstanding men. The first came with the appointment in 1839 at the age of twenty-nine of the Rev Peregrine Arthur Ilbert MA, of Trinity College, Cambridge, previously curate of South Milton, who built a fine Rectory, established a Primary School (1842), provided the church with a clock, and continued in this office for fifty-five years until his death in 1894. There was then a short period from 1895 to 1897 when the Rev Hon Reginald John Yarde-Buller MA (1864-1950) was rector, until the appointment in 1897 of the Rev Frank Egerton Coope MA (1863-1934), also a Trinity man and previously curate at Littlehampton, who remained until 1921, when he became vicar at Danehill in Sussex, and who published his book Thurlestone Church and Parish in 1913, and added a second enlarged edition in 1920.

The Lordship of the Manor of Thurlestone was a title of little substance, and the only property which was believed to have been once the actual Manor House of Thurlestone was Didwell House in South Milton, according to Rev Coope. To follow the Lordship beyond the Courtenays, however, and to assess its impact on the social framework of Thurlestone we have to examine the chequered history of the Brunskill family, beginning with Stephen William Fawcett Brunskill (1799-1854).

Born in Ravenstonedale, Westmorland, Stephen was the eighth of the ten children of William Brunskill and Ann Fawcett. They were not wealthy. William Brunskill was assessed for Land Tax in 1798 at 3s. 3¼d. out of a parish total of £74. 16s. 7d. Stephen would have to make his own way in the world - and he set out to do just that. He established himself as a draper and mercer, presumably having served an apprenticeship somewhere, possibly in London, before moving in the 1820s to the West Country, where he opened shop premises at 242 High Street, Exeter. His business prospered and in 1844 he married Susan Brooking Square from Dartmouth. Over a period of some thirty years he managed to amass a very substantial fortune from his drapery business and financial dealings, including the acquisition of the residence of Polsloe House in Exeter, and various other lands and properties in Devon extending to 437 acres with an annual rental income value of £1,160.

Stephen and Susan began their family with the birth of a son, William Fawcett Brunskill, in 1849. The following year, conscious that he had now "given hostages to fortune", Stephen wrote a long, careful and detailed will making plans for his family to be provided for in the event of his death. A second son, John Square Brunskill, was born in 1851, and in the census of that year both sons were shown living at the family home in Polsloe House, Clifton Road, Exeter, with their mother and four domestic servants.

Father Stephen at that time was away on business in London, staying at the "Golden Cross" hotel at St Martin's in the Fields, London (now 3 Duncannon St) and possibly visiting master tailor Thomas Price, whose premises were next door to the hotel.

A third son, Arthur Stephen Brunskill, was born in 1852. By this time, unfortunately, Susan had contracted tuberculosis and survived the birth of her third son by only twelve months before her death on 13 July 1853. Stephen made no further changes to his will in the ensuing twelve months, but then fell victim unexpectedly to typhus and died within four days on 6 July 1854.

In his will Stephen had nominated three men to be his executors and Trustees. They were Robert Hurrell (1808-1883), a Kingsbridge solicitor married to Stephen's wife's sister Frances Sarah Square (1811-1895); Charles Terrell Lewis (1821-1881) an Exeter actuary and Secretary of the West of England Insurance Company; and William Caird (1803-1879), an Exeter surgeon. The will was proved in the Prerogative Court of the Archbishop of Canterbury on 27 September 1854. Two suits were then instituted in the High Court of Chancery the same year for the administration of Stephen's estate, the execution of the trusts of his will, and for the appointment of a receiver and guardian for his three children.

On 16 December 1854 the Master of the Rolls intervened in these suits and ordered "divers accounts and enquiries to be taken and made". As a consequence of his findings, and by a further decree of the Court on 2 May 1855, John Henry Square (uncle) and Mary Brooking Haley (aunt), the wife of William Cholwich Haley (also a Kingsbridge solicitor), and Frances Sarah Hurrell (aunt), the wife of Robert Hurrell, were duly appointed guardians of the three boys, and £400 per annum was allowed for their maintenance and education.

Also in 1855, one of their first acquisitions made by the Trustees in accordance with the direction in Stephen's will to invest in "heritable estates" was the Buckland Tout Saints estate of 1200 acres, including Buckland House, and four other properties, which came on the market when the Clark family decided to dispose of it via Sotheby's, and which the Trustees acquired for the sum of £1,260. This purchase gives a very clear picture of the purchasing power of the £140,000 that came under the Trustees' control from Stephen's will, and which they used subsequently to acquire the Thurlestone Estate and other holdings from the Earl of Devon on 14 December 1868 for the sum of £36,000. Eight months later, in another court decree, John Henry Square was discharged from being one of the guardians.

Buckland House and estate were seen as a suitable home for the three Brunskill boys, though the property was in some need of repair and renovation. In the 1861 census they were all living with the Hurrell family at the bank in Fore Street, Kingsbridge, where Robert Hurrell also had his office. It was not until June 1863 that the court made an order allowing Robert and Frances Hurrell, together with the three Brunskill boys, to occupy the property rent-free, to have it repaired as required, and to have an annual sum of £850 for the boys' maintenance, education, and support.

To complete his education William Fawcett Brunskill was entered as a pensioner at Exeter College, Oxford in October 1868, though he did not obtain a degree and it is not recorded how long he stayed there altogether. He reached the age of twenty-one on

26 February 1870 and immediately set about enjoying his inheritance. He married Annie Elliott, aged sixteen, the third daughter of a Dartmouth GP, on 2 June 1871, and spent lavishly on her and their home at Buckland House. Their first son, also named William Fawcett Brunskill, was born on 18 February 1872, and following his father's example, William drew up his own will which was executed on 9 October 1872 leaving his entire estate to his wife, and appointing her as his sole executor, and appointing his wife, his uncle John Henry Square, and Edward Tindal Atkinson (a barrister who had married Jessie Elliott, Annie's elder sister) as guardians of his children.

However, before the end of that year his spending had been so excessive that in October 1872 he was obliged to declare himself bankrupt. The first intimation of the crash came in a report in the Western Daily Mercury, repeated in the Exeter & Plymouth Gazette of 17th October 1872.

> **REPORTED FAILURE OF A DEVONSHIRE GENTLEMAN.**— Many of the tradesmen and others of Kingsbridge, Dartmouth, and Totnes, and other neighbouring towns, including Plymouth and Torquay, are smarting under the intelligence which reached them on Tuesday morning from the Stonehouse Bankruptcy Court, to the effect that Mr. William Fawcett Brunskill, of Buckland Tout Saints, near Kingsbridge, had placed his affairs in the hands of his solicitors for the purpose of liquidation by arrangement or composition with his creditors. A general meeting of the creditors is to be held at the office of Mr. William Robert Harris, 40, Chancery Lane, London, on Tuesday, the 29th day of October instant. It is estimated that the liabilities to secured and unsecured creditors are over £30,000. The tradesmen of Kingsbridge will suffer severely, for the amount due to them is calculated to be over £5,000. The liabilities to the London tradesmen are also very heavy, Mr. Brunskill's *bijouterie* bill with Hancock and Co., the great jewellers, being between £4,000 and £5,000. All the horses, with the pack of foxhounds, together with their paraphernalia, will be sold at the Railway Hotel, Totnes, on the 24th instant. Such a calamity, by which so many tradesmen of neighbouring towns suffer, is seldom experienced. The affairs are in the hands of gentlemen who will do their best for the creditors, and it is hoped that the tradesmen will yet fare better than they now anticipate.— *Western Daily Mercury.*

Exeter & Plymouth Gazette, 17 October 1872

A London Solicitor, Frederick Whinney, of Harding, Whinney & Co, 8 Old Jewry, London, was quickly appointed to be his trustee in bankruptcy, and he lost no time in selling off at auction many of the items William Fawcett Brunskill had not so long ago acquired. The first auction, on 24 October 1872, of his horses and hounds, realised 1,100 guineas. The entire contents of Buckland House were then sold at auction on 17-19 December.

PRELIMINARY ANNOUNCEMENT.

IN BANKRUPTCY.

MR. JOHN TRIST has received instructions from Frederick Whinney, Esq., the trustee in the estate of W. F. Brunskill, to SELL at BUCKLAND HOUSE near Kingsbridge, Devon, on TUESDAY, the 17th, WEDNESDAY, the 18th, and THURSDAY, the 19th days of DECEMBER instant, all the HOUSEHOLD FURNITURE, Pictures, and Utensils; Billiard Table by Cox and Yemans, and all the fittings of a billiard-room complete; 2 Cows; 5 Horses; 3 Pigs; Outdoor Effects; Plants; large Cellar of Wine, including vintages of 1834 and 1847; a Brougham by Collyns and Oyns, and handsome Mail Phaeton by Laurie and Marner; Victoria, by Peters and Sons; Break, by Collyns and Oyns, Dog Cart by Collyns and Oyns, and small Dog Cart; Carriage Harness; Carts; Cart Harness, and other Effects.

Full particulars in handbills, and catalogues with fuller descriptions and order of sale may be obtained of the Auctioneer on and after the 13th instant at 6d each, returnable to purchasers.

Kingsbridge, Dec. 3, 1872.

Western Times, Friday 6 December 1872

Shortly afterwards, on 18 February 1873 a total of 1830 trees from the woodlands of the Buckland Estate were sold by auction in 32 lots at the Kings Arms Hotel, Kingsbridge, by Messrs Norton, Trist, Watney and Co.

While these measures were drastic enough, they were able to realise only a small fraction of the total debts incurred by William Fawcett Brunskill during his spending spree, and failed to account for the estimated total extent of his bankruptcy.

This was revealed and highlighted during a hearing at the Exeter County Court held on Wednesday 22 January 1873 before Judge Fortescue, as reported in the Western Times on the Friday of the same week, (See Appendix 1) though Whinney had been able to announce in the Morning Post on the Saturday before the hearing that a first dividend payment of 5 shillings in the pound would be made to creditors on Thursday 23 January 1873.

MR. BRUNSKILL'S BANKRUPTCY.

An application was made by Mr. Halse, the solicitor to the Trustee, with the view of securing his Honour's approval of a scheme agreed to by the creditors, in the matter of Mr. W. F. Brunskill. Mr. Halse mentioned that the bankrupt's secured debts amounted to £12,000, and the unsecured debts to £16,000 or £17,000 ; his assets amounted to between £4,000 and £5,000, and he had a life interest producing about £5,000 per annum. An unusually prompt and tolerably favourable realisation of the assets had enabled the trustee to pay off one-fourth of the debts, and the distinctive object of the scheme was to enable the trustee to hold the life interest, and carry on the estate until such time as the money should be accumulated by which the creditors might be paid the balance due to them. The scheme had received the almost unanimous approval of the creditors, there being but one objection made against it ; and although the rules did not require it, he had given notice that the application would be made, and he believed no one was present to oppose it.—His Honour sanctioned the scheme, believing it to be as good a one as could have been devised.—A motion was then made by Mr. Halse, that Mr. R. W. Head should pay to the trustee £1,893 in his hands, as receiver or agent of the bankrupt, arising from rents of estates of which the bankrupt was tenant for life under the will of the late Stephen Brunskill, which rents had accrued previous to the 26th Feb., 1872. It appeared that the money was claimed by the trustee under the bankruptcy and the trustees under the will, and the receiver was ready to pay the money to anyone who could give him a competent discharge for it. Some of the affidavits, however, did not appear to have been filed more than four days ago, and counsel's opinion having to be obtained upon them, Mr. Floud, who appeared for the receiver and the trustees under the will, said he had not had time to look into them, and could not in justice to his clients state their case to-day. Under the circumstances his Honour adjourned the further hearing of the motion for a month.

Western Times, Friday 24 January 1873

More cash was realised through the sale of the Ranscombe Estate, a mansion house and 120 acres of grounds, for £8000 to John Henry Square in July 1874. The process of identifying and validating the claimant creditors, and realising the funds to repay them from within the assets of the estate, kept Fred Whinney, the Brunskill Trustees and their solicitors busily employed during the next few years. Whinney was able to pay back the creditors in four further instalments, though the final one was not until December 1876, and the five dividends amounted to only a total of 15 shillings and sixpence in the pound.

During the four years 1873-6 William Fawcett Brunskill and his wife Annie had three more children, Hubert Fawcett Brunskill born in 1873, Elliott Ridgeway Fawcett Brunskill born in 1874, and Arthur Edward Fawcett Brunskill born in April but who survived only five months and two weeks before his death on 16 September 1875. His father survived him by a matter of weeks before his death from consumption (tuberculosis) on 5 December 1875. The three original Trustees did not live to see the next heir succeed, as William Caird died in 1879, Charles Terrell Lewis in 1881, and Robert Hurrell in 1883, but they had ensured that Stephen's legacy was preserved for his heirs to inherit.

William's two younger brothers, having both been educated at Harrow, and Exeter College, Oxford, and each having received £10,000 from their father's estate under the terms of his will, went on to make their own way in the world. John Square Brunskill qualified MRCVS at the Royal Veterinary College, London, in 1878, and carried on a successful practice in Bishops Stortford until his death in 1903. Arthur Stephen Brunskill was commissioned in the Army in 1874 and served mainly in the West Indies until 1891 when he returned as a Major to the UK to become adjutant of the 2nd Volunteer Battalion the Cheshire Regiment at Chester, where he died on 17 January 1893.

Three years after the death of her husband, Annie Brunskill married again, this time to Edward Irwin of Ireland, on 28 December 1878 at Loddiswell. This union was even shorter and less profitable than her first, as Edward Irwin, JP, of Derrygore, County Fermanagh, died intestate on 15 June 1880, and his property in the counties of Donegal and Fermanagh passed to his brother John Arthur Irwin who was his heir-at-law and administrator.

In the census of 1881 Annie Irwin, now twice widowed but still a young woman 26 years of age, and her son Elliott were staying with her sister Jessie and her barrister husband Edward Tindal Atkinson (now Elliott's guardian) at their home in Leeds. Her two older boys, William and Hubert, were now both boarders at Clifton College, Bristol, but William did not live to see the end of the decade, as he died at Warfleet, Dartmouth, on 27 August 1887.

His death left his younger brother Hubert as heir to the Brunskill Estates, and the 1891 census shows that the family had now returned to Buckland House where Annie, aged 36, was the head of the house and of independent means, with a household staff of five servants, and her two boys, aged 18 and 17, still pursuing their studies. Elliott was a boarder at Repton School, and went on to Trinity College, Cambridge. Hubert went up to Exeter College Cambridge, after Clifton in 1892, but when he came of age in 1894 he set about establishing his position as a country squire.

He married Hilda Turner of Ponsonby Hall, the second daughter of William Barrow Turner, JP, DL, a wealthy mine-owner, at Ponsonby Church, Cumberland, on Tuesday 2 June 1896, and began extensive repairs and renewals to Buckland House. Together, he and his wife "transformed the mansion to make it the centre of social life in the neighbourhood". Their two children Norah Fawcett Brunskill (b. 1897) and William Hubert Fawcett Brunskill (b 1899) were both born there. The couple entertained on a grand scale, and entered into County life to the full. Hubert was an athlete and a skilful and enthusiastic sportsman. He had played football for the Exeter College XI, and was captain of Devon County Cricket Club for three years 1904-7. He was also a keen huntsman and in 1902 became master of the South Pool Harriers, and later Master of the South Devon Hunt. Special kennels were built for the hounds, and dog shows were regularly held at the house.

They were an active and popular couple, and not just for their entertaining. A hunting magazine reported in 1911 "Mrs Brunskill most ably assists her husband in every detail of the hunt. Devoted to sport and hound work, she is always out, and keen from find to finish, no day being too long for her...In the Master's absence, she takes command in the field for the day."

Despite his father's bankruptcy, his grandfather's estate had been well preserved by the Trustees, and still covered a large acreage providing a substantial income. The schedule to the Brunskill Act of 1877 which concluded the Chancery suits had listed the estate's 2263 acres and its annual rental value of £6,055. The management of the estate was in the hands of solicitor John Square until his retirement, at which point it was taken over by Henry Lionel Jenkins, a retired tea planter, who had bought Clanacombe House from Miss Ann Square in 1874. Jenkins took a more active interest in the role and "the first thing he did was to cut the road straight across from Eason Town to join the Bantham Road, and next he turned the Malt House into two houses and started the nursery garden", according to his daughter Mary Emily. She believed it was her husband Ashton Gilbert Radcliffe "who first mooted the idea of a golf course on the Warren in 1895. He got the pro from Westward Ho to come down and prospect the land".

A detailed account of Hubert Brunskill's successful engagement in the establishment of the Thurlestone Golf Club appears in the fine history The Centenary 1897-1997 by Derek Roberts, who notes that it was Jenkins who chaired the originating meeting at which Hubert Brunskill was diplomatically elected as the club's first captain. It was also Jenkins who in 1897, according to his daughter, was responsible for coming up with the idea of turning tenant Samuel Shath Square's large Farm Barton farmhouse into a guest house for golfers when he relinquished the tenancy, and then advertising the premises on this basis. The Grose family, whose farming enterprise had run into difficulties, were attracted to this idea, and took on the tenancy of the premises (though Peter Pugh's 1986 book The Thurlestone Hotel maintains it was the family's idea). Derek Roberts' book includes details of Hubert Brunskill's ambitious but failed project to try and turn Thurlestone into another Bournemouth, through a £100,000 share flotation which was never taken up, and also mentions "his reputed proclivity for sizeable wagers at the races".

The golf course became a significant new focal point for Thurlestone, and attracted the attention of people looking to build fine new homes in the parish. The Bungalow, later to be known as Furzey Close, was one of the first, built by Hubert Brunskill for his own use, though he never actually lived in it. Hubert also built stables for himself at Bantham in what is now Clock Cottage, and also Whiddons where previously there had been a blacksmith's forge. With his financial difficulties increasing, Hubert Brunskill began to sell off parcels of land in Thurlestone Parish to wealthy people looking to build properties there. Halliday Harcourt's grand new house at Aune Cross was probably started around 1897. Mollycombe was built in 1902 by William Beer (and named after his daughter), and Heathfield followed in 1904, built by Henry Prowse.

The most imposing property to be built, however, was for one of Hubert Brunskill's aunts. Mary Catherine Elliott, his mother's younger sister, had married Charles Chantry Inchbald, a wealthy banker, in 1888. Returning to England from the Far East with their three young sons, they persuaded Hubert to sell them a prime site of undeveloped land extending from Thurlestone church to the top of Buckland Hill, and including one of the highest points in the parish, with stunning views in all directions. No expense was spared in the building and furnishing of The Grey House, which was begun in 1906 and completed in 1909. Another wealthy incomer was Alfred Nathaniel Clifford, who brought his American wife and their three children from London to live at Burnt House in Buckland (acquired by Jenkins for his son Francis, and rented out), where they first appear in the census of 1911. The Links Hotel, built by Sir Joshua Boyd in an attempt to compete with the Thurlestone Hotel, opened in 1913.

In the twenty years between the censuses of 1891 and 1911 the population of Thurlestone had risen from 324 to 419, and Rev Coope estimated it at 418 at the outbreak of war in 1914. Thurlestone would continue to grow as travel and communications improved, and more people came to appreciate it as a place to visit, to stay on holiday, and also to retire. But the war brought significant change to the parish, and the Lordship. Hubert Brunskill's financial situation had become critical, and on 1st July 1918 he sold his Thurlestone parish holdings and the Lordship of the Manor to Commander Charles Edward Evans RNVR of Nailsea Court, Somerset for just £26,000 - "a price much below its value", according to his agent Jenkins' daughter Mary.

Hubert Brunskill put the rest of his estates, including Buckland House and land amounting to 2000 acres, up for auction on Friday 12th August 1921 at the Globe Hotel, Newton Abbott.

The Brunskills then lived for a time at Minehead, but returned in the 1930s to Glazebrook House, South Brent. Hilda died in 1940, and Hubert lived on until his death on 17 May 1951 at Davids Moor, Ivybridge. Both are buried in East Allington churchyard along with the earlier Brunskills, and there are memorial tablets and stained glass windows in St Peter's church dedicated to the family.

Commander Evans did not need, or want, all the properties he had acquired, and immediately proceeded to recoup much of his outlay by selling off some of them in a public auction at the Thurlestone Hotel on Thursday 29 August 1918 (Appendix 2). Court Park Farm was bought in by the Stidston family, the existing tenants, ahead of the auction. The Thurlestone Hotel itself was bought in for £4,050 by the Grose family, despite competition from Chantry Inchbald, and they also acquired Brunskill's The Bungalow for £800. The golf course was evidently unsold at the auction, and was subsequently bought by the club members from Commander Evans for £4,700 in 1923.

At a further auction at the Thurlestone Hotel on 4 October 1919, the 4-acre field known as Merchants Field also went under the hammer.

This turn of events enabled much more of the parish to be owned by individual freeholders after more than 400 years of the Courtenay's absentee landlordship, and was directly attributable to the extraordinary work-ethic and financial astuteness of the self-made son of a Westmorland peasant farmer. The legacy of an Exeter tailor had left an indelible mark on the history of the Manor of Thurlestone, touched many of the families who lived there, and directly or indirectly laid the foundations for its continuing prosperity into the post-WW1 world. Stephen Brunskill himself never lived to enjoy the wealth he had created, but it was due to his work and his will that much of it eventually found its way into providing the foundations of the economic and social fabric of the parish of Thurlestone today.

Unlike those who gave their lives in the Great War he has no memorial here, but he deserves his own place in the history of the parish and the Lordship of the Manor, a title that was passed on from the Courtenays to the Brunskills, and then on to Commander Evans, whose family held it for nearly a century until its acquisition by Nicholas Johnston of Bantham Estates in 2015/16.

However, Stephen Brunskill's legacy was not the only factor in the transition of Thurlestone from sleepy agricultural village to desirable holiday and residential community. The opening of the Great Western railway branch line from Brent to Kingsbridge in December 1893 put Thurlestone within relatively easy reach of travellers from all over the UK, and the development of the motor car brought an increasing number of them to and through the parish, although this was seen as something of a mixed blessing. Under the Local Government Act of 1894 elected local parish and district councils came into being, transferring civil powers that had previously belonged to the church, and opening up new avenues for debate and action on local political and social issues.

In Thurlestone a public meeting was held on 4th December 1894 to elect the members of the new Parish Council. H L Jenkins was elected to chair the meeting, and an election took place from names put forward. The first meeting of the Parish Council was held briefly on Boxing Day 1894, at which the elected members - George Browse, William Snowdon, Henry Albert d'Angibau, George Robins, William Charles Masters, Albert Edward Stidston, and Richard Sherriff - were sworn in. Henry Albert d'Angibau of Buckland Park was unanimously elected to be the first chairman, Albert Edward Stidston to be the parish Clerk, and a Mr Balkwill to be the Treasurer. There was no other business recorded, and no further meeting until 26 July 1895.

D'Angibau continued as the chairman until 15 April 1897, when Halliday Harcourt, a newly elected member, was proposed by HL Jenkins and duly elected as chairman. A solicitor aged 31, with a residence, wife and family at Oaksey, in Wiltshire, Harcourt had built (or was in the process of building) a rather grand new home at Aune Cross, and was presumably a protege of HL Jenkins, who would probably have negotiated the sale of the land (which included Higher Aunemouth and some 60 acres) for this development. He was succeeded as chairman in April 1899 by HL Jenkins, receiving a unanimous vote of thanks for all his efforts during the previous two years. Jenkins remained as chairman for the next fourteen years, before being succeeded by Albert Edward Stidston in April 1913.

Sadly, Halliday Harcourt's enjoyment of his home at Aune Cross was somewhat short-lived. In a fall from his horse one day he suffered a head injury and severe concussion, which left him subject to epileptic fits and convulsions, and his health deteriorated. On Saturday 26 Sept 1903 his body was found in Stiddicombe Creek, and his physician, Dr L de Courcy Harston, who carried out a post mortem, found that death was due to drowning. At the coroner's inquest on Tuesday 29 September the jury returned a verdict of suicide while of unsound mind; that first he attempted to shoot himself with a revolver, and afterwards drowned himself.

From the turn of the century to the outbreak of war, Lionel Jenkins was a significant figure in the Thurlestone community. He owned the oldest and grandest property in the parish. As the agent for the Brunskill estate, he was well known to all their tenants in the parish, and became familiar with almost every inch of the lands within it, and the beaches and river estuary that bordered it. He was duty-bound to look after the Squire's interests, but in his other role as Chairman of the Parish Council for fourteen years he was also duty-bound to serve the interests of the community too. As time went by, it would not have been surprising if serving the community's interests had become the more urgent priority for him. His name will be forever remembered and associated with Jenkins Quay and the iconic thatched boathouse built at Bantham, one of the most photographed spots in Devon.

His obituary in the Western Morning News of Saturday 25 February 1922 is particularly revealing.

"The death of Mr Henry Lionel Jenkins of Clanacombe, Thurlestone, occurred on Tuesday night after a brief illness. Born on 22 February 1837, he was the second son of the Rev David Jenkins, who was for many years vicar of St Gorran. The Jenkins are a well known Cornish family, and Mr Jenkins only surviving brother is vicar of Tideford.

Educated at Marlborough College, Mr Jenkins went to India in 1853 to work under his uncle, Major General Francis Jenkins, the then Chief Commissioner and Governor-General's agent for Assam. He very shortly became a most useful and influential member of the Chief Commissioner's staff. Later he became a tea planter, trapped and trained elephants, and went in for big game shooting and research.

Mr Jenkins travelled extensively. Perhaps his greatest achievement was his exploration of a practicable route from Assam to Burma. He travelled with a small escort through an almost unknown country, making his way across the Patkoi Mountains, an exploit that will ever be a monument to his memory.

Mr Jenkins settled at Clanacombe in 1874. He was a man of rare ability and culture and a great horticulturist. He was devoted to sport, fishing and sailing in particular, and was very familiar with Bigbury Bay. For many years he was a member of the Avon and Erme Fishery Board and figured on the committee of the Devon Sea Fisheries, taking the keenest interest in the local fishermen and their concerns.

Mr Jenkins was a man of great discernment and forethought. While agent for the Brunskill property he planned the development of Thurlestone as a seaside resort. He first started an hotel, adapting an old and commodious farmhouse for the purpose.

With the assistance of his son-in-law, Mr Radcliffe, golf links were planned on the coast land, and on their opening the success of Thurlestone as a seaside resort was assured.

Mr Jenkins was a Liberal Unionist, and identified himself with the local and county organisations as long as he was able. He was for some time Chairman of the Thurlestone Parish Council.

Mrs Jenkins, who survives her husband, is a daughter of the late Col C W Short, Coldstream Guards, belonging to a younger family of the Shorts of Bickham near Exeter. Mr and Mrs Jenkins two children are Mrs Radcliffe, Thurlestone, and Lt-Col Francis Jenkins CMG, Coldstream Guards, now Colonial Secretary at Lagos, Nigeria.

Mr Jenkins older brother, the late Sir Francis Jenkins KCB, ADC to Queen Victoria, was well known in Plymouth and in Cornwall."

Meantime, in 1899 a group of Thurlestone worthies made a successful application for the village to be connected by telephone, and the first telephone exchange was established in the Post office, with the postmistress acting as telephonist. The parish was certainly seeing changes as the twentieth century arrived.

Thurlestone mourned the passing of Queen Victoria in 1901, and mounted a bust in her memory in the wall of the new school building; celebrated the coronation of Edward VII in 1902, and welcomed the first Old-Age pension payments in 1909. The death of Captain Scott and the Titanic disaster in 1912 were followed in October 1913 by a terrible tornado, which passed over Devon and Somerset and struck in Glamorgan, where six people were killed and 100 injured.

Worse was still to come. The assassination at Sarajevo on 28 June 1914 of Archduke Franz Ferdinand of Austria and his wife Sophie provided the excuse for Germany to set in train a series of events that thwarted all diplomatic attempts to resolve the situation peaceably. The Kaiser had hoped that Britain would remain neutral in the event of war, despite treaty obligations that required us to assist Belgium against just such an invasion. But all Lord Grey's efforts to secure a peaceful outcome came to nought, and the government had no option after German declarations of war against France on 3rd August and Belgium the following day other than to declare war against Germany effective from 11pm on 4th August 1914.

And so Thurlestone went to war.

Chapter 2

The Coming of War

The Coming of War

The news of the declaration of war created a mood of both excitement and anxiety throughout the country, led to a rush of panic buying of food stocks for the home (by those who could afford it), and saw scenes of jubilation and patriotic support as the Army and Navy reservists were immediately assembled and transported away to their various bases around the country. A national recruiting campaign for voluntary enlistment for the armed services, and particularly the Army, began without delay, and prompted an immediate response from the British public.

The towns saw a higher level of initial voluntary enlistment than rural areas. The harvest in Autumn 1914 was excellent, and farmers were keen not to lose their key labourers, maintaining they were being patriotic by producing the nation's food, and even offering them increased wages to stay. Devon proved rather backward in coming forward. The Devon branch of the Parliamentary Recruiting Committee took seven weeks after the outbreak of war to set itself up, and voluntary enlistment in Devon for the first two months was well below the national average. Dismayed by the lack of volunteers from the county, the Parliamentary Recruiting Committee issued a seven-page pamphlet addressed to the "Men of Devon" emphasising the emergency with the words "Never... has the Motherland been faced by a more tremendous task or threatened with dangers so terrible".

The British Expeditionary Force (BEF) of 80,000 men began to embark for France on 8th August, and completed its move of five divisions by 16th August. They fought a series of battles to defend the French left flank, being forced to retreat from Mons back to the outskirts of Paris before counter-attacking with the French at the Battle of the Marne and driving the Germans back to the Aisne River by 12th September. Thereafter the war settled into an attritional period of trench warfare that continued for three years until the big German push of spring 1918, which was finally checked by the end of July, and followed by the Allied 100 Days Offensive, in which with the help of newly arrived American troops the Germans were driven back to the River Meuse and ultimately capitulated, signing a humiliating Armistice at Compiegne on 11th November 1918.

In England the severe losses suffered by the BEF in the early battles required a huge voluntary recruitment drive to rebuild the British Army. On 25th August 1914 The Times had reported the news of the Battle of Mons, noting that "it has gone ill for the Allies" and warning that further bad news was to follow. There was a sudden and immediate upsurge of volunteers - over 10,000 on 25th August alone. Between 30th August and 5th September, 174,901 men joined the army, including 33,204 on 3rd September, the highest total for any day of the war. Kitchener had called initially for 100,000 volunteers, then a second 100,000, and on 10th September for 500,000 more. However, the surge of volunteers had subsided by the end of September.

Prime Minister Asquith sought Parliamentary approval for a further million volunteers in mid-November. But casualties continued to mount, and by mid-1915 volunteer numbers were continuing to fall. Although 2,466,719 joined the British Army voluntarily between August 1914 and December 1915, it was not enough to meet the Army's requirements and the National Registration Act was created, listing all the men fit for military service who were still available. On 27th January 1916 conscription was introduced for single men between 18 and 41. It was also applied to married men on 25th May that year. In 1918 the upper age limit was raised to 56. Over the final three years of the war conscription added a further 2,277,623 men to the British Armed Forces.

Against the background of these statistics, we can look at how the population of Thurlestone parish responded to the war. Rev Coope, writing in 1920, stated that "Thurlestone was a comparatively quiet place during the war. Our chief interest centred in our own men and women who went in various capacities to serve their country at home and abroad. As our population was about 418, it will be seen from the following list what a large proportion of the people served." He went on to name 98 men and 5 women, and also three others in reserved or ancillary work.

Names of Servicemen

Axworthy, William	Ellis, Albert	Moore, George
Beer, Capt William	Ellis, Harold	Moore, Henry, RN
Bonnor, Charles E	Fisher, H RN	Moore, JH
Broad, Geo	Fisher, Tom, RN	Moore, JT
Brunskill, Lt H	Foote, ES	Moore, Osmund
Bryant, George RN	Fox, George	Moore, Owen
Burns, William RN	Freer, Lt George,	Moore, Walter
Campbell, Lt H	Fulford, CH	Morgan, William
Clifford, A	Fulford,GR	Morris, Harcourt
Clifford, Lt GK	Grose, Lt H	Morris, Marshall
Clifford, Lt C	Grose, Lt J	Pope, George
Coleman, H RN	Hannaford, Harry	Pope, John
Connolly, Lt P,	Henson, J	Prettijohn, Ernest
Connolly, F,	Hill, CH	Rendle, A, RN
Coope Arthur,	Hubback,	Riley, M
Cope, Charles	Ilbert, Geoffrey A	Robins, George
Cox, Major G	Inchbald, Geoffrey	Robins, P
Creper, William	Inchbald, J	Rogers, J
Crispin, G	Inchbald, Peter	Rogers, R
Dyer. Albert	Ingram, Courtenay	Rundle, J
Dyer, Alfred	Ingram, Frank, RN	Sherriff, H
Dyer, Arthur	Ingram, Henry, RN	Square, Francis
Dyer, Bernard	Jackman, Robert	Square, H
Dyer, Frederick	James, Capt	Snowdon, E
Dyer, Wallace	Jeffery, William	Snowdon, George
Dyer, William	Jeffery, William B	Snowdon, JW, RN
Easterbrook, P	Jenkins, Francis,	Snowdon, S
Edgecombe, C	Johns, G	Steer, J, RN
Edgecombe, Edgar	Johns, J	Stidston, A
Edgecombe, TE	Masters, Frank	Wood, William,
Edgecombe, Wm	Masters, Owen	Woods, F, RN
Elliott, James	Moore, Arthur	Creswick, WB
Elliott, Joseph	Moore, Frank,	

There were also: Grose, EMC, worked in munitions factory
*Maud Moore, WAAC Evelyn Moore, WAAC
Hilda Clark, Gladys Clifford, *Winefride Coope, (Hospitals)
Monica Coope, OBE, Secretarial work, Ministry of Munitions
F.Hewett, YMCA France

There were, of course, a number of men from Thurlestone already serving in the armed forces, particularly in the Royal Navy, or members of the reserves and territorials. Even so, Coope's 98 named servicemen out of a total of some 400-odd parishioners represents a substantial contribution by Thurlestonians to the British war effort.

Thurlestone in 1913 - Rock Hill Corner

The next chapter is about the casualties - those whose names appear on the War Memorial, and who featured as the principal item in the Thurlestone at War exhibition in the Parish Hall in November 2014.

Chapter 3

The Casualties

The Casualties

The following pages are about those servicemen from Thurlestone who did not return from the war, and provide details of their family backgrounds and their war service records. Their names are the ones inscribed on the Thurlestone War Memorial.

In addition, where they had relatives who also served in the war, some details for them have also been included, rather than giving them separate pages in the following chapter, which is about the survivors. This was a matter of choice, and it was felt that this option provides a better context for individual relatives to be seen as part of their extended families.

Clifford, Gerald Kerrison (1895-1918)

This line of the Clifford family can be traced back to Avebury in Wiltshire in the late 17th century, but two hundred years later it had arrived in the Greater London area, with Thomas Pack Clifford (1788-1870) firmly established in Camberwell, where he was the parish Relieving Officer. He and his wife Mary Ann Hurst raised a family of nine - three boys and six girls - and this tradition was more than maintained by his eldest son, Nathaniel Joseph Christian Clifford (1806-1886), a carpenter. His first wife Jane Morris died shortly after producing a son Joseph in December 1824, and he then married a local girl Susannah Thornback on 8 October 1827 in the parish church of St Giles, Camberwell, and raised a family of ten children with her - six boys and four girls.

Their second son, Nathaniel Alfred Clifford (1831-1908) began his career in domestic service for over a decade with wealthy stockbrokers in London and evidently learned a few lessons about how to make money. In 1871, ten years after his marriage to Caroline Knott (also in domestic service for a stockbroker), they were running the York Hotel, Waterloo Road, Lambeth. By 1881 he was a wine merchant in Hastings, and by 1891 had retired to The Grange, Strawberry Hill Road, Twickenham, and was able to live "on his own means" there until his death in 1908, at which date his estate was worth £44,000.

Their only son, Alfred Nathaniel Clifford (1868-1935) became first an underwriter at Lloyds, living in 1891 with his American wife Helen Louise Breed (and two domestic servants) at Staines, where their three children - a daughter and two sons - were born. Later, between 1896 and 1901 he had taken on a manufacturing business and moved to 23 Priory Road, Hampstead (with three domestic servants). After his father's death in 1908 he was able to retire with his wife and three children to Burnt House*, West Buckland, and be of "independent means", employing local girl Pauline Moore as a housemaid.

Both sons, Gerald Kerrison Clifford (1895-1918), and Cecil Clement Horton Clifford (1896-1954), joined up as officer cadets and were commissioned into the London Regiment, and both were to see service in WW1. Their sister Gladys Helen Clifford (1892-1971) became a Red Cross nurse, so that all three children were involved in the war effort. While Gerald did not survive the war, Cecil returned to the family home at Burnt House when the war was over. His mother Helen passed away aged 56 within twelve months of his return, in December 1919, and the family moved from the parish the following year to The Cedars, Brixham, where father Alfred Nathaniel died on 12th April 1935, leaving a net estate of £7,303.   Cecil later married Malvina Joan Bernardinello (1916-2010) in 1943, and their descendants still live in Devon to this day, and have kindly supplied the family photographs for this research.

* "Burnt House belonged to the Polyblanks. Old PB was a churchwarden for many years. He wore a top hat and frock coat on Sundays. The village boys used to cheek him and call him Lord Churchland. As a matter of fact he was an old reprobate, very fond of the bottle, and he bullied his wife. When his sister-in-law "Mrs Gus", also addicted to drink, came to live with them poor old Mrs Polyblank had a thin time." (Mrs Radcliffe)

The Officer Training Corps provided an important supply of young men as the additional officers required for the New Armies being raised at the start of the Great War. In September 1914 Gerald Kerrison Clifford joined the Public Schools Special Corps, camped in the paddock at Epsom racecourse. On the disbanding of this unit, he joined the OTC of the Old Boys Corps, of which his father Alfred Nathaniel was an officer and an instructor. After training, he was able to obtain a commission as a Second Lieutenant in the Princess Louise's Kensingtons 13th Battalion of the London Regiment on 8th February 1915, "where his modesty, generous spirit and keenness soon made him beloved alike by officers and men."

In November 1914 the battalion was mobilised for war and embarked for France arriving at Havre and joining the 25th Brigade of the 8th Division. Second Lieutenant Clifford was for some time the Rail Transport Officer (RTO) at Arques, near St Omer in France, but was later involved in front line action and wounded in fierce fighting at Loos Wood. After recovery he returned to the Western Front, but was forced to go back into hospital in England again with pneumonia. He rejoined his regiment in 1917, but was again struck down with pneumonia and hospitalised at Reigate, from where he was discharged as cured.

He was promoted to full Lieutenant in June 1917, but with a recurrence of pneumonia he was subsequently treated for some time at the Prince of Wales Hospital for Officers in London, where his condition further deteriorated into tuberculosis of the lungs. He was pronounced unfit for further military service in January 1918, and spent his final weeks at home in Thurlestone, finally succumbing to the disease on 1st July 1918. "His courage and constancy made him many friends, and those who knew him loved him".

His funeral took place at Thurlestone on Thursday July 1918, the service conducted by Rev F E Coope, Rector, and he was buried in the churchyard, where a granite cross against the western wall of the churchyard surmounts a tablet with the simple inscription:

> Lieutenant Gerald Kerrison Clifford,
> late Princess Louise's Kensingtons
> 13th Battalion the London Regiment,
> the dearly loved elder son
> of Alfred and Helen Clifford,
> died 1st July 1918, aged 23 years

His younger brother Cecil Horton Clement Clifford was also gazetted as a Second Lieutenant in the same regiment on 26th April 1917 and attached to the 2/4 battalion. He survived the 1914-18 war, and also served in the 1939-45 war in the RAF Regiment.

His family still honour his life and service, and placed a card of commemoration on his grave to mark the anniversary of his death on 1st July 2018.

> (Some of the information and quotations in this text were taken from the obituary report in the Salcombe Gazette.)

Gerald Kerrison Clifford - Pictures

Gerald Kerrison Clifford

Gerald Kerrison Clifford at camp

Alfred N Clifford

Cecil H C Clifford

Grave and Cross
in Thurlestone Churchyard

Gladys Clifford & Red Cross nurses

Creswick, Wilfred Bertram

The Creswick family roots in Sheffield can be traced back to the 16th century, but it was at the beginning of the 18th century that the two brothers James (1789-1854) and Nathaniel (1791-1855) made their mark (literally) as silversmiths. Their hallmark was first registered in 1853 in both London and Sheffield, and examples of their work come up for sale at Bonham's and Christie's to this day. The brothers married two sisters, Hannah (1793-1864) and Elizabeth (1802-11869) Jubb, and raised large families in Sheffield.

Nathaniel's eldest son was also given the name Nathaniel (1831-1917), and he too made a very considerable mark in the city. He practised as a solicitor in Sheffield, but is perhaps better known for having co-founded the Sheffield Football Club (1857), the first officially recognised football club in the world, and co-authored the "Sheffield Rules" (1857) which became the generally accepted rules for the game of football. He was also very prominent in local military circles, being a co-founder of the Hallamshire Rifles (the 2nd West Yorks) in 1858 and serving as their Colonel until 1897, and was awarded CB (1897) and knighted for his services to the volunteer movement in 1909.

The youngest son, Wilfred (1846-1922), also opted out of the silversmith business and became a mining engineer, winning the Hermon Prize in 1974 for his essay on The Prevention of Accidents in Mines. He married Margaret Ann McNiven at Killin, Perthshire in 1885, and they had two sons Wilfred Bertram (1886-1916) and Alister Malcolm (1892-1963), who also became mining engineers. The family lived at Grove House, Walton, Wakefield where Wilfred was the Manager of the three mines of the New Sharlston Coal Company until, after Wilfred retired in 1913, they moved to Aune Cross House, Bantham. They remained there for the rest of their lives, and after father Wilfred's death in 1922, mother Margaret and brother Alister were well-known figures in the parish till their deaths in 1942 and 1963 respectively.

Wilfred Bertram Creswick was born at Sandal Magna, Walton, Wakefield, Yorkshire on 27 June 1886, and baptised in the parish church of Sandal Magna on 30 July 1886. He was educated at Giggleswick School, Settle, Yorkshire from 1898 to 1904, and was a member of the 1st Football XV. After leaving school he followed his father into mining engineering, gaining a First Class Certificate of Competency as a Manager of Mines in Jan 1910, and was further qualified as a Surveyor of Mines in Nov 1912. He had also applied for a commission in the 4th Territorial Battalion of the Kings Own Yorkshire Light Infantry on 30th April 1910. He married Jessie Woodward on 23 April 1912 at Worksop, Nottinghamshire, and the couple made their home in Heath, Wakefield, where their daughter Eva Joan was born in 1915. They may well have paid visits to Aune Cross, but it is doubtful whether Wilfred Bertram was ever actually a resident of this parish.

With such a strength of family connection to Volunteer Regiments it is not surprising that Wilfred Bertram Creswick made an early move in this direction, and in fact he was gazetted with a commission as Second Lieutenant in the 4th (Territorial) Battalion of the Kings Own Yorkshire Light Infantry on 30th April 1910. As such, he would have been called up and mobilised immediately on the outbreak of war in August 1914, and as early as 23rd October 1914 he is gazetted as being promoted to Captain.

His battalion moved on mobilisation from Wakefield to Doncaster and in November 1914 to Gainsborough. It then went to York in February 1915, and was sent to France to join the BEF on 12 April 1915, landing at Boulogne. Within a week the battalion had moved up to the front line and was being introduced to trench warfare in the Bois-Grenier sector. They moved into the front line as an entire battalion on 28th April. The first officer from the battalion to be killed was 2/Lt Roderick Gwynne of Filey on 23rd May. Wilfred Bertram was wounded the following day, 24th May, and went back briefly to the UK for treatment before returning to France in June.

Three months later, on 12th September 1915, he joined the 179th Field Company, Royal Engineers on attachment, and was involved in tunnelling and mining operations. The Germans had started this tactic in December 1914, and the British were quick to respond, with ad hoc Mining Sections at Brigade level. On 17th February 1915 the first British mine was blown at Hill 60 by Royal Engineer troops of 28th Division. The first eight Royal Engineer tunnelling companies were swiftly set up by Major John Norton-Griffiths soon afterwards, and they rapidly expanded their operations. It was dirty, dangerous work deep underground for the small teams of "clay-kickers", but they could earn twice the pay of miners back in the UK. The 179th was the ninth of these companies to be formed, and in October 1915 it moved into the Thiepval-La Boiselle sector of the Somme.

Wilfred Bertram was immediately into action for his company and on 30th November 1915 he was mentioned in despatches "for gallant and distinguished services in the Field" and was later awarded the Military Cross, gazetted on 15th January 1916. The work of these mining teams has been famously written about by Sebastian Faulks in his 1993 WW1 novel Birdsong, which was also made into a two-part television drama in 2012 by Philip Martin, starring Eddie Redmayne and Clemence Poesy. Wilfred Bertram was himself an experienced mining engineer as well as a trained soldier, so he was perfectly equipped for the task ahead. However, he was confronting enemy miners already more experienced in these new "dark arts", and especially in one of the darkest of them - the newly developing activity of counter-tunnelling and mining. He was one of three men killed on 10th April 1916 when the Germans exploded two countermeasures mines of 5000kg and 6000kg underneath the area in which they were working at La Boiselle. The two men who died with him were Sapper 102758 Stephen Devine (aged 40) and Private 14583 William Henry Cross, 10th Battalion, Essex Regiment (aged 42).

Wilfred Bertram Creswick's name appears on Sir Edwin Lutyens' Thiepval Memorial to the Missing of the Somme, and on the Thurlestone War memorial, and is commemorated at Giggleswick School. His medals have been donated by his grand-daughter-in-law Mrs Rosemary Sillars to the KOYLI Regimental Museum at Chequer Road, Doncaster. The two soldiers who died with him are also both commemorated at Thiepval and at Giggleswick School.

British tunnellers gradually gained ascendancy over the Germans, and mining warfare reached its zenith at the Messines Ridge in June 1917. After that, mining activity diminished as a more fluid war of movement developed in which siege methods became less relevant. The "gunpowder plotters" made way for the more mobile men in tanks and flying machines. Warfare moved on.

Creswick, Wilfred Bertram - Pictures

Capt. Wilfred Bertram Creswick

Mentioned in Dispatches

Giggleswick School

Thiepval Memorial

Military Cross & War Medals

Medal Roll Card

The Dyer Family

John Henry Dyer (1857-1905), like his father John Dyer (1816-1890), and his grandfather John Dyer (1792-18??), was born in the parish of Tor Moham, Torquay. "The parish of Tor-Moham, or Tor-Mohum, comprised about 2000 acres of land, occupying most of that bold promontory which projects eastward into the English Channel, about three miles in length, and two in breadth, to Hope's Nose, the point which divides Torbay and Babbicombe Bay. . ." (White's Devonshire Directory 1850). The family home was at 10 Church Street in 1851 and 1861, where John Henry and his three sisters, Emma Luscombe (1844-1906), Mary Elizabeth (1850-1915), and Harriet Louisa (1859-1941) were all born, but the family later moved to 23 Lucius Street, where they are to be found in 1871 and 1881.

John Henry did not follow in his father's footsteps as a mason, although he did begin to learn the trade of a plumber, but decided in 1873 at the age of sixteen to join the Royal Navy. He spent time in the training ships at Devonport (Ganges, Cambridge Royal Adelaide, and Topaz) and went from boy seaman, to ordinary seamen, and then able seaman by July 1878, when he joined HMS Iron Duke, and Audacious class ironclad, and sailed in her to Hong Kong where she was flagship of the China Fleet at the time of the 1881 census.

Returning to the UK in 1883, he transferred to the Coastguard Service, and on 23 April 1884 married a Cornish girl, Julia Bowcher, whose family lived at Manaccan on the Lizard peninsula. Their first child, William Henry, was born at Falmouth on 30 September 1885. They then moved to Ireland, where John Henry served at a number of places along the western coast, including Porthill, Doohooma, and Kilkee, and where their next four children were born. Francis Arthur John (Belmullet 1887) was followed by Violet Elizabeth (1890), Albert Bowcher (1892 Kilrush), and Alfred Ernest (1893 Kilrush).

John Henry returned to the UK in 1894 and continued to serve as a coastguard boatman from stations at Cadgewith, Challaborough, and Branscombe. The family continued to grow, with the addition of Thomas B (1898 Cornwall), Frederick C (1899 Thurlestone), a half-brother George Cuthbert (1902 Thurlestone), and Courtenay Percival (1904 Branscombe), until John Henry died of Bronchitis at Branscombe Coastguard Station on 10 December 1905.

Dyer, William Henry (1885-1918)

William Henry Dyer was keen to follow in his father's footsteps, and started as a boy seaman when he was just sixteen. On his eighteenth birthday he signed on for twelve years. William Henry Dyer joined the Royal Navy as a boy seaman when he was only sixteen, on 15 February 1901. He trained to be a signalman at HMS Impregnable until 30 May 1902, when he was transferred to HMS Vivid up to 30 September 1902. His next posting was to HMS Empress of India and, after a another twelve months, he was able to sign on at Devonport on his 18th birthday, 30th September 1903, for a period of twelve years. He was 5ft 4¾ins, with dark brown hair, blue eyes, and a fresh complexion. He trained as a signaller, rising to leading signalman, and had served in the Royal Navy continuously for seventeen years until his death on 21 August 1918, a month short of his thirty third birthday.

It was back to Vivid for three months before his next posting to HMS Challenger for a two year period up to July 1906. Then followed three months at HMS Argonaut, and then a series of postings between Cambridge (Wembury), Vivid (Devonport), Blake and Collingwood (Fareham, Hampshire), Pactolus, and Leander. HMS Vivid, commissioned in 1890, operated as a training unit until 1914, and became the Navy barracks at Devonport. The base was renamed HMS Drake in 1934. William Henry spent his entire career as a signalman, and subsequently leading signalman, including long periods at Royal Navy shore establishments, as a trainer for trainee signalmen. His character record was always Very Good throughout his entire service period of seventeen years, during which time he was awarded badges on five occasions.

His final posting was aboard HM Yacht North Star ll which was active in the Mediterranean, and had touched in at the harbour of Mudros, on the Isle of Lemnos, which was the British base for the Gallipoli expedition, and where the armistice between Turkey and the Allies was to be signed in late October 1918. Two months earlier the North Star ll had sailed away to return to the UK, and it was shortly afterwards that William Henry disappeared overboard on the night of 20/21 August and his body was never recovered. He was said to have been drinking heavily while at Mudros, but the circumstances of his death have never been satisfactorily explained. He was awarded posthumously the British War Medal and the Victory Medal.

Albert Bowcher Dyer (1892-1915)

Albert Bowcher Dyer was the first person from the parish to enlist to serve in the war. He attested and joined the 8th Battalion of the Devonshire Regiment on 26th August 1914 aged 21 as Private 10615. The 8th (Service) Battalion was formed at Exeter as part of the First New Army and then moved to Rushmoor Camp, Aldershot as part of the 14th Division. Training was carried out Aldershot and then Farnham. Back at Aldershot, the Battalion was mobilised for war and landed at Le Havre on 26 July 1915, and transferred to the 20th Brigade of the 7th Division, which engaged in various actions on the Western Front including the first Battle of Loos in 1915.

Albert Bowcher was severely wounded at Loos on 25 September 1915, when the 8th Devons suffered heavy casualties in the first wave of attacks towards Hulloch. Caught in a burst of machine gunfire, he was seriously wounded in the thigh by bullets and shrapnel. Bullets shattered his water bottle and one bullet tore off a button from his tunic. He was rescued and taken back to base, and from there to the Royal Herbert Hospital at Woolwich, where his mother visited him. He underwent four operations, but passed away on 2 November while still under anaesthetic from the fourth operation.

His body was conveyed to Kingsbridge station, and then taken by the 7th Battalion of the Devonshires to the church at Thurlestone, where it was received by the Rector, Rev Coope, and rested in the church overnight before burial on the Saturday afternoon. He was given a funeral with full military honours, attended by a detachment of 30 men of the 7th Devons under Captain H Hems. There was a large attendance of parishioners and others from the surrounding district, many of whom were unable to find space inside the church.

During the service the Rector gave a short address, taking as his text "Greater love hath no man than this, that he lay down his life for his friends". He pointed out that this was the first military funeral that had ever taken place in Thurlestone churchyard during the 800 years of its existence. The favourite hymn of Albert Bowcher Dyer, "Lead kindly light" was sung during the service. A volley was fired at the graveside by the men of the 7th Battalion, and their bugler sounded the "Last Post".

This was perhaps rather special treatment for a private soldier, but it may have been somewhat influenced by the letter which had been sent shortly beforehand by His Majesty King George V via the Keeper of the Privy Purse to his mother, Mrs Julia Dyer of West Buckland, which read:

> "I am commanded by the King to convey to you an expression of His
> Majesty's appreciation of the patriotic spirit which has prompted your
> five sons to give their services at the present time to the Army and
> Navy. The King was much gratified to hear of the manner in which
> they have so readily responded to the call of their Sovereign and
> their country, and I am to express to you and to them His Majesty's
> congratulations on having contributed in so full a measure to the great
> cause for which all the people of the British Empire are so bravely
> fighting."

The eldest son, William Henry, had been a regular in the Royal Navy since 1893; second son Francis Arthur John was serving in the Royal Engineers; fourth son Alfred Ernest was a stoker on HMS Warspite ; fifth son Thomas Bernard and sixth son Frederick Charles had both followed their brothers into the Royal Navy, while the seventh, George Cuthbert, was at Greenwich Hospital School, the cradle of the Navy, from which he too would go on to join the senior service.

It was a remarkable record of service, justly recognised by the King's letter, and with Private Albert Bowcher Dyer's funeral fittingly accorded full military honours by the Devonshire Regiment.

Note - Though George Cuthbert Dyer was too young to serve in WW1, he served in the Royal Navy right through WW2, and was one of the lucky 1000 survivors of HMS Repulse, sunk by Japanese torpedo bombers on 10 December 1941. He was released from the Navy in October 1945.

Elliott, James Whitting (1882-1919)

James Whitting Elliott carried the surnames of two families who were well known in the parish of Thurlestone for two centuries before the Great War. While there had been Whittings living in Thurlestone for at least two generations during the 18th & 19th centuries, there were none left by 1901. His father Joseph Elliott had been born in Buckland in 1851, worked as a mason, and lived his whole life there until his death in 1934, when he was buried in Thurlestone churchyard. Joseph had married his first cousin Selina Whitting in 1877, and they raised a family of nine children - four boys and five girls - who were well known throughout the parish. Selina appears to have been the last one of her Whitting line to remain in the parish, and she died early in 1919.

Although Joseph Elliott, his grandfather, was actually born at Holbeton in 1804, he married Mary Ellis Whitting, the daughter of a Thurlestone man (William Whitting) in South Milton (though she had been born in Newton Ferrers), and they settled in Buckland, where they raised four sons - William, James, Richard, Joseph - and one daughter, Elizabeth. All four sons married and raised their families in Buckland.

> William (b.1840) married Susan Moore and they had 6 children.
> James (b.1842) married Eliza Geach and they had a daughter Mary.
> Richard (b.1848) married Louisa Ellen Lethbridge & had 6 children.
> Joseph (b.1851) married Selina Whitting and they had 9 children.

Altogether, a total of twenty-two Elliott children were born in Buckland between 1871 and 1895. Elliott baptisms at All Saints were clearly a regular event for the rector!

Joseph Elliott, the youngest of the four sons, became a mason like his father, while his brothers were farm workers. He too, like his father, had four sons - three of whom were to see active service in the Great War - but also produced five daughters. They were :

> Etta (1878-1932) m. William Osborne Gidley in 1905,
> George Whitting (1880-1956) m. Florence Ellen Edworthy
> James Whitting (b.1882) m. Bessie Leah Wakeham in 1912,
> Bertha Harriot (1884-1939) m. William F Old in 1912,
> Joseph (1886-1953) m. Eva Herd in 1922
> Maggie (1887-1938) m. Frank Yole Heathman in 1910,
> Louisa (1890-1942) m. Edwin Thomas Auger in 1918,
> Mary Gladys (b.1890) m. William Diamond in 1921,
> William Arthur (b.1895) m. Margaret Dorothy Butt in 1919.

James Whitting Elliott, also a mason like his father, married Bessie Leah Wakeham at South Pool on 26 June 1912, and their son William George was born in Thurlestone at the end of 1913. Sadly, the boy outlived his father by only three months, and died on 13th April 1919, quite possibly from the same Spanish flu which had carried off his father a continent away, and 50 million others all around the world. After the war, widow Bessie married Thomas H Baker at Totnes in 1923 and had a daughter Rosemary (b.1925) and a son Roy (b.1930). As far as we know, there are no direct Elliott descendants living in the parish today, though they are still spread around in the county of Devon.

William Arthur's daughter, Kathleen Evans (nee Elliott) revisited Bantham in 1995 from her home in Exmouth, and kindly gave us copies of the attached pictures of her Elliott relatives. She had worked as a postwoman in Exmouth from 1941-46 and was paid £3.5s a week. Her daughter Margaret Evans now lives somewhere in the Manchester area.

James Whitting Elliott's detailed military service records have not survived; nor have we found a picture of him - in or out of uniform. All we know is that he joined the 1/4 Battalion, Devonshire Regiment, and served (as did his brother Joseph) in Mesopotamia in the Middle East. His battalion suffered badly from the heat in 1916, but on 3rd February 1917 they were in the forefront of the successful attack on the Hai bridgehead against the Turks at Kut that proved "the decisive day in the Salient" (official Eye-Witness) despite suffering heavy losses. There is no record of the part James played in the campaigns or why he came to be in Kantara Hospital in Egypt in January 1919, but it is quite likely that he was finally a victim of the epidemic of Spanish flu that took 50 million lives worldwide in 1919 (more than all the numbers killed in the war). He died on 23rd January 1919 and was buried in the Kantara War Memorial Cemetery.

During World War I Kantara, situated on the edge of the Suez Canal some 50 kilometres south of Port Said, was the site of Headquarters No. 3 Section, Canal Defences and Headquarters Eastern Force during the latter stages of the Defence of the Suez Canal Campaign and the Sinai Campaign of 1916. It became the main supply depot for all British, Australian and New Zealand operations in the Sinai from 1916 until final demobilization in 1919. A massive distribution warehouse and hospital centre was located in the town that supplied and supported the numerous units in the area.

James' mother Selina survived him by only two months, and his infant son William George by just three months - both possibly dying also from the flu epidemic.

George Whitting Elliott, the oldest of the four brothers, did not serve in the armed forces during the war, and was presumably either deemed to be in a reserved occupation or physically unfit for service. He does appear in the electoral register for Thurlestone through from 1913 to 1921. He is not mentioned in Rev Coope's list of all those who served in the war. However, Rector Coope singularly failed to include the youngest brother William Arthur Elliott in his list, so he was not infallible. George lived at 3 Bantham in 1939, by now widowed but still a fisherman.

Joseph Elliott, the third of the brothers, attested on 25 November 1915 at Newton Abbot, and was subsequently posted to the Royal Regiment of Artillery depot at Hilsea on 16 March 1916 as a driver. Within this Regiment he served with various units in various places with D Force in Mesopotamia, including "S" Battery, Royal Horse Artillery, and the 6th and 7th Cavalry Brigades, for the remainder of the war. He was more fortunate than his brother James, in that he survived, although he had to wait until 30 January 1920 before he eventually arrived home and was demobilised. He had to wait even longer to receive his British and Victory medals on 17 June 1921.

William Arthur Elliott, youngest of the four brothers, attested on 30 October 1915 and trained as a driver in the Army Service Corps. He was posted to the British Military Transport Depot at Rouen on 5 January 1916 and served throughout the war in France. The driving must have been long, arduous, and stressful, for he was admitted to hospital at Le Treport from 7 to 21 November 1916 suffering from debility, and had two weeks leave in January 1917. Then it was back to France for the remainder of the war, which he was fortunate to come through unscathed, and after which he returned to England to marry Margaret Dorothy Butt on 7 April 1919 before being finally discharged back to civilian life again on 18 August 1919.

Elliott, James Whitting - Pictures

Pte James W Elliott Medal Roll Card

Kantara War Memorial Cemetery

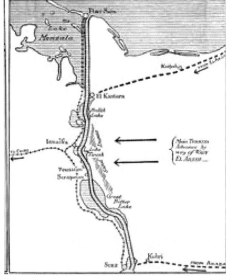

Kantara on the Suez Canal

Devonshire Regiment badge

**Joseph Elliott's daughters and daughters-in-law
at Under Cliff, Bantham about 1912**

Ellis, Harold John Henry (1896-1918)

The Ellis family has a long history in the South Hams. The family line of Harold John Henry Ellis can be traced back to the 18th century in the nearby village of Malborough, where Joseph Ellis married Mary Grose on 23 December 1801. They had ten children - three boys and seven girls - between 1803 and 1824. The eldest child, Robert Ellis, born in 1803, married a local Malborough girl Amy Clarke on 6 November 1828. They continued to live in Malborough and their seven children were all born there between 1829 and 1840, when their youngest, Philip Ellis, completed the family. However, mother Amy survived only another two years before she passed away, aged just 33 years, in the autumn of 1842.

Philip Ellis married an Aveton Gifford girl, Jane Pepperell, at Stoke Damerel on 30 October 1869, and set up home in Malborough where he worked as an agricultural labourer. They had three sons - Robert was born in 1870, followed by John Edmund in 1872, and Philip in 1878. By the census of 1891 the family had moved from Malborough to Buckland Bank, in Thurlestone parish, and the two younger boys had found local positions as farm servants. John Edmund lived in with farmer White at Whitley Barton. At nearby North Upton he met a young local lady, Elizabeth Ann Jackman, who was in domestic service there with the Perratons, and a year later they were married. By 1901 they had moved to the cottages in Thurlestone village, between William Snowden (gardener) and Nathaniel Moore (shoemaker, and also boarding James Coombes the golf professional) and had three children - Albert Edmund (b.1892), Harold John Henry (b.1896) and Eva Rosalind (b.1899).

A decade later, in the 1911 census, they were living in Glebe Cottage next door to the rector Rev Frank Egerton Coope, with the three children all still living at home. Albert Edmund (18) was now working on the golf links, Harold John Henry (15) was a farm horseman, and Eva Rosalind (11) was still at school. By now James Coombes had expanded his role as golf professional to include running the Sloop Inn at Bantham. And living nearby, acting as housemaid for visiting organist Helen Waddington Smith, was a young London "incomer" Ethel Cook. By the time the war came, three years later, the Ellis boys had changed their occupations. Albert Edmund gave his as "signal porter" when he enlisted, while Harold John Henry was also a porter, working for the GWR at Loddiswell station.

Harold John Henry was the first to join up, on 10 December 1914, and attested and took the oath at Kingsbridge in front of Ashley Froude JP, attesting officer. The same day he went on to Exeter, where he was duly approved and appointed to the Devonshire Regiment with the rank of private. His elder brother Albert Edmund had other pressing engagements, which delayed his enlistment by five months, but he was then duly attested at Kingsbridge in front of Hubert F Brunskill JP on Wednesday 5 May 1915, having married Ethel Cook on Monday 3 May, just two days earlier. Harold John Henry was able to get leave to attend the wedding at All Saints, and signed the register along with Robert Henry Jackman as witnesses.

Monica Coope, a daughter of the Rector, recorded "The Glebe Cottage, set in the Rectory wall, was in a sad state of disrepair, so father had it pulled down and built a new one, a pretty gabled dwelling with a good living room and airy bedrooms. Here came the Ellises to live and work for us, with their children. Harold was a young tearaway then, and we used to follow his devilries with bated and admiring breath. He grew up into a fine young fellow, and lost his life in WW1. Albert survived, and became a signalman on the GWR, but he too was fated to a sudden death, being killed by an express train on the main line at Cornwood, just as he was handing over the Right of Way Key to an engine driver in the up Line. Rosalind in due time became our maid at the Rectory, and has remained one of our dearest friends through all the years that have passed".

Harold John Henry Ellis of Glebe Cottage, Thurlestone, became Private Ellis H J H of the Devonshire Regiment on Wednesday 10 December 1914 at the Barracks, Exeter, and began a programme of basic training. After six months, however, and given his previous occupational experience with horses, he was transferred to 662 Company of the Army Service Corps on 9 June 1915 as a driver. He spent the next eighteen months with them before being transferred to the 48th Training Battalion at Prees Heath on 21 January 1917. Four months later, on 15 May 1917, he was posted to France to join the British Expeditionary Force, embarking on a troopship at Folkestone and reaching Boulogne the same day. Next day he arrived at Étaples.

After a fortnight in this notorious base camp Harold John Henry was transferred from the Army Service Corps to the Infantry, and posted to the 17th Battalion of the Manchester Regiment as a private with a new Regimental service number 42132. Following 14 days leave to the UK he rejoined the battalion in France, and stayed with them through the campaigns of the autumn of 1917 and the spring of 1918. He was employed on the narrow gauge railway that was used to move munitions up to the front line. Then in March 1918 the German army launched an all-out offensive in the Somme sector.

On the morning of 21 March, the 16th Manchesters occupied positions in an area known as Manchester Hill, near to St. Quentin. A large German force attacked along the 16th's front, being repulsed in parts, but completely overwhelming the battalion elsewhere. Though encircled, the 16th continued to resist the assault, encouraged by Lt-Colonel Elstob, its commanding officer. At one point, he sent a message to Brigade "The Manchester Regiment will defend Manchester Hill to the last." To his men he said "Here we fight, and here we die". And they did. Lt-Colonel Elstob was awarded a posthumous Victoria Cross. An attempt to retake the hill was later made by the 17th Manchesters with heavy losses, and it was during this battle on 22nd March 1918 that Harold John Henry Ellis was killed. He is commemorated in the Pozieres British Cemetery, Ovillers-la Boiselle, on the GWR Roll of Honour at Exeter St David's station (platform 5), and Thurlestone War Memorial.

Elder brother Albert Edmund Ellis followed a very similar path during the war. He too was drafted into the Army Service Corps as a driver, having taken with him a reference from farmer Albert Edward Stidston dated 30 April 1915. He too was posted to 48 Training Battalion at Prees Heath on 29 January 1917. The brothers will have been there together over a period of four months, during which time Albert Edmund impressed enough to earn first one stripe (11 April), and then a second (12 June). However, he too was then transferred to the Infantry, and posted to the 4th Reserve Battalion of the Kings Shropshire Light Infantry at Swansea on 15 December 1917, but as a private with a new service number 31349. Whether the loss of seniority rankled, or there was some other cause, but he was "Absent from Tattoo until 10.45 pm on 21 Jan 1918" - and awarded 4 days CB (confined to barracks). The following month came his posting to France to join the BEF on 28th February 1918, and he found himself in the thick of the fighting almost immediately.

"On the 21st March 1918, the 1st Battalion King's Shropshire Light Infantry were holding the ridge between Noreuil and Lagnicourt, when they were overrun by German forces, and by about 11 am over three quarters of the Battalion found themselves prisoners of war." (KSLI Facebook).   Albert Edmund was one of those taken prisoner that day at Lagnicourt, having suffered wounds to both arms from shell splinters. He was taken to a POW camp at Wahn-Limburg, south of Cologne.   Conditions at the camp were comparatively good and his wounds would have received medical attention there. He was eventually repatriated on 13th January 1919.

Ellis, Harold John Henry - Pictures

Pte Harold John Henry Ellis

Albert Edmund Ellis

Family Display of JHJ Ellis's Medals

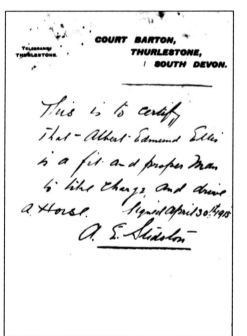

Reference from A E Stidston

Ilbert, Geoffrey Arthur

The lineage of the Devon Ilbert family is recorded in "A Genealogical and Heraldic History of the Commoners of Great Britain and Ireland, enjoying Territorial Possessions or High Official Rank but Uninvested with Heritable Honours" by John Burke, published in London in four volumes (volume four) in 1838. At that date the estates were Bowringslea and Horswell and their latest owner and family representative was William Roope Ilbert, who had inherited them from his uncle in 1826. His younger brother was the Reverend Peregrine Arthur Ilbert, born and baptised in Quebec in 1810, who married Rose Anne Owen at Tiverton in 1840 and was Rector of All Saints, Thurlestone from 1839 to 1894.

Rev Peregrine Arthur Ilbert was the father of eight children, all born at Thurlestone, and brought up in the Rectory on Main Street. They were:

Courtenay Peregrine (1841-1924) married Jessie Bradley (5 daughters)

Arthur (1843-1899) married Beatrice Alice Porter (2 children)

Marian Lucy (1844-1938) married Robert Campbell (3 children)

Owen (1846-1896) married Mary Elizabeth Elder (4 children)

Willoughby (1848-1928) did not marry

Donald (1850-1941) did not marry

Helen (1854-1934) did not marry

Lewis George (1856-1940) married Ann Barrack (1 daughter)

Owen Ilbert read classics at Corpus Christi College, Oxford from 1865-70, graduating BA in 1870 and MA in 1872. He married Mary Elizabeth Elder in Rochford, Essex in 1875, and their first child was a daughter, Rose Dorothy, born in 1877 at Crowthorne, Berkshire. Owen Ilbert followed a career in teaching, becoming assistant master at Tonbridge in Kent, where their three further children, all boys, were born - Peregrine Edward (1878-1938), Owen Lewis (1880-1968), and Geoffrey Arthur (1883-1917).

In 1884 the family moved to Crediton, where Owen Ilbert was to be Headmaster. His wife died there in 1888, and with his own health deteriorating, Owen left for New Zealand in December 1891 to become classics master at Auckland College and Grammar School. The three boys followed him in 1893, but their father's health failed to improve and he died in October 1896 in Auckland.

Rose Dorothy Ilbert married George Gordon Coulton at Kingsbridge in July 1904. He was a lecturer at Cambridge, where they lived, and where she died on 29 March 1959.

Eldest son Peregrine Edward Ilbert remained in New Zealand, married Ida Mildred Wilson, and lived in Waikato, North Island, until his death in March 1938.

Second son Owen Lewis Ilbert returned to UK and studied electrical engineering at Chelmsford before moving to Shanghai, where he married Gertrude Margaret Howard Monypenny, a minister's daughter, on 24 September 1907. After retiring he lived in USA and UK until his death in Surrey in 1968.

Geoffrey Arthur Ilbert went to Auckland Grammar School, where he played for the cricket XI, but had little inclination for an academic career. He joined the Royal Navy as a lieutenant in the Royal Marines Light Infantry in January 1902, but failed to qualify in the gunnery course at HMS Excellent. After eighteen months with the RMLI, he then joined the Royal North West Canadian Mounted Police and spent three years as a "Mountie". Returning to New Zealand, he decided to stay there and learn all about sheep farming, perhaps encouraged by his eldest brother. The records show that he worked as a labourer and storekeeper in Te Araroa, Bay of Plenty, between 1911 and 1914.

Geoffrey Arthur Ilbert married Mate Kino Ariare at the Auckland Registrar's Office on 20 November 1911, although by the time he enlisted in October 1914 he declared himself to be single on his Attestation Form. He was killed in action on the Western Front on 28 February 1917. He is buried in the Royal London Rifle Brigade Cemetery Comines-Warneton, Hainaut, Belgium, half a mile beyond the village of Ploegsteert.

A memorial plaque in Thurlestone Church is inscribed:

In memory of Geoffrey Arthur Ilbert (Private) acting stretcher-bearer, 1st Auckland Infantry Batt (New Zealand) youngest son of Owen Ilbert, grandson of the Rev P A Gilbert, who gave his life for his fellow men 28 February 1917 and is buried at Ploegsteert in Flanders aged 33.

See Chapter 6 for a more detailed look at the Ilbert family history as compiled by Michael Day.

Geoffrey Arthur Ilbert - Pictures

Geoffrey Arthur Ilbert

**Geoffrey Arthur Ilbert's gravestone in the
London Rifle Brigade Cemetery at
Ploegsteert, Belgium**

Inchbald, John Chantry Elliott (1894-1917)

The roots of the Inchbald family (with various spellings) lie in Boroughbridge, Yorkshire and can be traced back through a line of yeoman farmers to 1700. This branch of the family descends from Rev Dr Peter Inchbald (1777-1838) of Adwick Hall, near Doncaster, which he ran as a school for boys. In 1815 he married Sarah Shipton of Whixley, and they had twelve children.

Their third son, William Inchbald (1818-1893), a scholar of mathematics at St Catherine's College, Cambridge, became a teacher and rector. In 1851 he was teaching mathematics in the grammar school at Kingsbridge, where he married a Dartmouth girl, Elizabeth Elliot (1822-1902), daughter of Dr William Elliott. They had three sons, William Elliot, Henry, and Charles Chantry Inchbald, during the following four years while he was second master at Crediton grammar, before a move to Cheltenham College where he was assistant master and clergy for 25 years. He returned to Kingsbridge in 1881 before a final move to Paignton, where William died in 1893 and his widow Elizabeth in 1902.

The youngest son, Charles Chantry Inchbald (1856-1940), was educated at Cheltenham College and went straight from school into the London office of bankers Comptoire d'Escompte de Paris. After a bout of cardiac asthma he took a convalescent trip to China, where he joined Comptoire's branch in Shanghai. Over the next twenty years he remained in China, where he amassed considerable wealth through banking, investments, and brokering deals. He came back the UK to marry his cousin Mary Catherine Elliot in Kingsbridge in 1888, but the couple returned to Shanghai for the birth of their first son, Pierre (Peter) Elliot Inchbald in 1890. Their second son, John (Jack) Chantry Elliot Inchbald, was born in Plymouth in 1894 on another visit to UK, and the youngest, Geoffrey (Geoff) Herbert Elliot Inchbald, in Hong Kong in 1896.

The family returned to England in 1900 and Charles Chantry Inchbald became general manager, later chairman, of the Russo-Chinese bank in the City of London. With the fall of Czar Nicholas in 1917 the bank collapsed, and Charles felt personally responsible to those people he had persuaded to invest in it. He refunded them out of his own pocket, significantly depleting his own wealth. During his time in the City the family lived in Cheam, but as a holiday and retirement home Charles Chantry built The Grey House high on the downs at Thurlestone.

The Grey House

The Grey House phone number was Thurlestone No.2: the post office being Thurlestone No.1. They all loved the house and the beach and estuary. It was their "Arcadia" where the boys learned to swim, shoot, fish, and handle a boat from their boathouse, built in the crook of Bantham Ham. The boys played with lead soldiers - "the battles could go on for two or three days" - a foretaste of their military service in WW1. Their mother died at the house in 1925, and it was sold in the 1930s, and later became The Downs Hotel. It burnt down in a dramatic fire in 1960, was rebuilt, and is now apartments.

Charles Chantry Inchbald married again in 1933 to Audrey Lilian Boyce in Rochester, Essex, who had previously given him two more sons, Hugh G Inchbald (1918-1941) and Norman Charles Inchbald (1920-1970). Charles Chantry Inchbald died in Bromley, Kent aged 84 in 1940.

The three eldest sons all served in WW1, and Jack, still single, was the only one not to survive and return home.

Pierre Elliot Inchbald left active service at the end of 1917, convalescing in Scotland. He married Esme Lyle Bingham in 1918, and returned to the army as an instructor before retiring to become a stockbroker. He was recalled to the army in WW2, survived that war too, and died at his home, Wraxall Manor, Dorchester, in 1958.

Geoffrey Herbert Inchbald returned from the war on a hospital ship, married Evelyn Rosemary Ilbert in 1919, read Law at Oriel College, Oxford, later rose to become senior partner in the City law firm of Bischoff & Co., and died in London aged 85 in 1982.

John Chantry Elliot Inchbald, known as Jack, attended Cheam School, Winchester College, and went up to New College, Oxford in 1913 with a Classical Scholarship. He volunteered immediately war broke out, and was commissioned into the 9th Battalion, Devonshire Regiment. He arrived in France in May 1915 and saw extensive action at Loos and on the Somme. The Regimental History refers to his deeds at Loos in September 1915, and the attempt to capture Cite St Elie, when he and his men became embroiled in hand-to-hand fighting, "with the Germans on top of them and all mixed up". After a spell in the reserve echelons he was called up again to the front in July 1916.

On the night of 30 September 1916 Jack led a trench raid at night into the enemy lines, inflicting numerous casualties, and losing only two of his own men. It was probably this action that led to his Mention in Despatches in the London Gazette of 4 January 1917. Jack was killed in action in the advance to the Hindenburg Line, leading his No 2 company in the attack in the early morning of 2 April 1917 when the 8th and 9th Devons captured Écoust-St Mein, near Bapaume, in a blizzard. German snipers and machine gun fire contributed to battalion losses of 16 killed, 68 wounded, and 8 missing. It is believed he fell victim to a machine gun position located in the cemetery and protected by uncut wire which proved "very troublesome".

John Chantry Elliot Inchbald is buried alongside four subalterns who died with him and commemorated on a headstone in the Honourable Artillery Company Cemetery, Écoust-St Mein, and is remembered in the War Cloister at Winchester College. His memorial in Devon is a stained glass window in All Saints, Thurlestone, which has an inscription in Latin by his Winchester headmaster, Montague Rendall:

> In memory of their treasured son John Chantry Elliot Inchbald, scholar of Wykeham College and Devonshire Regiment Captain, who died at Bapaume aged 23 in 1917, this beautiful west window was placed by his parents.

The window in three sections depicts Sir Galahad flanked by Sir Bors and Sir Percival, three knights of the Round Table - believed to signify the three Inchbald brothers, with Jack looking over the shoulder of Sir Galahad.

Eldest brother Pierre Elliot Inchbald spent two years at Woolwich as a Gentleman Cadet in the Royal Military Academy, and became a professional soldier, commissioned into the 36th Brigade Royal Field Artillery attached to the 2nd Infantry Division. He was mobilised as a Lieutenant at Aldershot and arrived in France with the BEF on 19 August 1914. Within two months he was one of four officers named in General French's first dispatch to be awarded the Military Cross, a new decoration for gallantry announced on the same day the awards were made. His battery was heavily engaged in the battle of Mons, and was the last to retreat to safety on 20 September 1914 as the Germans surrounded them. He fought on for three years without any significant break, gaining the rank of Major, and somehow survived the war unharmed, but not unscathed. He was blown up more than once, saved by a silver cigarette case that stopped a bullet, and suffered severely from shell shock and battle fatigue which brought his war service to an end.

Geoffrey Herbert Elliot Inchbald joined the Berkshire Yeomanry in May 1915 straight from Winchester College as an Officer Cadet. He sailed from Liverpool on 16 January 1916 for Egypt. He had volunteered for the No 8 Company, Imperial Camel Corps, which was to engage in fighting the Turks and defending the Suez Canal. In heavy fighting in April 1918 he took a bullet in the left forearm fracturing both bones. After three months in hospital in Alexandria, the arm had not healed and he was suffering from undiagnosed malaria. He returned to UK on a hospital ship still suffering from the effects of tropical diseases.

Geoffrey's younger son Lieutenant Anthony Ilbert Inchbald of the Grenadier Guards died of wounds in Italy on 6 December 1943 in fighting to cross the River Garigliano. He is buried in the Minturno War Cemetery some 50 miles north of Naples.

Inchbald, John Chantry Elliott - Pictures

John Chantry Elliott Inchbald

Geoffrey H E Inchbald

H.A.C. Cemetery, Ecoust-St.Mein

Charles Chantry Inchbald

Moore, Arthur Owen (1899-1918)

Arthur Owen Moore sprang from a long-established Thurlestone parish family who can be traced back through several generations to the mid-18th century in the parish, and to his third great grandparents Roger and Jane Moore, whose son George was born in January 1753. George Moore, his second great grandfather, and Ann had seven children between 1780 and 1792, all baptised at All Saints. The oldest, James Moore, his great grandfather, and Mary had four children between 1806 and 1816. Their youngest son was George Moore (1816-1888) who married Sarah Gillard (1829-1904) from South Pool in 1847.

George Moore (Arthur Owen's grandfather) was a farm worker who lived in the cottage next door to the Sloop Inn at Bantham. His wife Sarah survived him there by sixteen years, and both were buried in All Saints churchyard. They had three children:

(1) Edwin Gillard Moore (1847-1938), a policeman, married Selina Scoble (1849-1931) and lived and worked in Plymouth, where they had six children, three of whom became teachers in Devonport.

(2) Amelia Jane Moore (1850-1940) married Edwin James Pinhay (1848-1901) at Stoke Damerel, and they lived in Dodbrooke, where they had three children.

(3) Nathaniel Gillard Moore (1859-1932) and his wife Emma lived in one of the Church Cottages in Main Street, Thurlestone, where they had James Coombes, the first golf professional at Thurlestone, as a lodger in 1901.

Nathaniel Gillard Moore, a cobbler (boot and shoe maker and repairer) and Emma had a large family of nine children - four sons and five daughters - all born in Thurlestone.

(1) Amelia Moore (1877-1940) was baptised at All Saints on 1st July 1877. She went into service as a nursemaid and cook and died in December 1940 in Plymouth.

(2) Henrietta Moore (1880-1942) married William John Cole, a builder, in 1904 in Kingsbridge and they had three children all born at Ugborough before 1911 when the family lived at Avonwick. Henrietta died in 1942 at Totnes.

(3) John Henry Moore (1881-1981), a groom and coachman, married Kate Blewett Roberts (1883-1976) in 1906 in Cornwall, where they had two sons, and from where they emigrated to South Dakota, USA in 1920. John Henry died in 1981 aged 100 years and 9 months.

(4) Bessie Ann Moore (1885-1951) was a maid for Colonel Newport at Whiddons Cottage, Bantham in 1901 and married Henry J Dicks in 1914. She died at Taunton.

(5) Edith Moore (1887-1969) was a servant to Amy Coope at West Buckland in 1901 and to three unmarried sisters in Plymouth in 1911. She died in Torbay.

(6) George Frederick Moore (1890-1956), a farm worker, married Elizabeth Ethel Oldridge in 1919 and lived in Kingsbridge. Their only daughter Elizabeth Esme Joyce married William Edwards in 1942 and they had two children, Karen (1944) and Paul (1952). Paul has kindly provided the images of the medals awarded to Arthur Owen Moore that have been handed down through the family.

(7) Evelyn Moore (1892-1968) married Jim Steere, who for many years operated the Bantham Ferry across the Avon estuary, and died in Plymouth in 1968.

(8) Arthur Owen Moore (1899-1918) enlisted at his earliest opportunity in 1918 and was killed in action in France on 11 August 1918, three months before the Armistice.

(9) William Nathaniel Gillard Moore (1902-1988) was born on 3 June 1902 at Thurlestone and died in Kingsbridge in July 1988.

Arthur Owen Moore was clearly impatient to join up in 1918 when he became of age and he may perhaps have gone to visit his brother in Cornwall to escape any parental pressure to the contrary. At any event, it was at Penzance that he enlisted in 1918 (date uncertain) and began his service as Private 45826 of the Hampshire Regiment, and presumably underwent his basic training with them. In this training he would have met up with another youngster, Leonard Hugh Hull, from Corsham, Wiltshire, who enlisted at Chippenham a day or two earlier and was assigned the number 45814.

Both these lads were then transferred to become Private 44257 Hull and Private 44279 Moore of the 2nd/4th (Princess Charlotte of Wales) Royal Berkshire Regiment. The Regiment was nicknamed "The Biscuit Boys" because of the close proximity of Brock Barracks, their headquarters in Reading, to the Huntley and Palmer biscuit factory.

On 11 April 1918 the 2/4 Royal Berkshires were at Amiens, and entrained for Berguette before marching to St Venant, and occupying a front line position near Robecq. From 25 May to 31 July they moved back to Linghem Camp for training, sports, etc., until moving to Bourecq, where they relieved the 1st Duke of Cornwall's Light Infantry in support line in the Nieppe Forest sector. On 9th August they relieved the Oxfordshire battalion in the right front line of the Brigade. The next day their Capt Horace Benjamin Goater (aged 43) was killed by a German sniper. The Battalion War Diary records what happened on the following day, 11th August 1918.

" Infantry Brigade attacked enemy line, objective being to cross the PLATE BECQUE and establish a bridgehead. Infantry Brigade attacked with 2/4 R Berks on Right, 2/5 GLOSTERS on Left, 2/4 OXFORDS in Support. Zero hour 4.15am. Attack advanced and crossed stream at broken footbridge. Two platoons were to cross higher up by plank bridges which had been put in position during the night but had been destroyed by shell fire and remaining forces were subjected to heavy machine gun fire. No progress over the river was made by Battalions on flanks and our forces withdrew about 9.30am with no ammunition left. The attack was carried out in a most gallant manner but was not successful as the scheme was a weak one.

Everything depended on silencing enemy machine guns sufficiently to enable the crossing of the stream to be effected: our barrage appeared not to affect enemy machine guns which were at work immediately our advance started."

The two young boys who had enlisted almost simultaneously earlier that year, and whose military paths had run together throughout the year, were both killed in action on this day, and the bodies of Privates Arthur Owen Moore (aged 19) and Leonard Hugh Hull (aged 19) lie side by side with Captain Horace Benjamin Goater (aged 42) in graves in the CWGC Communal Cemetery Extension, Merville, Nord-Pas-de-Calais, France.

There were two Moore third cousins also lost in the war.

(1) **Ernest James Moore**, son of Rhoda and Lucius Osmond Moore of West Alvington, died of wounds on 6th May 1916 in India, with the 2nd Battalion Dorsetshire Regiment. He is remembered on the Kirkee Memorial, India, and on the West Alvington War Memorial.

(2) **Archibald James Moore,** eldest son of Mary and Edmund Moore of 2 Duke St, Kingsbridge, who died 20th May 1915, aged 19 at Exeter, serving with the 3rd Battalion Devonshire Regiment.

Lucius and Edmund Moore were brothers (sons of James Moore and Mary Beavil) who had lived at Bantham and Buckland in their youth.

Leonard Hugh Hull's sister Effie gave her only son the forenames Leonard Merville in memory of her late young brother and his final resting place.

Moore, Arthur Owen - Pictures

WW1 Victory Medal and British War Medal, known as "Mutt and Jeff", awarded to Arthur Owen Moore

Royal Berkshire Badge

Brock Barracks, Reading

The cemetery at Merville where Arthur Owen Moore and Leonard Hugh Hull where laid to rest

Moore, John Thomas Dolton (1881-1916)

John Thomas Dolton Moore's branch of the Moore family can be traced back to Roger Moore, born on 10 October 1742 and baptised at All Saints, Thurlestone. Roger married Elizabeth Yabsley there on 5th December 1769. Her Yabsley line stretched back from Thurlestone through Malborough to the 14th century in South Huish. Their son Richard Moore was born 1776 and married Hannah Clark on 9 June 1801 in All Saints. They lived in Bantham, where they had nine children:

Betsey (b.1801) married William Lidstone and they had 8 children

Thomas (1803-1882) married Susan Eastley and they had 6 children

Hannah (1805-1881) married Philip Pinwell and they had 2 children

Roger (1808-1900) married Mary Hardey and they had 3 children

Richard (1810-1886) married Margaret Rudd and they had 9 children

Walter Clark (b.1813-1831) unmarried

John (b.1819) married Jane Pound and they had 2 children

Maria (b.1822) married Robert Jackman and they had 4 children

Amelia Jane (1822-1844) unmarried, had a son, and died four months later

George Henry Moore (1844-1925), the illegitimate son of Amelia Jane, was brought up by his grandparents, and his aunt Hannah and uncle Philip Pinwell in Bantham, in the cottage next door but one to the Sloop Inn, and remained living there after his grand-parents, uncle, and aunt had all passed on. He worked as a farm labourer all his life. In 1871 he married Elizabeth Ann Dolton, a Bantham girl, and they had seven children: Amelia Jane (1872), Henry (1873), Bessie (1874), John Philip (1876), George Henry (1877), John Thomas (1881), and Francis George (1887).

Of these children only Bessie, John Thomas, and Francis George survived to 1891, and their mother died in 1889. George Henry married again to a widow, Keziah Perring on 8 August 1891, and they had four children by 1901: Amelia Jane (1893), Walter Norman (1895), Maude (1896) and George Henry (1899), so that in 1901 there were nine people living at the cottage, including two children of Kezia's first marriage, Frederick William Perring and Henrietta Perring.

John Thomas Moore may have felt the domestic scene was becoming rather too crowded with regular new additions to the household, and he was able to find an escape route by joining the Royal Navy as a boy seaman when he was just fifteen years old. At the completion of his "twelve" he must have volunteered for further service, as his record of duty on ships is unbroken. In 1915 he took the plunge, and married 25 year old Plymouth girl Alice Kingwell Elliott in East Stonehouse, Plymouth. Their marriage did not last long. An accident ended the life of John Thomas Moore on 8 April 1916 and Alice became a war widow. The British War Medal and Victory medals awarded posthumously to her late husband were little compensation. But she did not remain a widow for very long, marrying John C May early in 1917 at East Stonehouse, Plymouth.

His younger brother Francis George Moore, who had been an apprentice blacksmith with Mr Ingram in 1906, enlisted in 1907 and served three years before joining the reserves. In 1911 he was working as a jobbing gardener in Haslemere, Surrey. After the war he married Amy Rosina A Williams in Kingsbridge in 1919. Their daughter Eileen Frances Moore born 20th January 1921, married Leonard George Tucker in Kingsbridge. They had four sons, with three of them still living in Kingsbridge.

Frederick William Perring emigrated to Canada in June 1911, and on 15 November 1915 attested for the Canadian Overseas Expeditionary Force, claiming to have over 2 years previous military voluntary service, and again on 23 August 1916 at Regina, stating he had been honourably discharged from the 68th Battalion Canadian Expeditionary Force. He survived the war and eventually died in Davidson, Saskatchewan, on 13 August 1962.

John Thomas Dolton Moore was only fifteen years old when he first joined the Royal Navy as a boy seaman (second class) at the Devonport based training ship HMS Impregnable on 21st January 1897. He was only 5 ft 2 inches tall. By the time he had completed his training as a boy seaman (first class) he grown 3 inches to 5 ft 5 inches, and had spent time aboard HMS Thunderer, HMS Arrogant, and HMS Ramillies. On his eighteenth birthday, 16 September 1899, he signed on for twelve years as an ordinary seaman (191741), and was posted to HMS Devastation. This was the first capital ship to be built without sails, designed by Sir Edward Reed, and with turret guns mounted on top of the hull rather than inside it, allowing a 280 degree arc of fire. Its picture became very familiar throughout the UK as the ship depicted on England's Glory matchboxes.

John Thomas Moore was promoted to the rank of able-bodied seaman during his three years with this ship, and subsequently saw service in a range of Royal Navy warships, including HMS Empress of India, HMS Nile, HMS St George, HMS New Zealand, and HMS Leander, as well as shore based periods at HMS Vivid at Devonport before the outbreak of WW1. While his conduct throughout was usually "very good", it was not an entirely unblemished record, with a couple of disciplinary cases, one for refusing to obey an order. His final posting was to HMS Wallington, an Auxiliary Patrol Depot headquarters at Immingham, from which he was assigned to one of its North Sea patrol vessels HMS Avon, a much smaller vessel than the big battleships in which he had mostly served.

HMS Avon was a C class, three funnel, 30 knot destroyer assigned to the 7th Destroyer Flotilla and deployed to the Humber Patrol in September 1914 for anti-submarine and counter-mining patrols. At the beginning of April 1916 the ship was in dry dock at South Shields for repairs. The last entry on John Thomas Moore's service record is "Died 9th April 1916 in Ingham Infirmary from injuries sustained by a fall into the dock." The event was reported in the local (South Shields) Shipping Telegraph on Tuesday 11 April as follows:

> An inquest was held this afternoon at the South Shields Police Court Buildings before the Deputy Coroner, Mr R A Shepherd, concerning the death of John Thomas Moore aged 35, an able seaman, who died at the Ingham Infirmary on Sunday from injuries received by falling into a dock bottom the previous night.
>
> Henry Allen Freer, a Chief Petty Officer, gave evidence of identification. He said that on Saturday last the deceased man got leave to go on shore for an hour. Witness saw him come back at 9.30pm. He saw the deceased

appear to stagger backwards, throw up his hands, and go over the rail into the bottom of the dock. The ship's deck was quite clear at the time and there was nothing that the man could trip over. Witness had no suspicion that the man was under the influence of drink, and there was nothing whatever in his appearance to suggest such a thing. The jury returned a verdict of accidental death.

John Thomas Moore was buried at South Shields (Harton) Cemetery, and is commemorated on the Royal Navy Memorial at Plymouth, as well as on the Thurlestone War Memorial.

His younger brother, Francis George Moore, had enlisted in the Royal Engineers in 1907. As a trained reservist, he was mobilised on the outbreak of war as a Lance Corporal on 5 August 1914 and went to France with the BEF. On 1 May 1915 he was awarded the Croix de Guerre (reported in the London Gazette). This award was only instituted on 8 April 1915 to recognise acts of bravery in the face of the enemy, and Francis George Moore was one of the first recipients. On 21 December 1916 he was commended for gallantry and distinguished service in the field and Mentioned in Dispatches (London Gazette of 16 May 1917).

Moore, John Thomas Dolton - Pictures

HMS Avon - John Thomas Moore's last ship

CWGC Headstone in Harton Cemetery at South Shields

Harton Cemetery

Pope, Samuel George (1889-1916)

The family connections of Samuel George Pope can be traced back to William Pope, born in the parish of Thurlestone in 1754. He was married to Elizabeth in All Saints church on Christmas Eve 1777, and they had nine children. The third of these nine children was John Pope who married Mary Whiting on 27 June 1806, also in the parish church. After their marriage they lived in West Alvington before moving to Kingsbridge. By the census of 1841 they were living in Market Place, Dodbrooke, with their four children Betsey, Robert, Mary, and George.

By 1851 John Pope, an agricultural labourer, was widowed but remained at Market Place, Dodbrooke, with his unmarried daughter Mary, aged 26, a charwoman, and her illegitimate 3 year old son Robert Pope. John himself died within a few years, and Mary then married John Clark, a widower twenty years older than herself on Christmas Eve 1859 in All Saints, Thurlestone. They lived at Bantham, where John was an agricultural labourer, and Mary ran a small grocery shop. John Clark died in 1873 and Mary continued to run the shop until the late 1890s, but by 1901 she was on parochial relief.

Robert Pope found work as an agricultural labourer, having been a farm servant with Edwin Winzer at Buckland Park in 1871. At the age of thirty he married a Lifton girl Bessie (Betsey) Matthews from Tinhay, near Launceston, in Plymouth in 1878. After the marriage they lived next door to his widowed mother in Bantham, where they had five children, of whom four survived - Mary (b.1878), John Clark (b.1880), Hannah (b.1882), and Samuel George (b.1889). Robert died in 1900, and his mother Mary a year later, and both are buried in All Saints churchyard. Samuel George (known as George in the census returns of 1901 and 1911) continued to live with his widowed mother, and he and his elder brother worked as farm labourers locally. His sister Hannah married Philip Johnston Jeffery in 1911, and they had two children - Robert, who died in 1922 aged 6, and Blanche, born 1917, who married William Henry Bickle in September 1943.

Samuel George married Mary Ellen Bevill in 1913. She was a Loddiswell girl (one of twin sisters) who in 1911 was working as a servant, along with her younger sister Eva for the Mackenzie family farming at Buckland Parks. They had little more than a twelvemonth together before the war broke out and separated them forever. After her husband's death Mary Ellen remained a widow for five years until 1922 when she married a second time, to Haytor James Triggs Torr (aged 38, and three years her junior), the youngest son of James Torr and Charlotte Triggs, who with their eight children ran the family milling business at Clyng Mill, Kingston. Mary Ellen had no children by her second husband but remained in Kingston until her death on 12 June 1955, at the age of 74, and was buried in Kingston churchyard.

Samuel George's older sister Mary remained single all her life and died on 27 March 1955 at 8 The Cottages, Bantham, aged 77. His brother John Clark married Mary E Shore in 1920 and died in Plymouth in 1964 at the age of 84. They had one son, John William C Pope, who was born on 1st March 1925, and seems to have remained a bachelor, living for a time in Totnes, and whose death is recorded in the Teignbridge district in November 1995. Samuel George Pope enlisted at Newton Abbot shortly after war was declared in 1914 and trained with the Devonshire Regiment before being transferred to Taunton where he became Private 27061 Pope of the 7th Battalion (Prince

Albert's Own) Somerset Light Infantry formed in September 1914 as part of the Second New Army (K2). Altogether there were eighteen battalions that were formed by this regiment during the war. This new battalion immediately went into training at Woking attached to 61ˢᵗ Brigade, 20ᵗʰ (Light) Division, and then moved away to Whitley Camp at Godalming. In March 1915 there were further moves; first to Amesbury and secondly to Larkhill, where the battalion was mobilised for war and shipped across the English Channel to Boulogne, landing there on 23 July 1915. Over the next five months they were engaged in trench familiarisation and further training in the Fleurbaix area.

In 1916 the 7ᵗʰ battalion was involved in many actions that took place on the Western Front throughout the year. These included the battles of Mount Sorrel, Delville Wood, Guillemont, Flers-Courcelette, Morval, and Le Transloy. Sadly, no service record for Samuel George Pope remains extant with the exception of his medal roll card, so it is not known if, when, or where he was personally involved in front line fighting. The major battles of the year had been concluded, or shelved by the end of November 1916 as winter weather began to take hold.

If Samuel George Pope may be considered fortunate to have survived a whole year of the Western Front conflict, his luck ran out on 13ᵗʰ December 1916 when he was killed in action. His body was never recovered to enable interment in a specific local cemetery, and so he is remembered on the Thiepval Memorial, Somme, which was constructed to record the names of those that lost their lives in the Battle of the Somme that have no known grave. It carries the names of more than 72,000 officers and men of the United Kingdom and South Africa who died in the Somme battle sector before 20 March 1918. Over 90% of those commemorated died between July and November 1916.

Samuel George Pope is also remembered on the Thurlestone War Memorial, and recorded in the Memorial Book of Remembrance for those who lost their lives while serving in Somerset County Units. The book is leather-bound with 220 vellum pages and is held in a glass case in St Martin's Chapel in Wells Cathedral and contains a Roll of Honour of nearly 11,300 men. The title page carries the following tribute by the Rt. Rev. George Wyndham Kennion, the Bishop of Bath and Wells:

> "All whose names are inscribed in the pages of this Roll of Honour were numbered among those who at the call of King and Country left all that was dear to them, endured hardship, faced danger, and finally passed out of the sight of men by the path of duty and self-sacrifice, giving up their own lives that others might live in freedom. Let those who come after see to it that their names be not forgotten."

Samuel's older brother John Clark Pope, enlisted on 9 June 1917, six months after Samuel's death, as a Private in the newly formed Agricultural Company Labour Corps posted to Devizes and Exeter. This Corps was for men who were medically unfit to serve at the Front - and John suffered from tuberculosis. Despite this illness, he survived the war, married, and reached the age of 84 before his death in 1964.

Pope, Samuel George - Pictures

Samuel George Pope

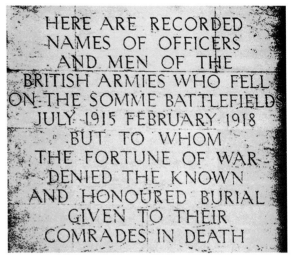

HERE ARE RECORDED
NAMES OF OFFICERS
AND MEN OF THE
BRITISH ARMIES WHO FELL
ON THE SOMME BATTLEFIELDS
JULY 1915 FEBRUARY 1918
BUT TO WHOM
THE FORTUNE OF WAR
DENIED THE KNOWN
AND HONOURED BURIAL
GIVEN TO THEIR
COMRADES IN DEATH

Thiepval Memorial Dedication

Medals awarded to Samuel George Pope

Somerset Light Infantry Badge

Wood, William Ernest (1867-1915)

James Wood (1781-18) was born in Chivelstone. In 1803 he married Grace Cranch, born in South Pool, and their family of five children were brought up there. Their son William Wood (1804-1874) worked as an agricultural labourer and lived all his life in various properties in South Pool. He married Sarah Evans in 1828 and they had thirteen children between 1828 and 1851 - seven boys and six girls. A remarkable photograph of this remarkable family survives, and is shown overleaf. The sixth of these children was Peter Wood (1843-1911). He earned his living as an agricultural labourer, mainly in the South Pool area, and married Ann Quick in 1865. They had eight sons and a daughter. Peter died in 1911 at Dittisham and is buried in St Cyriac churchyard, South Pool. The fifth of their nine children was named William Ernest Wood, born 31st May 1867 at South Pool.

William Ernest Wood grew up in South Pool, and began work as a labourer. He decided to join the Royal Navy and signed on for 12 years in April 1898. After another six years as a bachelor he married Edith Louise Rowe in 1904 and they had two children - Ronald Peter, born in 1907 at Devonport, and Marjorie Alice, born in 1909 at West Alvington. During his twelve years in the Navy, William served as a Stoker on numerous ships, and completed his service as a Leading Stoker in April 1910, at which point he was transferred to the Royal Fleet Reserve at Devonport.

On leaving the Navy in 1910, William secured the job of Steward at the Thurlestone Golf Club (which had opened in 1897), and was living with his family in one of the Church Cottages in Fore Street in 1911 at the time of the census. His wife Edith did not survive that year, however, and was buried in Thurlestone churchyard. Peter married again in June 1914. His new wife was a local girl Mary Emily (Edith) Stone, but they did not have long together before William was called up from the Reserve on 2nd August 1914, and was killed in action on 13th May 1915.

His widow Mary died in March 1978 in Torbay, having never remarried. His son Peter Ronald died in March 1981 in Plymouth. His daughter Marjorie Alice married Maurice Noyce in 1941 at Kingsbridge.

William's youngest brother, William Henry Wood, married Sarah Ellen Rendle and lived in Modbury. During the war he was a Private in the 1st Battalion Duke of Cornwall's Light Infantry and died in Flanders on 13 April 1918. He is remembered on the Ploegsteert Memorial and also on the Modbury War Memorial.

Traditionally, many young men enlisted in the Services as a means of escape from a working life as an agricultural labourer with little prospect of advancement, and the Royal Navy base at Plymouth was conveniently to hand for men of the South Hams. William Ernest Wood decided to make a career at sea, and signed on in April 1898 for twelve years. He became a Stoker, and served on various ships between spells of duty at HMS Vivid II, the shore-based establishment at Plymouth and forerunner of HMS Drake.

These ships included HMS Hermes (a Highflyer-class cruiser), HMS Blenheim (a Blake-class armoured cruiser), HMS Vulcan (a depot ship), HMS Orion (an armoured corvette), and HMS Royal Arthur (an Edgar-class armoured cruiser). During his entire service he displayed exemplary conduct and was of "very good" character throughout. He was promoted to Leading Stoker, and completed his "twelve" on 7th April 1910, transferring into the Royal Fleet Reserve the following day.

William was called up from the Reserve on 2 August 1914 (two days prior to Britain's declaring war against Germany) and served on the battleship HMS Goliath until the end of the year, attaining the rank of Petty Officer. He rejoined the ship on 2 February 1915.

In April 1915 HMS Goliath was ordered to the Dardanelles to join the Mediterranean Fleet as part of the ill-fated Gallipoli campaign of 1915-1916. The plan, put forward by Winston Churchill, was for British and French Forces to capture Istanbul, capital of the Ottoman Empire, thus gaining a sea route to Russia. The action took place in the entrance to the Dardanelles Strait, the exit from the Sea of Marmara and Istanbul to the Mediterranean Sea. The Royal Navy was to land an amphibious force on the Dardanelles peninsula, silence the Turkish forts and use its ships to force through the Strait. Unfortunately, intelligence had not shown that the Turks had mined the Straits.

HMS Goliath and HMS Cornwallis (a Duncan-class battleship) were ordered to support the French general in command and on the night of 12-13 May 1915, HMS Goliath anchored in Morto Bay off Cape Helles, together with HMS Cornwallis and five destroyers, in foggy conditions. Around 1.00am the Turkish torpedo-boat-destroyer Muavenet-I Milliye, manned by a combined Turkish and German crew, eluded both the destroyers Beagle and Bulldog and closed on the battleships.

She fired two torpedoes which struck HMS Goliath in quick succession causing a massive explosion. The first torpedo hit close to her forward 12 inch gun turret and she began to list to port. The second torpedo struck close to her forward funnel. The ship continued to turn over, and was nearly on her beam ends when a third torpedo hit near her aft 12 inch gun turret. She turned turtle, briefly floated upside down, and then sank bow first, taking down with her 570 of her 750-strong crew. William was one of them.

Petty Officer William Ernest Wood is commemorated on the Plymouth Naval Memorial on The Hoe, and also on the War Memorial at South Pool, the place of his birth. His name was added to the gravestone of his first wife in the churchyard of All Saints, Thurlestone, in remembrance.

The Gallipoli operation proved a costly failure, with losses in the Dardanelles totalling some 220,000 Allied casualties. Churchill was demoted from First Lord of the Admiralty, resigned from the government in November 1915, and departed for the Western Front, where he commanded the 6th battalion of the Royal Scots Fusiliers from 1st January to 6th May 1916, when he was recalled to London.

Wood, William Ernest - Pictures

**Memorial to William Ernest Wood on the headstone in All Saints Churchyard
- the grave of his first wife Edith Louisa who died July 16th 1911**

HMS Goliath

Chapter 4

The Survivors

Axworthy, William Henry (1877-1946)

The information about the family background of the William Henry Axworthy resident in Thurlestone in 1901 and 1911 and 1915 is somewhat fragmentary and elusive, and a bit of a genealogical puzzle. He appears to have been the grandson of Philip John Pedler Axworthy, a gunsmith and tidewaiter (customs officer) born in Poplar, London, who married a Mary Ann Toms, from Plymouth, on 1 Dec 1841 in St Andrews Church, Plymouth (though his occupation is given as tailor, the same as hers). Philip was the son of William Axworthy, a Bideford born tailor who had his business in the Strand, London, in 1815 and whose children were born in London, before they all relocated to Plymouth.

In the 1851 census Philip and Mary Ann live at 33 Frankfort Street, Plymouth with their three children Fanny (8), Cordelia (6), and Philip (4). Philip's occupation given as tidewaiter. In the 1861 census they have moved to Raleigh Street, next door but one from the Victory of China beerhouse, and after a gap of 13 years another son Reginald (10 months) has been added to the family. After the death of husband Philip in 1864 Q4, the widow Mary Ann Axworthy (tailoress) and her family are boarders at 6 Henry Street in the 1871 census, with the exception of daughter Cordelia (absent) and son Philip who had died in 1866.

However, Cordelia has returned to the family in 1881 when they are now living at 10 Summerland Place, St Andrew, Plymouth, where Mary Ann Axworthy, widow of Philip, has a boarding-house at which her two daughters Fanny and Cordelia were dressmakers, son Reginald (21) a billiard marker, and new grandchildren Rosina (6) and William (4) were scholars. The parents of these two grandchildren are not identified, and the assumption is that each is a child of an unmarried daughter of widow Mary Ann Axworthy, either Fanny or Cordelia. Ten years later in the 1891 census the family are no longer living together. Cordelia died 1885. Fanny died 1900.

If William Henry Axworthy's mother had indeed been Cordelia, and his father a sailor drowned at sea, it would certainly fit the entry found in the Thurlestone baptismal register for 1887, where a boy of this name was baptised (his age believed to be about 9) with the annotations "father sailor drowned at sea, mother also dead".

Thurlestone Baptism Register Entry 27 March 1887

Who was looking after the boy, or who brought him to Thurlestone to be baptised, is not recorded, and he does not appear in the 1891 Thurlestone census. A possible sighting for William Henry Axworthy in 1891, however, is in 13 Cromwell Road, Sutton, Plymouth, where he lives in a single room, works as a labourer, and gives his age as 18 and birthplace as Wembury. Confirmation was subsequently found on his birth certificate, which shows Cordelia as his mother, no father, and a birthdate of 27 March 1877 at 10 Summerland Place, Plymouth.

The Naval Records show that a William Henry Axworthy signed on for 12 years in the RN at Devonport 21 Feb 1898 as a Stoker, no. 287353, giving a birth date of 20 March 1875, and served on the newly launched dreadnought HMS Niobe from 6 Dec 1898 to 9 Nov 1900, when he was invalided out. The vessel had been involved in the South African War and he was awarded Queens South Africa Medal No. 3612.

HMS Niobe

Queen's South Africa Medal

He next appears as a gardener boarding with Bessie Pope and her sons at Thurlestone in the 1901 census, aged 24. He then married Susan Ellen Elliott of Buckland (1874-1961) in 1910, and they are living there with father-in-law William Elliott in 1911, when William Henry is working as a mason's labourer.

They appear on the Electoral Roll in Thurlestone for 1915 (though not for 1913 or 1914), and again in 1918, when William Henry is absent (on naval/military service). This is when he served in WW1, though unfortunately his service records for the period cannot be found. Even so, he would have been entitled to the British War and Victory medals. He returned safely and continued to live in West Buckland through 1919 to 1929, after which he and Susan Ellen moved to Bantham., where they appear in the 1939 census at 5 Bantham Cottages and WH worked as a labourer for Evans Estates.

William Henry Axworthy died in Plymouth in 1946 Q4, and his widow Susan Ellen Axworthy died in Launceston in 1961.

The Beer Family

William Beer (1861-1942), the well-known Kingsbridge solicitor, built Mollycombe as one of the first of the "new" houses in Thurlestone in 1902, though it seems to have been used as a second or holiday home. In 1859 his father, William H Beer, a Kingsbridge merchant, had married Fanny Elizabeth Hurrell, the daughter of Robert Hurrell (1810-1883) and the 48 year old Frances Sarah Square (1811-1895) so he was well connected to the Brunskill family. Their son William was educated at Oxford University and qualified as a

Mollycombe

solicitor. In 1902 his elder son William Robert was 7, and his younger son George Hurrell Bentham was just 3. It seems very likely that the boys spent a lot of holiday time at Mollycombe, enjoying the beaches and the seaside, perhaps even attending church service on Sundays. So one can understand why Rev Coope included William Robert Beer on his list of parishioners who served in WW1, but not why he did not also include younger brother George Hurrell Bentham, who also saw military service. Both brothers are therefore included here.

Beer, William Robert (1894-1983)

Born 17 Sep 1894, at Dodbrooke, the first son of William Beer and Annie Beatrice Bentham. The Beer family lived at Victoria Place in 1891 but had moved to Mill St by 1901. William Robert was educated at Blundell's School, Tiverton, where he appears as a boarder in the 1911 census. After Blundell's he continued his education at Wellington College.

On 19th April, 1914 the London Gazette announced that William Robert Beer (late Cadet, Blundell's School Contingent, Junior Division, Officers Training Corps) was appointed to be Second Lieutenant in the 5th (Prince of Wales's) Battalion, The Devonshire Regiment. Two years later, on 14th November, 1916, the London Gazette announced that "The KING has approved the admission of the undermentioned gentlemen cadet from the Cadet College, Wellington, to the Unattached List for the Indian Army: *To be 2nd Lieutenant.* William Robert Beer." A fortnight later, on 27th November, 1916, 2nd Lt. William Robert Beer was attached to the 7th Gurkha Rifles.

34th Poona Horse Badge

His Medal Roll Card shows that he was a Lt. in the 34th Prince Albert Victor's Own Poona Horse of the Indian Army, a regiment which was sent to France at the outbreak of war and fought on the Western Front, their first action being the First Battle of

Ypres. On 2 November 1914 the regiment was sent to reinforce the 2nd Gurkhas in the Neuve Chapelle sector on arrival they discovered that the Gurkhas defences had been breached and overrun. The Poona Horse was asked to recapture the position. The Regiment launched a counterattack in daylight and without any artillery support. The Commanding Officer Lieutenant Colonel Swanston who was leading the attack was killed. In France the regiment would be involved in the Battle of Givenchy, Battle of La Basse, Battle of Armentiers, Battle of the Somme (1916), Battle of Flers–Courcelette and Battle of Cambrai (1917). In February 1918, the Poona Horse and all the other Indian cavalry regiments in France were deployed to Palestine to join General Allenby's forces. Lt William Robert Beer thus qualified for the 1914/15 Star as well as the British War and Victory medals. He stayed on in the Indian Army after the war and was made Captain in 1922.

Returned to the UK, where he married Elsie Clara Rainey (nee Bowles) at Paddington in June 1934. He returned to Kingsbridge where he practised as a solicitor, living at Widdicombe House in 1939. His wife died 25 March 1966. William Robert Beer's final home was at Blue Waters, Churston Ferrers, Brixham, Devon, where he died on 28 April 1983, aged 89.

George Hurrell Bentham Beer (1898-1980)

Born 27 June 1898 in Kingsbridge, and educated at Blundell's School, Tiverton. Deciding early to become a professional soldier he attended Royal Military College and was gazetted 2nd Lt in the Devonshire Regiment on 16 August 1916, Lt in Royal Tank Corps 16 Feb 1918. Served in Mesopotamia from Nov 1917 to 31 Oct 1818. Awarded British War & Victory Medals.

His service after the war took him to West Africa, where he served with the West African Frontier Force from 1 June 1921 to 25 Sep 1924; and also with R.W.A.F.F. from 26 June 1927 to 14 Sep 1928. He was promoted to Captain on 26 April 1928. Back in the UK a year later he married Margaret Gilroy on 5 Oct 1929 at Hemel Hempstead, Herts. Served on the North West Frontier in India 1936-1937, and was made Major on 14 Oct 1937. Retired with the rank of Lt. Colonel. Died at his home at Home Orchard, Bovey Tracey on 10 Nov 1980.

Royal Tank Regt Badge

Bonnor, Charles Edward (1887-1948)

Son of George Bonnor (1856-1939) and Francis Jane Barnes (1850-1935) who were married in Burghill, Herefordshire in 1881. Charles Edward was their second son, following George William (1882-1927) and preceding their daughter Mary Elizabeth (1885-1962). She was followed by a third son, Frederick (1887-). Charles Edward left home after school and became a bank clerk, and in 1901 was in lodgings in 8 Daneville Road, Camberwell, London. Ten years later he is still a bank clerk, and still single, but now boarding at 79 Stockwell Park Road in Lambeth. At that time, his parents were living at Hill Top Farm, Rochford, Tenbury, Worcs. with son Frederick working the farm, and daughter Mary helping in the house.

In 1915 George acquired the freehold of Buckland Parks, and lived there with his wife and daughter until 1920. in 1915, leaving in 1919. Meantime, Charles Edward attested in London on 21 July 1915 and joined the Army Service Corps to be trained as a motor driver and given the number DM2 112535. He served with 244 company ASC served in the Mediterranean, and Salonica, but suffered from Myalgia and was treated in No. 31 Casualty Clearing station and the Hospital ship Essequibo.

H.M. HOSPITAL SHIP "ESSEQUIBO"   (*Publication Officially sanctioned by the Lords Commissioners of the Admiralty*)

He was finally discharged as no longer fit for military service on 29 November 1918. Awarded British War and Victory medals in 1920. No Bonnor resident in Thurlestone after 1920.

Died 24 April 1948 at 48 Whiteford Road, Plymouth.

Broad, George (1890-1972)

George was born 2 May 1890 at Tideford, Cornwall, the first of the three sons of Samuel John Broad (1861-1933), blacksmith, and Elizabeth Pound (1861-1941). A second son, Samuel John, was born in 1893. Samuel and Elizabeth moved their family to East Buckland in 1894/5 and it was here that daughter Mary was born (1895) and followed by Alfred (1902) to complete the family. Samuel was now earning a living as a land agent rather than a blacksmith.

On his eighteenth birthday George made his way to Devonport and signed up for twelve years in the Royal Navy with the service number 272223. With his background experience in metalworking he trained as an Engine Room Artificer, in which capacity he served in HMS New Zealand (1910-1911) and then on HMS Cumberland (1911-1916).

ERA Badge

HMS Cumberland was one of 10 Monmouth-class armoured cruisers built for the Royal Navy in the first decade of the 20th century. She was assigned to the 2nd Cruiser Squadron of the Channel Fleet upon her completion in 1903. After a refit in 1907–08 she became a training ship in the Home Fleet. She was sent to West Africa after the beginning of WW1 in August 1914 and captured 10 German merchant ships in September. For the rest of the war HMS Cumberland was deployed on convoy escort duties and patrolling for German commerce raiders.

Figure 2 **HMS Cumberland**

After leaving HMS Cumberland in 1916 George was assigned to training duties at HMS Vivid and was eventually demobbed on 31 Jan 1919. His entitlement to the Star, British War and Victory medals was confirmed when he was working on HMS Hawkins, a new cruiser launched in 1917, prior to its commissioning in July 1919.

George died Sept 1972 (Kingsbridge).

HMS Hawkins

Brunskill, Hubert Fawcett (1873-1951)

The life and family background of Hubert Fawcett Brunskill have been covered in an earlier chapter The Brunskill Legacy. His various duties and responsibilities within and around the county of Devon precluded him from taking up a full-time military role immediately in the armed services. He was an attesting Officer at Kingsbridge in May 1915. Nevertheless he first joined the 5th Volunteer Battalion of the Devonshire Regiment and was given the rank of Captain. Later he transferred to the Royal Wiltshire Yeomanry as 2nd Lt on 18 July 1915, and by the end of the war in 1918 he was listed as a Captain in the Royal Wiltshire Yeomanry.

His medal roll card indicates that he served with the British Expeditionary Force from 3 June 1916, and was awarded the British War and Victory medals, as well as being

Medal Roll Card for Hubert Fawcett Brunskill

eligible for the Silver Wound Badge (5.07.18), though this last award is not confirmed in the Ancestry record of Silver Wound Badges issued.

Bryant, George Alfred (1871-1936)

George Alfred Bryant was born 5 October 1871 at Millbrook, Portsea Island, but his young life was disrupted when his mother died before he was 8 years old, and in the 1881 census he was a schoolboy having to live with his widowed father George Bryant in the workhouse at South Stoneham, Hants. George wasted no time once his eighteenth birthday came round and enlisted in the Royal Navy on 5 Oct 1889 at Portsmouth for 12 years, with the service number 40366, having already spent time in the mercantile training ship HMS Warspite. He served in a wide range of ships as an able seaman before promotion to leading seaman in 1900.

George Alfred Bryant married Fanny Lawrence, daughter of Thomas Restell Lawrence and Thirza Bussell on Portsea Island in 1900 Q1 (2b, 660). Their daughter Elsie M F Bryant was born 4 months before the 1901 census, in which she and her mother are staying with her parents at 46 Monmouth Road, Portsmouth.

On completion of his "12" he then joined the Coastguard Service, and progressed from boatman to Chief Petty Officer at stations along the south coast, including Challaborough (1909) and Hope Cove (1910-1914). In 1911 the family were at the Bantham Coastguard station, and that census reveals that two other children had born since 1901 had not survived. A new son William George was born at Bantham and baptised at All Saints, Thurlestone on 16 Nov 1913.

George Alfred re-enlisted in the Royal Navy in August 1914, and spent five years as a Leading seaman and then Petty Officer aboard the battleship HMS Collingwood, taking part in the battle of Jutland. HMS Collingwood was a St Vincent-class dreadnought battleship built for the Royal Navy and commissioned in April 1910. She spent her whole career assigned to the Home and Grand Fleets and often served as a flagship. Prince Albert (later King George VI) was assigned to the ship on 15 September 1913 and spent several years aboard her before and during WW1 He was aboard at the Battle of Jutland in May 1916 when HMS Collingwood was in the middle of the battle-line and lightly damaged a German battle-cruiser. Shortly afterwards, during the attack of the German destroyers, the ship fired her main armament at a damaged destroyer without success and dodged two torpedoes that missed by 10 yards behind and 30 yards in front. This was the last time she fired her guns during the battle.

HMS Collingwood

In 1919 George Alfred returned to Hope Cove Coastguard and on 1 May 1919 transferred into the Coastguard Service. George and Fanny appear in the 1919 Electoral Roll for Thurlestone, but then moved on as George was relocated to other Coastguard stations. He eventually retired back to his native Portsmouth where he died in December 1936 aged 64.

Burns, William John (1877-1945)

Born at Hope Cove, Devon on 4 September 1877, the fifth child of James Burns, resident Coastguard at Hope Cove, and Elizabeth Holmes. In the 1891 census the family is still living at Hope Cove, though father James is now a retired Naval pensioner.

William John could not wait till his eighteenth birthday to join the Navy and enlisted at Devonport on 3 October 1894 (giving a false age) for 12 years. Given the service number 278187 he served as a Stoker in ironclads and dreadnoughts, including HMS Royal Sovereign in the Mediterranean Fleet. Completed his 12 years and joined the Fleet reserve in 19 Oct 1906. By then he had married Edith Mary Brooking (born 16 March 1877 at Stokenham) at West Alvington Parish Church on 21 June 1899, and they had produced three daughters, Winifred May (born April 1902 at Mutley, Plymouth), Edith Irene (born 7 August 1906 at West Alvington), and Katie Doris (born September 1907 at Churchstow), and were living at Buckland Parks at the time of the 1911 census, with William John working as a farm labourer in 1911.

However, the call of the sea seems to have been too strong and William John decided to re-enlist on 30 Oct 1911 for another term of 5 years. However, with the war intervening, he served right through WW1 until being demobbed on 8 May 1919. He served briefly in HMS Cumberland before joining HMS Virginian, an armed merchant cruiser with the 10th Cruiser Squadron on Northern Patrol and North Atlantic convoys. He was awarded Star, British War, and Victory medals.

HMS Virginian

The family remained in West Buckland, and feature on the electoral rolls through to 1921. Eldest daughter Winifred May married a Kingsbridge WW1 veteran Arthur Reginald Carne (private in the Devonshires and then the Machine Gun Corps) in March 1925. Second daughter Edith Irene married a William G Pepler (born 19 January 1903) in Kingsbridge in 1939/40. In the 1939 census they were living at 8 Seaview Terrace, Thurlestone. William John is described as "disabled in the last war", and the recently married Peplers are living with them, with William G working as a gardener.

William John died in 1945, his wife Edith Mary surviving him until September 1959.

Campbell, Hugh Elphinstone (1874-1943)

Hugh Elphinstone Campbell was born on 30 June 1873, with the birth registered in Croydon in July 1873, and baptised at St Peter's, Mitcham, Surrey, on 28 July 1874. He was the son of Robert Campbell, barrister (1832-1912) and Marian Lucy Ilbert (1844-1938), and younger brother of Ilbert Lewis Campbell (1872-1939). Marian Lucy Ilbert was the elder daughter of Rev Peregrine Ilbert of Thurlestone.

Hugh was educated at Marlborough College (from which he was expelled for shooting one of Lord Ailesbury's stags in Savernake Forest), and Edinburgh University (1890). After University he went out to China, where he traded as a silk merchant, and became managing director of the firm Ilbert & Co, Merchants, of 22 Kiangse Road, Shanghai, with a long background of business in China.

Hugh married Ethel Marion Warren (1880-1951), daughter of Sir Pelham Warren KCMG, Consul-General at Shanghai, on 10 Oct 1905. Their first son, Hugh Donnithorne Campbell was born in Thurlestone and baptised at All Saints on 7 June 1908. However, after their return to China the boy died on 8 September 1910 at Port Edward, Weihaiwei.

Ethel Marion returned to the UK at the beginning of the war and appears on the Thurlestone Electoral registers from 1918-1921.

Hugh continued to work in China and was gazetted 2nd Lt in the Labour Corps on 3 Aug 1917. He was appointed to 110 Co. Chinese Labour Corps as a 2nd Lt, and served in France with them from 27 October 1917 to 24 February 1919. He was awarded the British War and Victory medals.

The Chinese Labour Corps, after much political fence-sitting by the Chinese Government, eventually supplied some 140,000 workers to serve in France, usually routed through Canada in uncomfortable railway wagons. After their arrival in France they were sent to ports, mines, farms and munitions factories. They repaired roads, transported supplies, and dug trenches near the front lines, risking German artillery shells, and provided vital support for depleted front-line troops during a critical stage of the war. Many stayed on after the war and settled in European countries.

After the death of their first son, Hugh Elphinstone and Ethel Marion had three more sons. Robert Elphinstone Campbell (1912-1968) was followed by Peter Donald Campbell (1916-1942), and Alan Hugh Campbell (1919-2007). Hugh had retired from running the family business, Ilbert & Co, in China, after the end of the war and had bought and rebuilt a large house, with a notable sub-tropical garden, called Combe Royal, in South Devon, near Kingsbridge. When Ilbert & Co ran into difficulties in the late 1920s, the family's affluent lifestyle underwent some contraction and they had to leave Combe Royal.

After leaving Combe Royal they returned to Bantham House, Bantham, where Hugh Elphinstone died on 17 Jan 1943. His widow Ethel Marion lived on at Sunny Ridge in Thurlestone and died 12 April 1951 in South Hams Hospital.

Coleman, Henry (1865-1934)

Henry Coleman was born at Antony, Cornwall, on 7 August 1865, a younger son of John (an excavator) and Mary Coleman. He joined the Royal Navy as a Boy seaman at Devonport on 5 January 1881 and some of his early training was aboard HMS Implacable, which had been originally a French ship of the line, the Duquay-Trouin, launched in 1800. She had fought at, and survived, the Battle of Trafalgar only to be captured by the British at the subsequent Battle of Cape Ortegal.

The Stern of HMS Implacable on display at the National Maritime Museum

After completing training he signed on at Devonport in 1883 on his eighteenth birthday, as No. 115307 and served continuously until 1893, including two years aboard the battleship HMS Howe, rising from ordinary seaman to leading seaman. He then then joined the Coastguard service, serving at Portloe, Cawsand, and Challaborough until Sep 1908, when he was transferred to the Reserve.

Henry Coleman married Annie Sleep, a Liskeard girl, at Stoke Damerel in 1890, and they appear in the 1891 census living at 17 Duke Street, Stoke Damerel. By 1901 they were resident in Bantham, at the Coastguard station. After retirement from the Coastguards in 1908 Henry was taken on by Charles Chantry Inchbald of The Grey House to act as his caretaker, and they appear in the 1911 census at the Lodge. During the period up to the war Henry taught the Inchbald boys all about sailing and handling boats, and the local waters.

Rejoined 2 Aug 1914 before the outbreak of war on, and served as PO (training) at Devonport until invalided out with chronic rheumatic arthritis on 29 Nov 1917. He was awarded the Star, British War, and Victory medals.

Henry Coleman's death was registered at Kingsbridge in 1934.

The Connolly Family

Patrick Connolly and his wife Lucy Isabel (nee Kenningham) were both "incomers" when they arrived in Thurlestone to take up the positions of Postmaster and Primary School teacher respectively. Patrick was Irish and a Roman Catholic, while Lucy was the daughter of Joseph Kenningham, who had moved from Hull in Yorkshire to become a lay vicar in the choir of Salisbury Cathedral. Lucy was baptised in the cathedral in 1859, and was educated at a private school in Wells. She took up a post as a certificated schoolmistress in Salcombe in 1881.

Lucy Isabel Kenningham married Patrick Connolly in 1895, at both Kingsbridge and Totnes. Their two sons were born at Hope Cove and then the family moved from Hope Cove to Thurlestone in 1897, when Lucy was appointed the teacher at the primary school in Fore Street, and two years later Patrick became the Postmaster at Thurlestone following the installation of the Telegraph service. Sadly, Patrick died in September 1900 in hospital after an operation, and was buried in Thurlestone churchyard on 13th September, the service being conducted by the Roman Catholic vicar of Dartmouth. Three days later their new baby daughter Margaret Eileen was baptised in Thurlestone church by Rev Coope on 16th September.

It was a traumatic introduction to the village, and no easy task for a widow with a new-born baby and two young boys aged 3 and 4 to look after, as well as cope with a full-time teaching post at the Primary School. Lucy was clearly very capable and well-regarded, for she was still teaching at Thurlestone in the 1911 census, and daughter Margaret Eileen was a scholar living at home. But the two boys had left home the year before to join the Merchant Navy in Cardiff as indentured apprentices to a Charles Nicholson. Lucy was still living in Thurlestone in 1915 but had moved to Bantham in 1918 and was there in 1919 and 1920 but not in 1921, when she had reached retirement age for lady teachers.

Lucy Connolly (top right) and her Thurlestone pupils c. 1904

Connolly, Frederick John (1897- ?)

Frederick John Connolly

Frederick John Connolly, the younger son, was born on 24 February 1897 at Hope Cove, and moved later that year to Thurlestone with the rest of the family. Attended the primary school where his mother taught, and in July 1910, three months after his elder brother left home to join the merchant navy, he followed him to Cardiff and was indentured as a seaman apprentice to the same mariner, Charles Nicholson, for 3 years on 26 July 1910.

He made rapid progress. By 1915 he had achieved his 3rd mate's ticket, and served in that capacity on the Anglo-Mexican (125666), the Boynton (101918), and the Tayabi (96383). He was awarded his 2nd mate's ticket on 17 December 1915. Frederick John then served on the SS Corby (115220), and went on to gain his 1st Mate's ticket on 30 July 1918, finally achieving his Masters on 2 February 1920, while aboard the SS Larchol (140323), a 210 ft oil tanker completed in August 1917 by Lobnitz & Co, Renfrew for the Admiralty, and registered in London. It served as a Fleet Auxiliary vessel. He was awarded the Mercantile Marine Medal and the British War Medal after the war was over.

Frederick John married Sophia Roose (b. 6 June 1897) from 33 Grenville Road, Plymouth in St Jude's church, Plymouth on 13 August 1918. They had a son Frederick Roose Connolly, born 1921, who joined the clerical class at the Admiralty in 1938 and who married Doreen Vera Mary Grimshaw at St Mary's, Plympton on 2 June 1956. He died 4 June 1994, at 37 Minster Way, Bath. Their son Richard J Connolly was born at Bath in Sept 1960.

Master's Certificate

Patrick Joseph Connolly (1896 -?)

Patrick Joseph Connolly

Patrick Joseph Connolly, the elder son, was born on at Hope Cove on 1 January 1896. When the family moved to Thurlestone he attended the Primary school where his mother was the schoolmistress, and lived at the schoolhouse with his mother, brother, and sister in 1901 after the death of his father.

At the age of fourteen he left Thurlestone for Cardiff where he became an indentured seaman apprentice on 22 April 1910 to a Charles Nicholson for 3 years. At the beginning of 1915 he was serving as 4th Mate aboard the SS Chopra (121321) until July, during which time he was awarded his certificate for 2nd Mate on 14 Jan 1915. He then served as 3rd Mate on the SS Colaba (121287), a coaster with a crew of 12, until the end of the year. Seven years later he qualified for his certificate as 1st Mate on 14 Jan 1922, and finally achieved his Master's ticket on 15 May 1927.

He was awarded the Mercantile Marine Medal and the British War Medal in 1922.

Mercantile Marine Medal

Master's Certificate

Coope, Arthur Egerton (1889-1981)

Son of Elizabeth Jenkinson and Rev Frank Egerton Coope, born on 10 October 1888 at Eastbourne where his father was chaplain at All Saints Convalescent Hospital before his appointment as curate of Littlehampton.

Educated at St. Edward's School and Keble College, Oxford, Arthur was resident in 1911 at Thurlestone where his father was Rector. He graduated in the summer of 1911, and entered the Colonial office as an Eastern Cadet. Later that year he sailed for Penang on 17 November 1911 aboard the SS Malwa. Under the terms of the Anglo-Siamese Treaty of 1909, the Thais relinquished their claims over Kelantan to Great Britain, and Kelantan thus became one of the Unfederated Malay States with a British Adviser. Arthur became one of the first British Advisers in Kelantan, the northernmost Malay state.

He joined the Malay Volunteer Rifles but no record of his war service 1914-1918 has been found. However, it would not have been without incident. There were a number of local uprisings, disturbances, and rebellions in this period, and Arthur would almost certainly have seen action during these events. Unfortunately, no details are available.

He was appointed Magistrate in 1928 at Ipoh, a city with average monthly temperatures of 82°F, and average monthly rainfall of 8 inches. and Collector of Land Revenue of Penang, Malaysia in 1930s. Arthur became engaged to Mary Winifrede Mills (born 1909, the daughter of Charles Harold and Eugenie Mills of Callencroft, Mumbles, South Wales) on 16 March 1931 in Singapore, and they returned to England where they were married a month later at St Barnabus Church, Kensington, London, on 15 April 1931. He was 42, and she was 21, living at 129 Mount Street, London, W14, and his father Rev Frank Egerton Coope officiated at the wedding.

In 1935 he was awarded the Kings Silver Jubilee Medal. Later, he lived at 9 Netherhall Gardens, Camden, Hampstead with brother JFE Coope and at 62 Long Lane Ickenham Uxbridge in 1953. He died in 28 November 1981 still at 62 Long Lane, Ickenham, Uxbridge. His former wife, Mary Winifrede, died one month later, on 30 December 1981, though by this date her surname had changed to Hall, which indicates that they had been divorced.

King's Silver Jubilee Medal

Cope, Charles (1892 -?)

Born in Ebrington Street, Kingsbridge 1892, son of George Cope, a merchant seaman and master of his own boat, and his wife Mary. Charles worked as a postboy, and then a labourer and was living with James Morgan, a market carrier, in Buckland in the 1911 census. Charles would have learned how to handle horses in this role, and this might have prompted his next move.

Charles decided to become a regular soldier and enlisted in the Royal Artillery at Totnes on 5 Dec 1912 (giving his occupation as a groom), and was given army number 1008651. Served as a gunner in India early in 1914 and then saw service in France in 1914,16,17,19. In 1914 he wrote home letters from France to his father, and some of these were published in the Kingsbridge Gazette. After his long service in France, Charles was one of the lucky ones to come through the conflict unscathed, and was transferred to section B army reserve 31 May 1919.

WW1 Royal Field Artillery Gun Team

He married Mary Bain Tappenden (born 28 Feb 1900 and baptised Sherford on 13 September 1908) on 9 October 1920 at Kingsbridge. They had two children, Charles T (born 19.5.21) and Eileen M (born 2.6.22) at Kingsbridge. Charles completed his twelve years military service and was discharged from the army on 4 December 1924. He was awarded the 1914 Star, British War, and Victory medals. (Royal Artillery Attestations).

In 1926 and 1931 Charles and Mary were living at 1 Church Steps, Fore Street, Kingsbridge. In the 1939 census they had moved and were living as lodgers at Brentmoor House, Shipley Bridge in Totnes, the home (now demolished) of William Ambrose Pritchard, and Charles was working as a lorry driver.

Brentmoor House, Shipley Bridge

Mary Bain died in December 1981.

Cox, Gerald Aylmer (1863-1929)

Gerald Aylmer Cox was born in Portsmouth in June 1863, the son of General Edmund Henry Cox RMA (1829-1893), whose family home was in Hampshire but who moved to Uffculme, Devon, in 1891. Gerald followed his father into the Royal Marines, and was gazetted as Lieutenant in the Royal Marine Light Infantry on 5 September 1882. Ten years later he was promoted to Captain, and two years later he married Dorothy Rebecca Mahon on 19 April 1894 in Plymouth. He was gazetted Major on 15 March 1900.

He retired from active service in 1907 at his own request, but took up an appointment as Recruiting Staff Officer Royal Marines Bristol from 1908 to 1913, during which time he lived at Keynsham.

On 30 July 1914, as war was about to be declared, he was appointed to the RMLI Reserve of Officers, and relocated from Keynsham to Bantham, taking up residence at Higher Aunemouth. There is no record of what role he played in RMLI during the war, but he was promoted to temporary Lt. Colonel in 1916, and the electoral register for Thurlestone in 1919 shows him to be absent on military service.

Gerald Aylmer and his wife Dorothy Rebecca continued to live in Bantham until his death on 19 Dec 1929 at Back of Beyond, Bantham, leaving estate of £1780 to his widow.

Creper, William

Although this man is listed by Rev Coope, I have been unable to find any evidence of his ever having resided in Thurlestone, and no evidence of any military service records.

Crispin, George Henry (1890-1960)

George Henry Crispin was born on 8 December 1890 at Beeson, Stokenham, son of Thomas and Charlotte Crispin, Farm Labourer at Beeson, Stokenham. He does not appear in either the 1901 or 1911 Thurlestone census, or later Electoral rolls.

As an agricultural labourer, however, George Henry may have worked in Thurlestone at some time between 1901 and 1911, but this is only supposition in attempting to explain how Rev Coope came to include him in his list.

He enlisted on 10 Jan 1911 at Devonport and was given the service number K 9826, beginning his naval career as a stoker. He was promoted to Leading stoker and served through war in HMS Donegal. Refitting at the beginning of the war, she was assigned to Sierra Leone for convoy protection duties as part of the 5th Cruiser Squadron. She was transferred to several different cruiser squadrons of the Grand Fleet in 1915 where she escorted convoys to Archangel, Russia. In mid-1916 she was assigned to convoy escort duties in the Atlantic.

During 1914-1916 George Henry Crispin and Charles Edwin Edgecombe were both stokers and shipmates together aboard HMS Donegal, though there was twenty years difference in age between them.

HMS Donegal rejoined the 4th Cruiser Squadron on North America and West Indies Station in 1917 and continued with convoy duties until the end of the war. After leaving HMS Donegal, George Henry served as Leading Stoker on HMS Benbow and HMS Emperor of India, both ships being involved in the allied intervention in the Russian Civil War in the Black Sea in 1920-21.

HMS Benbow   **HMS Emperor of India**

After the war he was awarded the Star, British War and Victory medals. He continued in service until 23 April 1927, having also received in 1926 his Royal Navy Long Service & Good Conduct Medal.

He was still single and living with his widowed father in Dartmouth in 1939, andeventually died in Torbay Hospital on 7 September 1960.

Easterbrook, Philip Henry (1872-1969)

Philip Henry Easterbrook was born on 29 November 1870 at Tormoham, Torquay, the second son of the eleven children of John Easterbrook, a fisherman, and his wife Charlotte Mary Blank Stone. He enlisted at Devonport before his seventeenth birthday, stating an incorrect date of birth as 9 June 1872, and given service no. 142892. His

Naval Service record therefore includes his time as a boy seaman, but begins his 12 year adult service with effect from 9 June 1890. So his continuous service record shows that he spent his initial training aboard HMS Lion, an 1847 ship of the line, from 1 November 1887 to 15 May 1889, and then in HMS Ruby until December 1890. He then served until May 1892 aboard HMS Aurora, an Orlando class armoured cruiser assigned to the Channel Squadron, during which time he was promoted from ordinary to able-bodied seaman.

HMS Aurora

His next ship was HMS Narcissus (1892-1894), and then HMS Endymion, an Edgar class cruiser (1895-1896) He then spent three years with HMS Royalist, being promoted to Leading seaman, before deciding to transfer to the Coastguard Service at Holy Island in Northumbria in 1900. In the same year Philip married Emma Jane Wollacott in October at Northumberland (Banns were read 23, 30 Sep, and 7 Oct 1900 at St Peter's Hammersmith, London). He was serving as a Coastguard boatman at Holy Island in the 1901 census, and continued there until 1903 when he moved to the Eyemouth station in Berwickshire.

Holy Island Coastguard Station

They had four children Phyllis Evelyn L (1901-1997), Henry Norman Cecil (1902-2006), born in Northumberland, and Mildred Ivy Eileen (1903-1990) and Gertrude Rosalind (1904-1980), born in Berwickshire. Tragedy struck the family with the death of wife Emma Jane on 11 September 1905 in Eyemouth, Berwickshire, leaving Philip with four children less than five years old to look after. He was transferred to the Southern area from November 1905 until September 1911, living first at Fortuneswell, and then at Grove Point, Portland.

Gertrude stayed with an uncle, Edwin Setter in Springfield Road, Torquay; Mildred with another uncle Sidney Bragg (a PO in the RN) at 18 Orchard Cottages, Hele, Torquay, and the other children were living with various relatives around the Torquay district.

Promoted from Leading boatman to Petty Officer, Philip then served from 1911 to 1914 at Hope Cove and Bantham coastguard stations. He then married Mary Ellen Ash a 41 year old spinster and daughter of Bantham coastguard William Ash on 16 Nov 1912 at All Saints church and son Philip Henry was born in 1914. They lived in a Coastguard cottage at Bantham in 1914 through to 1919, but in the Electoral Roll Philip was shown as absent on military service in 1918.

He served aboard the battleship HMS Vanguard from August 1914 to Sept 1915 but then returned to Coastguard duties based in Devonport and then Hope Cove until completing his service in September 1919. He was fortunate not to serve longer on HMS Vanguard, which blew up at Scapa Flow on 9 June 1917 with the loss of 843 of the 845 men aboard.

HMS Vanguard

Philip and Mary Ellen were not resident in the parish after 1919. Philip was awarded Star, British War, and Victory medals.

They lived at 20 Robinson Row, Salcombe from 1929-1939, later returning to live in Torquay where he died in 1969, aged 98.

Edgcombe, Charles Edgar (1899 – 1940)

Charles Edgar Edgcombe, born 12th June 1899 and baptised at All Saints on 2 July 1899, was the eldest son of the three sons of Charles Edwin Edgcombe and Sarah Elliott. Edgar (as he was known) had two younger brothers, Cecil Laurence and Ronald Elliott. Both were too young to serve in WW1, and only Ronald survived WW2. The family home was at 1 Kathleen Cottages, West Buckland.

Edgar joined the Somerset Light Infantry as a teenager during WW1 and served in France where he was wounded on two occasions. By the end of the war in 1918, he had transferred to the Royal Berkshire Regiment. After being demobilized, he re-enlisted as a regular. His battalion left England in 1919, spent two years in the Middle East and six years in India (1921-27). Edgar moved up through the NCO ranks and was made Sergeant in 1924.

Whilst on leave in 1928, Edgar married Annie Sheriff, and their only child, daughter Iris M V, was born in Kent in 1938 Q1. Sherriffs and Edgcombes were both families of long standing in the parish, and would have known each other well. Though Annie was born and lived in London, she used to visit her grandmother in Bantham, where she fell for Edgar.

Marriage at St Paul's Church, Lorrimore Square, Newington, London

In 1940 Edgar, now Company Quartermaster Sergeant, was posted to France and sent his last postcard home on 12 May 1940. Only 11 days later, he was killed in fighting at St. Omer, and is buried in the Longuenesse Cemetery there.

Longuenesse Cemetery, St. Omer

Edgecombe, Charles Edwin (1870-1947)

Born Aveton Gifford 7 May 1870, the son of Thomas Edgecombe, a road repairer, and Irena Dare. He enlisted in the Royal Navy at Devonport on 1 Apr 1890, signing on for 12 years, and served all his time as a stoker, rising from ordinary level to Petty Officer. His service number was 155440, and after training he served on HMS Edgar for the three years 1893-6. On his return home he married Sarah Elliott, daughter of William and Susan Elliott, on 23 December 1896 at All Saints, Thurlestone.

1896. Marriage solemnized in the Parish Church in the Parish of Thurlestone in the County of Devon								
No.	When Married	Name and Surname.	Age.	Condition.	Rank or Profession.	Residence at the Time of Marriage.	Father's Name and Surname.	Rank or Profession of Father.
120	Dec 23.	Charles Edwin Edgecombe	26	Bachelor	Sailor	Aveton Gifford	Thomas Edgecombe	Labourer
		Sarah Elliott	28	Spinster	Servant	Brook Cottage Buckland Thurlestone	William Elliott	Labourer

Married in the Parish Church according to the Rites and Ceremonies of the Church of England after Banns by me, R J Garde Buller, Rector.

This Marriage was solemnized between us, Charles Edwin Edgcombe / Sarah Elliott — In the Presence of us, Thomas Edgcombe / Susan Ellen Elliott

Charles served on HMS Cornwall during 1904-6 and (after her refit) also from 1907-1910 on the North American and West Indies station. His last ship before completing his 12 was HMS Bellerophon (1911-12) and he was aboard her during an exercise of the combined fleets of the Med, Home and Atlantic when on 26 May 1911 she was lightly damaged in a collision with the battlecruiser HMS Inflexible.

HMS Cornwall

HMS Bellerophon

Their son Charles Edgar Edgecombe was born 12 June 1899, second son Cecil Laurence in 1904, and third son Ronald Elliott in 1910. They lived at 1 Kathleen Cottages, West Buckland. When his 12 years were completed Charles was transferred from active service to the Fleet reserve from 14 April 1912. Charles was immediately recalled at the outbreak of war and served in HMS Donegal through the war (1914-18). At the beginning of war HMS Donegal served with 3rd Cruiser Squadron at Sierra Leone, but in January 1915 joined 6th Cruiser Squadron, Grand Fleet, and then, in November 1915, 7th Cruiser Squadron escorting convoys to the White Sea (Archangel). With 2nd Cruiser Squadron from May 1916, then 9th Ccruiser Squadron in September. Went to North America and West Indies Station in September 1917 but returned to Devonport in June 1918, where she paid off.

HMS Donegal

HMS Edgar

Charles then rejoined his old ship HMS Edgar for seven months prior to his demob on 27 March 1919. After the war he was awarded Star, British War, and Victory medals.

The family continued living in West Buckland, as shown by the electoral registers for 1919, 1920, and 1921. By 1939 Charles and Sarah had moved to Bantham.

Charles died in 1947 and Sarah in 1960.

Edgecombe, T E (1881- ?)

In addition to the three Edgecombes already covered, Rev Coope lists a fourth - a T E Edgecombe, who has proved difficult to pin down. No family connections have been found, and he does not appear in either the 1911 Thurlestone census or any of the Electoral registers from 1913 to 1921.

Nor is his military service record available. The only clue to his wartime activity comes from Forces War Records website, which provides the following details:

First Name: T
Surname: Edgecombe
Age: 35
Notes in Admission Number Column: 2a
Index Number of Admission: T1851
Rank: Private
Service Number: 2946
Years Service: 2 years
Months With Field Force: 1 year 4 months
Ailment: Pneumonia
Date of Transfer From Sick Convoy: 15/12/1916
Number/Designation of Ward: A 7
Religion: Church of England
Notes written by FWR when Transcribing: Disembarked at Bombay 20/12/1916.
Regiment: Devonshire Regiment
Battalion: 1/4th Battalion
Archive Reference: MH106/1938 MH106/1938 can be found at The National Archives in Kew, and contains First World War Representative Medical Records of H.M.A.T Ship Assaye: 17/04/1916 - 11/01/1917. British Troops Territorial. H.M.Hospital Ship ASSAYE Mediterranean Expeditionary Force.

There may possibly be more information in the National Archives under the reference MH106/1938, but it has not been digitised and is unaccessible on-line.
It can only therefore be supposition that this T Edgecombe, born 1881, and an early volunteer for the Devonshire Regiment, is the one Rev Coope knew.

Edgecombe, William Henry (1875-1951)

Born in 1878 at South Milton, the son of William Henry Edgecombe and Emma Jane Adams, but living at Foxhole in Bigbury in 1881 as his father, an agricultural labourer had found work there. However, by 1891 the family had returned to South Milton. In 1901 William had moved to Plymouth to work as a dock labourer, and was staying with his married sister Emma Thornton at 7 Vanguard Terrace in Devonport.

Four years later he married Beatrice Olive Jackman at All Saints, Thurlestone, on 10 June 1905 and was living there working as a gardener, and providing a home for his widowed mother-in-law in the 1911 census. Continued living in Thurlestone right through the war, except when he volunteered for army service with the Devonshire Regiment from November 1915 until his discharge through wounds on Boxing Day 1917. A private (regt number 24674), he served in France, and was badly wounded when shot in the hip and left stranded in No Man's Land for three days before managing to crawl to safety under the cover of darkness. He was awarded the Silver badge for the wounded (medal no. 498989) and subsequently the British War Medal and the Victory Medal. But he was disabled for the rest of his life.

After the war William and his wife stayed in Thurlestone and William continued to try and work as a gardener and at the Thurlestone Golf Club. Sadly, his wife Beatrice Olive died in the summer of 1934, and was buried in Thurlestone churchyard. The following year 1935 William married again, this time to Nellie Coombes, the 33 year old daughter of James Coombes, the Thurlestone Golf professional and proprietor of the Sloop Inn at Bantham. They returned to his home village of South Milton by 1939 to live at Mill Mead in Mill Lane, and William is described as "incapacitated" on the census return, though he was able to do a little gardening at Horswell House.

William Henry Edgecombe died in 1951 and is buried in the churchyard at South Milton. His widow Nellie died in Torbay in 1979.

Elliott, Joseph (1885-1953)

Joseph Elliott, the third of the four sons of Joseph Elliott and Selina Whitting, was born at Buckland 13 December 1885 and baptised at All Saints on 24 January 1886, together with his sister Bertha Harriot, who had been born nearly two years earlier on 12 April 1884.

Page 10

BAPTISMS solemnized in the Parish of _Thurlestone_
in the County of _Devon_ in the Year 18*86*

When Baptized.	Child's Christian Name.	Parents Name.		Abode.	Quality, Trade, or Profession.	By whom the Ceremony was performed.
		Christian.	Surname.			
1886 January 1st No. 73.	Margaret Elizabeth daughter of	Charles Henry & Margaret Harrietta	Burridge	Workhg Thurlestone	Gentleman	Henry Evans Associate Curate of Churleston Kingsbridge
Jan 24th No. 74.	Bertha Harriet daughter of	Joseph & Selina	Elliott	Buckland	Mason	Peregrine H. Ilbert. Rector.
Jan 24th No. 75.	Joseph son of	Joseph & Selina	Elliott	Buckland	Mason	Peregrine H. Ilbert. Rector.

Copy of the Baptism records for Bertha and Joseph Elliott

He attended the local school, and became a fisherman and pilot, living with his parents and siblings in the 1911 census at the family home in Bantham to which they had now moved. There is no record of the date his brother James enlisted, but his younger brother William Arthur enlisted on 30 October 1915, so Joseph may have been the third and last of the brothers to join the armed forces, which he did on 25 November 1915.

He attested at Newton Abbot, and was subsequently posted to the Royal Regiment of Artillery depot at Hilsea on 16 March 1916 as a driver with the Regimental number 130112. Within this Regiment he served with various units in various places with the Mesopotamia Expeditionary Force from 1916 through to 1919., including "S" Battery, Royal Horse Artillery, which took part in the attempts to relieve Kut, and the 6th and 7th Cavalry Brigades. Each cavalry brigade had one battery of Royal Horse Artillery; each battery being equipped with 6 x 13 or 18-pounder field guns, for a total of 30 guns.

The 7th (Indian) Cavalry Brigade took part in the Second Battle of Kut, including the Advance to the Hai and Capture of the Khudaira Bend (14 December 1916–19 January

1917), the Capture of the Hai Salient (25 January–5 February 1917), and the Capture of the Dahra Bend (9–16 February). It then took part in the Pursuit to Baghdad and a number of actions later in 1917. In 1918 it took part in the Affair   of Kulawand (27 April), the Action of Tuz Khurmatli (29 April), the Action at Fat-ha Gorge on the Little Zab (23–26 October 1918) and the Battle of Sharqat (28–30 October 1918). If Joseph had managed to avoid illness in this period, he would have been involved in plenty of action in these campaigns.

An 18-pounder gun crew in Mesopotamia

He was more fortunate than his brother **James**, in that he survived, although he had to wait until January 1920 before he eventually arrived home and was demobilised on 30 January at Woolwich. He had to wait even longer to receive his British War and Victory medals, which eventually reached him on 17 June 1921.

Joseph married Eva Herd in the first quarter of 1922 at Totnes, and they settled in Bantham, where Joseph resumed his role as a boatman and fisherman until his death in 1953 aged 68 years.

Elliott, William Arthur (1895-1962)

William Arthur Elliott, youngest of the four brothers, attested on 30 October 1915 at Kingsbridge, claiming his occupation as motor driver. A week later he found himself at the Army Service Corps camp at Osterley Park. However, he failed a driving test, and was sent for training to become a driver in the Army Service Corps. At his attestation he was required to sign the following:

I understand that I am being enlisted for the duration of the war for General Service in the Army Service Corps with a view to being trained as a Motor Transport Driver, and that my pay will be 1s 2d (one shilling and two pence) per diem, until such time as I am passed by the military Authorities as a qualified motor driver, from which date I am to receive in addition Corps pay at 1s 2d (one shilling and two pence) per diem...

He evidently qualified successfully, completed his driver training by the end of the year, and as private DM2/137646 (MT) he embarked aboard the SS Caesarea at Southampton on 4 January 1916, having been posted to the British Military Transport Depot at Rouen, and served throughout the war in France.

He had a number of postings to different units in his first few weeks before settling for a year with 66 MT Company. This was followed by month-long postings to 17th Corps, and 335 and 654 MT Company. The driving must have been long, arduous, and stressful, for he was off sick with synovitis in October 1916, and then transferred to hospital at Le Treport with debility for the month of November. In December he was posted to the MT vehicle Reserve Park and then granted two weeks leave in January 1917.

The Clayton 3-tonner - a typical WW1 truck

Then it was back to France for the remainder of the war, with postings back to 654, 886, 406, and 282 MT Coys, followed by a fortnight's home leave in March 1918. More postings from 282 to 403 and finally back to 886 saw him through to the Armistice, and fortunate to come through relatively unscathed. He was granted more leave to return to England to marry Margaret Dorothy Butt on 7 April 1919 at the Chapel of Holy Trinity, Littleham-cum-Exmouth, before being finally discharged back to civilian life again on 18 August 1919 from 1 Coy, 39 Division. His discharge papers record him as "a hard worker" and he had earned a Good Conduct medal to go with his British War and Victory medals.

A daughter, Kathleen Dorothy, was born on 22 January 1920, and after living in Bantham and West Buckland until 1926 the family then moved to Exmouth, where they were living at 5 Elm Road in 1939, and William Arthur was still working as a lorry driver. He died in 1962 aged 68 years.

Fisher, Henry

The only connection between Henry Fisher and Thurlestone was in the years 1914-1919 when he was stationed at Bantham and occupied one of the Coastguard Cottages. Both Henry Fisher and his wife Alice Eliza were absent on military service (NM) in 1918, and it is likely that they were resident throughout the war, having first appeared in Bantham in the Electoral register in 1914. In 1919 Henry was resident but Alice Eliza still absent (NM). Both had left the parish in 1920. It seems that Henry Fisher may have died at Portland in 1938. No further details could be found.

Fisher, Thomas

It is a similar story with Thomas Fisher, who had no connection with Thurlestone before his appearance in the 1918 Electoral register as resident at the Coastguard Station, Bantham, though absent on military service. He is still there in 1919, and still absent on military service. By 1920 he has left the parish and moved elsewhere. No further details could be found.

Foote, Edward Sydney (1899-1996)

Edward Sydney Foote was born at Whitley Barton, Thurlestone on 21 February 1899, and baptised at All Saints on 7 April 1899, son of Sidney Albert Foote, a farmworker from Sandford, Devon, and Eliza Bartlett Edgecombe, from Churchstow, who had married in 1889, and settled in Thurlestone. Edward was their fifth child, and was probably rather spoiled by his four elder sisters Hilda Annie (b. 1891), Alberta May (b.1892), Eva P (b. 1894), and Elsie M (b.1898). of Whitley Cottage. He would have attended the local school in Thurlestone, and probably helped out on the farm until signing on for military service on 24 January 1917 at Newton Abbot three days after his eighteenth birthday.

He was assigned to a Training battalion with the service number 14006, and was then transferred to the Royal Warwickshire Regt as private no 50765. Following his training period he was sent to France on 7 May 1918 to join the 10th Battalion Royal Warwickshire Regiment. He saw front line action with them, as the 10th RWR were in the forefront of the pursuit to the River Selle, with a night attack to occupy the village of Haussy and push forward to the River d'Harpies west of St Martin. It was probably here that Edward Sydney suffered slight gunshot wounds to the face and left hand on 22 Oct 1918, and was admitted to Number 3 Canadian General Hospital at Boulogne on 8 Nov 1918, three days before the Armistice. He was discharged from hospital, and finally returned to England 17 February 1919 and demobbed on 20 Mar 1919. He was awarded the British War and Victory medals.

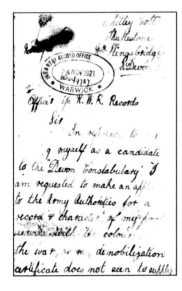

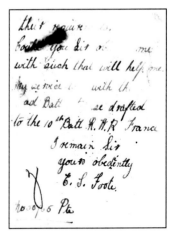

Edward Sydney returned to live with his parents at Whitley Cottage, and appears there with them in the 1919, 1920, and 1921 Electoral Rolls. Edward wanted to join the Devon Police Force on returning from the war, and wrote to his Regiment for a reference as to his character and good conduct. This he clearly received, to the satisfaction of the Devon Constabulary, as his address in 1939 is recorded as Police Cottage, New Road, Brixham.

Edward Sydney married Alice May Milford (b. 10 June 1904) in June 1928 at Okehampton. They had two children, Ivor A J Foote (b. 1932) and Barbara J Foote, (b. 1936) and later moved to Honiton.

Fox, Edward Lawrence (1861-1938)

Edward Lawrence Fox was born on 14 April 1861, the fifth of six sons of Henry Fox of Furzedon, Plympton St Mary, and Mary Charlotte Russell. After school he attended Cavendish College, Cambridge, from 1879, graduating BA in 1882, and then went on to study medicine at St Bartholomew's Hospital in London, obtaining M.R.C.S. (1885). Cavendish College awarded him M.B., B.C. and M.A. (1887) and M.D. (1891). He also graduated M.R.C.P. from Barts in 1891. After spells as a House Surgeon, at the Children's Infirmary, Liverpool, and at Stanley Hospital, Liverpool, he returned to the West Country and was for more than 25 years Physician to the South Devon and East Cornwall Hospital, and to the Royal Eye Infirmary.

As part of the pre-war preparations by the military Edward was gazetted on the 22nd June 1909 (his appointment dated 29 Sept 1908) to be available on mobilization as Lt. Col. (RAMC) 4th Southern General Hospital. During the Great War, 1914-19, he was in charge of hospitals at Tavistock and Plymouth, but there is nothing in military records about his service. However, his name appears in the Electoral Register for Bantham from 1913 onwards, as the owner of a property named Aune Down.

His principal residence was at 9 Osborne Place, Plymouth, and it was from here that Edward married Clare Elizabeth Walding, (b. 10 May 1892) the youngest daughter of Thomas White Walding, a Hunt Tailor of 23 Market Place, Rugby, Warwickshire, on 21 May 1921 at Holy Trinity Church, Plymouth. He was 60, she was 39. Clare had attended the Physical Training College at Kingsfield, Dartford, run by Martina Bergman-Osterberg, a Swedish physical training instructor and women's suffrage advocate. The couple evidently spent most of their time at Aune Down after Edward retired and it was here that he died in 1938. After his death Clare continued to live there along with a housekeeper Ellen Jeffery.

Mrs Clare Fox took a keen interest in community activities and natural history and became an influential figure in the parish. She collected together and organised an impressive and important Bantham Exhibition of Village History 2000 BC - 1953 AD, after which a number of the exhibits were gifted to the Torquay Museum. She died a few years later in 1958.

Gerald Dudley Freer (1866-1935)

Gerald Dudley Freer

Gerald Dudley Freer (1866-1935) MRCS, LRCP, was the son of Leacroft Freer of The Beeches, Red Hill, Stourbridge. After qualifying at Barts Hospital as a physician and surgeon he went out to the Far East, where he held senior appointments in Malaya and Singapore. He married Frances Maude Taylor from Bakewell, Derbyshire, in St Andrews Cathedral, Singapore, on 15 Aug 1896, and went on to become Colonial Surgeon Resident, Penang, in 1898.

He was one of the founders and the first principal of the Straits and Federated Malay States Government Medical School from 1905-9, following which he was appointed Senior Medical Officer for Selangor 1909.

Frances Maude came back to England for the birth of their son in 1898, but evidently returned with him to Singapore as neither of them appears in the 1901 census in the UK.

However, she returned to England with him in 1911 to enter him at the Royal Naval Cadet College, Osborne, Isle of Wight, where he appears in the 1911 census, while she stayed with friends in Hove. Gerald Dudley returned to England some time later, before the outbreak of war, and established a residence at South View, Thurlestone, where he appears on the Electoral Roll in 1915.

On 16 October 1914 he was appointed Captain RAMC, attached 2nd Wessex Field Ambulance, aged 48. The 2nd Wessex Field Ambulance went to France with the 8th Division in November 1914, and it is likely that despite his age Gerald would have gone with them, or joined them shortly afterwards as the casualty lists rocketed, as in the next (1918) Electoral Roll for Thurlestone he is noted as absent on military service.

A Field Ambulance (FA) consisted of ten officers and 224 other ranks including several Army Service Corps personnel. A field ambulance column consisted of ambulance wagons, water-carts and forage-carts for carrying medical stores, a cook's wagon, and GS wagons for stores and baggage, and 52 riding and draught horses. In addition, a soldier on a bicycle carried orders and messages within the unit.

Each field ambulance was divided into three sections, designated 'A', 'B' and 'C', and there was also a Bearer Division and a Tent Division. In battle conditions the tent division formed a main dressing station, and men from the bearer division brought in the wounded from front-line Regimental Aid Posts (RAP). During a big offensive, field ambulance units formed a chain of medical posts between the aid-posts and Casualty Clearing Stations (CCS).

This postcard picture depicts an unnamed field ambulance unit on parade. Some ambulance wagons are drawn by two horses and one wagon by four. In addition, there are several GS wagons and also limber-type carts on display. The date and location are unknown, but the photo was probably taken early in the war just before the unit left for France.

Gerald Dudley survived the war, and briefly returned to South View, Thurlestone, in 1919 but then moved to The Chalet, Milton Road, Brixham, in 1920.

By 1923 he had moved again, to Hillside House, Wrotham, Kent, and it was from here

Hillside House, Wrotham

that he and Frances Maude attended the wedding of their son George at Funtington Parish church. But this was not their final residence, as they moved once again to 6 Forest Road, Branksome, Bournemouth, where Frances Maude died on 18 June 1933.

Gerald survived her by only nineteen months, and passed away at The Old Manor, Salisbury, in February 1935.

Freer, George Francis Dudley (1898-1967)

George Francis Dudley Freer

George Francis Dudley Freer, born 20 Jan 1898 at Holmwood, Woodford Green, Essex, was the son of Gerald Dudley Freer MRCS, LRCP, a distinguished physician who held senior appointments in Malaya and Singapore, and Frances Maude Taylor.

He returned with his mother to Singapore, where he spent his early schooldays. He will have been made aware of, and probably influenced by, the naval exploits of one of his ancestors, who served as Flag Lieutenant on HMS Victory at the Battle of Trafalgar, and made a brass and oak tea-caddy from wood from the Victory's deck, which was handed down through the family to his mother. It is therefore not surprising that he was entered into the Royal Naval College at Osborne, Isle of Wight, in 1911 or shortly beforehand. Cadets spent two years at Osborne before going on to the Britannia College at Dartmouth. It was probably the proximity to Dartmouth that accounted for his father's decision to take up a residence in Thurlestone around 1913.

Having passed out as midshipman, George was quickly into action in the war, and aboard the battleship HMS Lord Nelson he was at the forefront of the landings on West Beach, Gallipoli on 25/26 April 1915 where he "behaved with exemplary skill, courage, and coolness under heavy fire", and was awarded the Distinguished Service Cross for bravery, gazetted on 16 August 1915. He suffered a fractured tibia in May 1915 and spent time in hospital in Egypt and Haslar. He was promoted to sub-lieutenant in July 1917, and to Lieutenant in June 1919, before joining the destroyer HMS Winchelsea in 1922.

HMS Lord Nelson

Distinguished Service Cross

It was while a serving officer on HMS Winchelsea that George married Harriette Ruby Bryant, a Canadian from Broadway, Winnipeg, at Funtington Parish Church on Saturday,

18 August 1923. It was quite an occasion, as reported in the Observer and West Sussex Recorder the following Wednesday:

HMS Winchelsea

Naval Wedding - Picturesque Ceremony at Funtington
Bridegroom Descendant of Trafalgar Admiral - Canadian Fruit Ranch as Present

The pretty little church at Fruntington was, on Saturday afternoon, the scene of a picturesque naval wedding, the contracting parties being Miss Harriette Ruby Bryant, daughter of Mr and Mrs H Bryant of Broadway, Winnipeg, Canada and Lieutenant George Francis Dudley Freer DSC, RN, HMS Winchelsea, only son of Dr and Mrs Gerald Dudley Freer of Hillside House, Wrotham, Kent, and cousin and godson of Miss E Marian Cochrane of "Sennicots" near Chichester. The bridegroom, who served with distinction in the late war, is a great great grandson of the Admiral Browne, who served with Nelson, and among his mother's wedding gifts was an oak and brass tea-caddy bearing the date October 21st, 1805, which was constructed by Admiral Browne out of pieces of wood from the portion of the deck on which England's immortal naval hero fell.

Many distinguished guests, including a number of naval officers, had been invited to the wedding, and there was a large gathering at the church. While the congregation was assembling, Mr Philip Dore FRCO, organist of Queen's College, Cambridge, and formerly assistant organist at Chichester Cathedral, who presided at the organ, played the Prelude in C Sharp Minor by Lyon, and also extemporised.

The weather behaved kindly for the occasion. It was fine before the commencement, and following a heavy shower during the service the sun broke through the storm clouds just as the bridal party was emerging from the church to the stirring strains of Mendelssohn's Wedding March. Four naval officers formed an archway of crossed swords for the happy couple to pass under, and roses were strewn in their path, while there was a merry peal on the bells. The officers referred to wer Lieutenants Tate and Huntington-Whitley of HMS Vernon and Lieutenant Chads and Lieut-Commander H Owen of HMS Winchelsea. The duties of best man were carried out by Lieut R H Longsdon, HMS Excellent.

Following the ceremony the guests were entertained at Sennicots, the home of Miss E Marian Cochrane, where the magnificent wedding presents were on show, and later, amid a host of good wishes, Lieut and Mrs Freer left for the honeymoon which is being spent in France.

Having completed 18 years service he was placed on the retired list as Lieutenant Commander on 23 April 1929. George returned to service as a Munitions Inspector of Naval Ordnance for the early part of WW2 before being retired on medical grounds in October 1941. Harriette died in 1956, and George in 1967.

Fulford, Lewis George (1896-1971)

Lewis George Fulford was the elder of two sons of Charles Lewis Fulford (1861-1942) and Emma Kate Witt (1858-1943), born 6 March 1896 at Peper Harrow, a village near Godalming, Surrey. His father had worked variously as a beer house keeper, labourer, and gamekeeper, in Wiltshire, Kent, Northampton, and Surrey and in 1901 the family (father, mother, four of five daughters, and two boys) lived at Wellcopse Cottage, Chipstead, Surrey. By 1904 they had moved to Eastling, Kent, where a third son William was born.

By 1911 however the family had moved to Fore Street, Kingsand, Cornwall, and were clearly struggling. Father was an unemployed woodman, four daughters had left home - Minnie was a living-in servant in Purley, Surrey; Mary and Ethel were servants to a Robert Ford in Sidmouth; Elsie was a servant at Woodmansterne, Surrey, and married Joseph Sparkes at Epsom in the same year - Lewis George was a grocer's errand boy, the younger boys were at school, and daughter Hannah helped her mother in the house - which had four rooms. In 1913 Hannah, too, left home to marry Arthur George Everson, a soldier in the Royal Garrison Artillery, in Plympton.

Lewis George was the next to go. By 1915 he had moved to Plympton and was working as a horse driver at Battisford Farm, and it was from there that he attested at Plymouth on 3 November 1915 for the Royal Engineers (Signals) service number 77529. He was nineteen years old. At some point between 1915 and 1918 his parents relocated to a cottage in West Buckland, and were to live there for the rest of their lives - nearly another thirty years.

Lewis George completed his training at Fenny Stratford Signals Depot in the UK and embarked for France on 3 July 1916 aboard the "Toronto" as part of the 11th Division with the WW Cable Section. He served with Cable Sections as a driver, including having spent a week in hospital in July 1917 until joining the 56th Division Signals Company on 27 July 1918 with the rank of pioneer, having passed the test for being a Mounted Field Lineman, and awarded 1st GC Badge. On 14 September 1918 he was granted two weeks leave to the UK, rejoining his unit on 29 September 1918.

On 5 October 1918 he was charged with neglect of duty in that he was absent from the Piquet Line when on Night Cable Picquet, and was awarded two days of open arrest. On the 19th October he was admitted to the 2/1 London Field Ambulance for a day, and allowed back to his unit on 20th October. On 7 December 1918 he was awarded the Military Medal - authorised by XXII Corps Orders. The award was gazetted 22 July 1919, supplement number 31469, page 9363. He received his Military Medal on the 7th October 1919.

After returning to the UK and his parents at West Buckland, he married Beatrice Maria Woodman (1898-1947) at Plympton in September 1922. Sometime later they moved to Salisbury. After her death he married his second wife Daisy Bertha Janet Williams (1891-1979) in 1949 at Salisbury, Wilts, where he died in 1971.

Awarded the "Military Medal."

FRANCE

Corps *R. Engineers*

Regimental Number *77529*

Surname *FULFORD*

Christian Name *George Lewis*

Rank *D⁴⁴. Pmr.*

Date of Gazette *11065*

Registered Paper *28/12/856* Schedule Number *524831 4*

Extract from War Office Records

WW1 Military Medal

The Rev Coope also included on his list of Thurlestone parishioners who served in WW1 the name of Lewis George's younger brother Charles Henry Fulford, but I have been unable to trace any military service records for him. unable to trace any military service records for him.

The Grose Family

William John Grose (1861-1921) and his wife Margaret Amelia (1859-1945) had made the transition from farming to hotel-keeping in 1897 when they became tenants of Farm Barton, previously in the hands of Samuel Shath Square and his family. Although it was quite a struggle in the early years, the Grose family were determined to make a success of their new venture, and set about making the Thurlestone Hotel a memorable experience for visiting golfers and holiday-makers alike.

Their four sons - William Richard (b. 1888), John Howard (b. 1890), Ernest Melville Cuthbert (b. 1892), and James Frederick (b. 1895) - were still at school during the first decade of the Hotel's progress, with the two younger boys both boarders at Kingsbridge in 1911. When the war came in 1914 they were all of an age and liable for military service after conscription was introduced in 1916. However, by then all four had begun their own careers, with William Richard a schoolmaster in South Africa; John Howard had completed an engineering apprenticeship with GWR and was a qualified Civil Engineer; Cuthbert was working for his parents in the hotel; and James had started with Lloyd's Bank.

William Richard Grose (1888-1979)

Immediately after graduating from Keble College, Oxford, with a degree in chemistry William Richard went straight to South Africa where he established himself as a schoolmaster. At the outbreak of war William Richard was keen to assist the war effort and made two separate applications to join the armed forces, only to be twice turned down for failing his medical examination. This was due to his eyesight, which had always been poor even from his childhood. After returning to the UK he married Muriel Balkwill in 1932 and they made their residence at Swallows in Thurlestone, with William Richard returning to work in the family business. He died in 1979 at the age of 91.

John Howard Grose (1890-1956)

After attending Kingsbridge Grammar School John Howard joined the Great Western Railway in 1906 and moved to Swindon, where he completed a mechanical engineering apprenticeship. He left GWR to take up a post as Inspector of Railway material with the Crown Agents for the Colonies from 1913-1915, before being appointed as Assistant Inspector for Munitions areas from 1915 to 1917. During this period he passed the examination for Associate membership of the Institution of Civil Engineers on 12 March 1915 while living in Leeds. He also married Mary Emily Cock, an Ivybridge girl, in Sculcoates at the beginning of 1916. All this time he was itching to serve in the armed forces, but was denied permission by the Ministry in view of his important role at home in the war effort. He eventually forced the issue by resigning his post in 1917 and was granted a commission as temporary 2nd Lieutenant in the Royal Engineers on 25 June 1917.

He was sent to France, where his railway experience was able to be used to good effect in organising railway operations for the transportation of men and materials, and the maintenance of the rail system that ensured supplies to the front line. After the armistice he was kept on for nine months, evidently involved in the logistics of repatriating all the men, machines, and supplies that had accumulated in France by the end of the war. He returned home on 23 August 1919, and spent some time working at the Hotel before the death of his wife in Paignton in 1930. Shortly afterwards he moved to Killiney, Dublin, where he married a Plymouth girl, Mabel Deacon, on 2 January 1932. They had three children there and it was in Killiney that John Howard died on 18 October 1956, aged 66 years.

He was awarded the the British War and Victory medals for his wartime service, but had to wait until 1935 before he actually received them.

Ernest Melville Cuthbert Grose (1892-1971)

Ernest Melville Cuthbert Grose, known as Bert, was born on 12 June 1892, and attended Kingsbridge Grammar School at Tresilian. Unfortunately, while still a schoolboy (and evidently an adventurous one) he was seriously injured in a fall while attempting to get some seagull eggs. He broke both his ankles and suffered spinal injuries which confined him to bed for six months. The damage to his legs and spine left him somewhat shorter than his three brothers, and also meant that he was unfit for military service in WW1. However he volunteered to work in a munitions factory in Yorkshire where he worked first in Hull and secondly in Leeds.

During his time in Yorkshire he met his bride to be Nora Jackson and they were married in Goole in March 1919. Their two children, Peter and Jim, were born in 1920 and 1925 respectively. Bert became a director of the Thurlestone Hotel and continued to be involved in its operations until his death on 4 July 1971 at Greenbank Hospital in Plymouth.

James Frederick Grose (1895-1991)

James Frederick Grose, known as Jim, was born on 22 February 1895 and followed his brothers in attending Kingsbridge Grammar School. After leaving school he joined Lloyds Bank (who were then the Hotel's bankers), and continued with them until enlisting for service in the Royal Flying Corps. He was gazetted as temporary 2nd Lieutenant for duty with the RFC on 5 September 1916, and sent for flying training to 31 RS Wyton aerodrome in Cambridgeshire on 4 January 1917. After three months he was recommended for Flying Officer, and on 30 April 1917 his appointment was confirmed with his service number 214849 and he was posted to 48 Squadron in France.

Jim was the only Thurlestonian to serve in the RFC/RAF during the WW1, and although we know little about his service it does have a number of interesting aspects. The first was his squadron.

No. 48 Squadron was formed at Netheravon on the 15th April 1916 and posted to France on the 8th March 1917. It became the first unit of the then Royal Flying Corps to be equipped with the Bristol F2a two-seater fighter/reconnaissance plane. The Squadron accounted for three hundred and seventeen kills during the First World War, and possessed no fewer than thirty-two aces. Topping this list, with twenty confirmed kills, was the Squadron's New Zealand-born commander, Keith Park who, during the Battle of Britain in the Second World War, commanded 11 Group of Fighter Command, upon whom the full weight of the Luftwaffe's offensive was directed.

Nevertheless, 48 Squadron's first sortie with the new Bristol F2a was not a success. The first numbers of F2a planes were flown to France in March 1917 and began their first offensive patrol on April 5th, which resulted in disaster and almost ended their production. Six of 48 Squadron's new Bristols, led by Capt. W. Leefe Robinson V.C, were sent to patrol over Etouai where they were ambushed by five Albatros D IIIs led by the Red Baron, Manfred von Richthofen. Unaware of the F2a's fine maneuverability, Robinson and his men attempted to hold flight formation and use their rear gunners as defence (which was standard practice at the time for two-seater aircraft in formation). Four of the Bristols were shot down, including that of Leefe Robinson, who survived but was captured, and a fifth was badly damaged. Richtofen noted in his combat report that the Bristol appeared "to be quick and handy" but summarised that the Albatros DIII was superior in speed and ability. Following the limited success of the Bristol F2a, an upgraded version called the F2b quickly followed with the 275hp Rolls Royce Falcon III engine. This could reach a maximum speed of 123 mph, 10 mph faster than the F2a and was three minutes faster at reaching 10,000 feet, and 48 Squadron RFC began to receive replacement F2b's for its F2a's as early as May 1917.

The Bristol F2b two-seater

This was "Bloody April". During April 1917 the British lost 245 aircraft, 211 aircrew killed or missing, and 108 as prisoners of war. The German Air Services recorded the loss of 66 aircraft during the same period. This was the air war in which Jim Grose found himself on arrival at 48 Squadron on 30 April 1917. As an inexperienced pilot the odds were heavily stacked against him - his life expectancy was little more than one week. Nevertheless, somehow he survived the whole of the month of May, until a terse RFC casualty report entry for 30 May 1917 reads as follows:

> "A3324 Bristol Fighter burnt on aerodrome on offensive patrol.
> 2nd Lt J F Grose Ok / 2nd Lt H Munro Ok"

Jim Grose was confirmed in the rank of Flying Officer in June 1917, but then appears to have left 48 Squadron, ceased to belong to the RFC, and was transferred to the Royal Warwickshire Regiment on 1 November 1917 (National Archives AIR 76/198/156). This National Archive entry was made retrospectively in September 1918 and contains few details. This may well be because the 48 Squadron records were destroyed in August 1918.

"On the evening of the 24th August 1918 a "concert party" was being held by 48 Squadron at the Bertangles Aerodrome. It was a bright moonlit night and the German Schlachtstaffel 16 launched a nocturnal air raid on the aerodrome by 5 German bombers. One of the Gotha bombers scored a direct hit on the middle hangar lighting up the whole aerodrome making it an easy target. The Germans continued to bomb the aerodrome for a further 15 minutes destroying 5 of the Squadron's hangars and causing a large explosion. During the raid most of the Squadron's Bristol Fighters (15 in total) and all their heavy transport (plus all of the Squadron's records) were destroyed. More tragic to the squadron was the heavy loss of personnel with 8 men being killed and a further 28 wounded. The air raid on Bertangles caused the heaviest loss suffered in these circumstances by the British air services throughout the entire war. 48 Squadron were transferred to the 11th Wing, 2nd Brigade at Boisdenghem, on the Second Army Front. The unit was back flying over the front two days later." (From Sgt Reginald White's blogspot.co.uk)

Jim Grose's subsequent military service with the Royal Warwickshire Regiment is unknown, but he clearly survived until being demobilised, and returned to his old job at Lloyds Bank after the war. He married the splendidly named Phyllis Victoria Theodosia Harmon Hanson at Dorking on 9 April 1921, and they had two children; William J (b. 1925) and Christopher AS (b.1926) both born at Bromley in Kent. Jim went on to become the Bank manager at Harpenden, Herts, and it was there that he died in a Nursing Home on 30 Oct 1991, aged 96.

Hannaford, Harry Hamilton (1880-1969)

Harry Hamilton Hannaford was born in Bantham, and baptised at All Saints church on7 December 1880, the younger son of John William Hannaford (1849-1931), the inn keeper of the Sloop Inn, and Mary Jane Widger (1851-1931). His elder brother Harold John Hannaford (1879-1966) had been born a year earlier, and they were joined by a sister Mabel Evada Gertrude Hannaford (1884-1936).

The Sloop Inn, Bantham, c.1900

The Hannafords had farmed in East Buckland, North Upton for several generations at a 120 acre holding known as Harris's Farm, and John William, who had been the inn keeper at the Sloop Inn for over ten years, gave up the licensed trade to take over this farm when his father Joseph retired. He was there in the 1901 census and again in the 1911 census, when both his sons were also working on the farm. By then daughter Mabel had left home in 1904 to marry Josias Moore of Thurlestone, son of Jonas Moore, at All Saints church on 26 April that year.

In the 1914 electoral register John William is shown as owning a property named Julian's Court in Thurlestone as well as Harris's farm. His two sons are shown as joint tenants of Julian's Court and West Downs (perhaps a part of the former Harris's Farm). In 1915 John William is still shown as the owner of Julian's Court and Harris's tenement, and his two sons joint owners of Julian's Court and West Downs. It was in 1915 that Harry Hamilton found a bride, when on 24 May 1915 he married Ethel Mary Gillard at West Alvington church.

There were no electoral registers published for 1916 or 1917, and so the next one, in 1918, shows that John William, his wife, and son Harold John are all living at Julian's Court. Harry Hamilton and his wife are shown living in Bantham, though Harry is absent on military service. Unfortunately there is no record of his military service, which must have been a victim of the blitz, but he is back safely in the 1919 and 1920 electoral registers again with his wife at Bantham, while his parents and brother continue living at Julian's Court.

In 1921 the scene changes, and Harry and his wife move into Julian's Court in Thurlestone, while his parents and brother Harold John have moved to Norton Farm, Churchstow, and they are still there in 1926. By 1939 Harold John had moved back to Thurlestone, where he was a smallholder at Harris Farm, and Harry Hamilton and his wife are living at Park Cottage, West Buckland (which may be the same as Julian's Court) and he is working as a groundsman at the golf club. Their son JW Harry, born24 June 1916, is a regular soldier. Brother Harold John seems to have been excused military service, and with Harry Hamilton's records having perished there is unfortunately no military testament to record for him, except that he did join the forces. Perhaps younger family members or relatives may be able to provide details of Harry's military service, as he survived until 1969, outliving his brother by just two years.

Harcourt, Cecil Jepson Halliday (1892-1959)

CJH Harcourt

Cecil Jepson Halliday Harcourt was born on 11 April 1892 and baptised 26 May at Bromley, Kent, the only son of William Halliday Harcourt, solicitor (1866-1903) and Grace Lilian Jepson (1870-1960). His only sister, Mabel Halliday Harcourt, was born three years later, in 1895, also at Bromley, Kent.

He began school at Fonthill School, East Grinstead, Sussex, and at the age of twelve was entered at Osborne Royal Naval College for two years (1904-6), prior to a further two years at Dartmouth Royal Naval College (1906-8).

Prior to his Naval College years, Cecil's father Halliday Harcourt had been active in Thurlestone. He bought the land at Aunemouth and began the building of his grand new home, Aune Cross, around 1897 and served as chairman of Thurlestone Parish Council from 1897 for two years until 1899. He still maintained his family home at The Hawthorns, Oaksey, in Wiltshire until after the 1901 census, but his death in 1903 left his wife as head of the family.

Grace Harcourt waited only two years before marrying again, to George Marshall Morris in 1905 in Ramsey, Minnesota, USA. They continued to live at Aune Cross while Cecil was at the Dartmouth Naval College, but put the house on the market for auction in 1910, and the 1911 census finds them living at Thornes, Pennsylvania Park, Exeter.

Cecil would have had limited time away from his naval duties to enjoy the facilities of the home at Aune Cross, but he made firm friends of the Ilbert boys and probably the Inchbalds too. His mother recollected that he was more often than not either on the water, or in it, swimming or sailing. Peter Inchbald has an amusing account of an occasion when his uncle Geoffrey and his friend Cecil Harcourt entered the Inchbald's 16 ft cutter in a sailing event at Salcombe, and sailed the boat round there from Bantham, finishing up with their boom through the porthole of the committee launch.

His naval college training ended at Dartmouth in 1908 when he won the naval mathematical prize, and from midshipman he was promoted to sub-lieutenant in 1912 and lieutenant in 1913. He changed his name at this time from Harcourt to Harcourt-Morris, but reverted to just Harcourt in 1920. During WW1 he served as a lieutenant in HMS Centurion under the command of Sir Roger Keyes. His records show that he was Lieutenant Commander in HMS Centurion at the Battle of Jutland.

After the war he married in 1920 the English pianist Evelyn Suart, now widowed, who had given the British premiere performance of Rachmaninoff's First Piano Concerto with the Queens Hall Orchestra conducted by Henry Wood on 4 October 1900. His two new step-daughters were also musically inclined - the beautiful Diana, a talented ballerina, married Yehudi Menuhin in 1947, while Grizelda married the pianist Louis Kentner in 1945.

Cecil's own career continued to go well. He was Lieut-Commander in several destroyers until he became Commander in 1926, and was promoted Captain in 1933. He was lent to the Australian Navy in 1936 and commanded her destroyer flotilla for two years, came home in 1938, and the next year became Director of the Operations Division of' the Naval Staff at the Admiralty, a post he filled for two and a half years.

In 1939, he was appointed Director of the Admiralty's Operations Division. In 1941 he was Flag Captain of the Home Fleet, while commanding HMS Duke of York. For his work at the Admiralty he was made a C.B.E. and became Rear-Admiral in 1942. From 1942 to 1944 he took part in the North Africa campaign, the capture of Tunisia, Pantelleria, Lampedusa, and Sicily, and the landing at Salerno. In 1944 he became Naval Secretary, and in 1945, he was Flag Officer Commanding 11th Aircraft Carrier Squadron, with his flag in HMS Colossus.

He became famous after he personally took the surrender of Japanese forces (under Vice-Admiral Fujita and Lieutenant-General Tanaka) in Hong Kong. He became the head of a provisional military government in Hong Kong from September 1945 to April 1946, serving as administrator until civilian rule could be established. He was knighted during this time, in December 1945, and became Vie-Admiral in 1946.

In 1947 he became Flag Officer (Air) and Second in Command Mediterranean Fleet. In 1948, he became Second Sea Lord and Chief of Naval Personnel as well as a Lord Commissioner of the Admiralty, and in 1950 was made Admiral, and Commander-in- Chief, The Nore, before retiring in 1952.

After his wife Evelyn's death in 1950 Admiral Sir Cecil Jepson Halliday Harcourt GBE, KCB married again in 1953 to widow Stella Janet Waghorn. He died 19 December 1959 on his way to St Stephens hospital SW3 from his home at 140 Rivermead Court, London SW6. His mother, Grace Lilian Harcourt, died six months later on 26 June 1960 at Dartmouth.

Henson, William John (1883-1957)

William John Henson, later known usually as John, was born in Farncombe, just north of Godalming, Surrey on 29 October 1882, and baptised 31st December at the parish church of St John, Farncombe, the son of Frederick Henson, a frame knitter and hosier, and Agnes Matilda Lee, a South Milton girl born in 1841.

They had been married in London in the parish church of St George, Camberwell on 26 July 1868, and went to live in Farncombe, near Godalming in Surrey. The burial records for the parish church of St John, Farncombe record:

Henry George Henson - born about 1868 - buried 5 October 1870
William Henry Henson - born about 1873 - buried 21 February 1874
George Henson   - born about 1871 - buried 16 September 1876

Another son, Frederick William was born in 1869, and appears in the 1871 census but disappears thereafter. Ten years later, in the 1881 census, he is not mentioned, but the family now has a daughter Edith (b.1873), daughter Laura (b.1875), a son Arthur (b.1878) and another daughter Mary Ann (b.1880).

Then William John was born 1882, but sadly another daughter Esther Myra died in October 1884 aged just 8 weeks, and their mother Matilda Agnes died just a week later. Frederick moved quickly to find a new mother for his young children, and a wife Emily appears in the 1891 census, and the family has moved to Witley, just south of Godalming, and children Edith, Arthur, and Mary Ann, have been joined by Amy (b. 1881), George (b. 1888), and Lily (b.1890). William John is not with them.

Ten years later, the 1901 census finds the family at 7 Victoria Road, Godalming, now consisting of Frederick and Emily, and children Amy, George, and Lily, who have now been joined by William E (b. 1892), Alfred (b.1894), Gertrude (b. 1897), and Arthur A (b. 1899). By the next census, they are still at the same address, but father Frederick has died (1904), and Emily is now Emily Topham (widow) and George, Lily, William, and Gertrude, have been joined by a step-sister Ruby Topham.

While this extended family was expanding all the time in Surrey, John was not a part of it. He was sent to the south west to his aunt Betsey Jane Prowse (nee Lee), married to Robert Prowse, a farmer and contractor living at Malborough, and John's name appears there in one of the Lower Town cottages in both the 1891 and 1901 censuses. His occupation in 1901 was that of a contractor/roundsman, but unfortunately he got his name in the local paper when he was "fined 10 shillings for ill-treating a horse" on 3 May (Western Times 4 June 1901).

He married Caroline Horn Saunders, daughter of Roger Saunders, thatcher of South Milton, and Mary Ann Horn, in South Milton in 1905, and they lived in Malborough until after the birth of their daughter Marie Corelli Rose in 1907.   By the time of the 1911 census they had moved to a cottage in Bantham, and John was working as a gardener. He was mentioned in Coope for digging up artifacts from his garden once used as tokens in the Sloop Inn. They continue to appear in the electoral registers through 1913, 1914, and 1915. John is shown as absent on military service in 1918 only, and is back in 1919, 1920, and 1921. No military service records for him can be identified, however. They are probably another victim of the blitz. In 1939 they were living at Aune Cliff, Aune Cross with John still working as a gardener. He died in 1957. Widow Caroline died in Plymouth in 1967.

Daughter Marie Corelli Rose Henson married Walter Caleb Wooldridge in 1933 and in 1939 they lived at The Nest, Bantham. He was a jobbing gardener. A daughter Rosemary was born 1934, and married Albert (Bert) G Jeffery in 1959. They lived at No. 1 The Watch, Bantham. Bert was a popular and familiar figure with his bicycle in and around the parish for many years, as he too was a gardener looking after many of the residents' gardens. He died in 2017. Son Robert and daughter Diane still live in the South Hams.

Hill, Charles Henry (1892-1970)

Charles Henry Hill was the son of William Kendall Hill (1851-1938), a London policeman originally from Frogmore in South Devon, and Elizabeth Wales. He was born at Bethnal Green on 8 Dec 1892, and first appears in the 1901 census when the family were living at 539 Wharncliffe Gardens, St Marylebone. He was still of school age when the family moved back to live at Woodbine Cottage in Thurlestone after William retired from the police, sometime before 1911, and completed his education in Kingsbridge before taking on a printing apprenticeship.

**His father,
William Kendall Hill**

His nephew, the late and much missed Kendall McDonald, in his book Just A Cottage describes Charles Henry's war service in characteristic style:

Charles Henry Hill

"By the time the 1914-18 war came Charlie Hill was such a Devonian that there could be only one regiment for him - The Devonshires.

Private, later Corporal C. Hill, No. 230754 of 'A' Company of the 1/5th Devons saw quite a lot of that war. He fought 'Johnny Turk' in Palestine, was there when Gaza fell and pushed on to Jerusalem. Was switched suddenly to the British Expeditionary Force in France and, because of such a sudden change of climate, fell an easy victim to the influenza which killed as easily as a bomb or bullet.

Once recovered from this it was back to the trenches and his 'Blighty one' - he took a small piece of shrapnel in his right shoulder and was evacuated just before the end of the war to England. Once discharged, he tried to join the Great Western Railway, but nothing seems to have come of it and so he became a postman. He had one extra qualification that is not required of any postman. He could always tell when it was going to rain - the shrapnel left in his shoulder would start to ache hours before!"

Charles Henry Hill was awarded the British War and Victory medals. He was demobbed on 26 March 1919, and became a postman covering South Hams villages out of Kingsbridge riding an ancient motor-cycle. Charles married Violet Beatrice Bevell on 16 July 1931 in Brentford, and they set up home in Just-a-Cottage in Thurlestone, where he lived until his death in March 1970. This subsequently became the holiday home of Kendall McDonald, his nephew.

Hubback, Arthur Benison (1871-1948)

Arthur Benison Hubback

Arthur Benison Hubback was born 13 April 1871 in Liverpool, the first child of Joseph Hubback, a merchant, City Magistrate, and former Mayor of the city, and Georgina Benison, his third wife and a widow, whom he had married in Scotland on 13 April 1869. He was 56 years old, and she was 28. They had four more children before Joseph's death in 1883. He evidently left the family well-provided for, as in 1891 they were living in Falkner Square, Liverpool with a governess and three servants. Arthur attended Fettes College on a scholarship (1884-1887), and was then articled as an apprentice to the Liverpool city architect Thomas Skelmerdine.

He was appointed chief draughtsman of the Selangor public works department, Malaya, in 1895, and went on to have a distinguished career in major public building works in Malaya and Hong Kong, from mosques to railway stations, becoming a Fellow of the RIBA in 1909.

He was also a keen cricketer, and captained the Selangor cricket team, though he could not equal his brother Theodore who, keeping wicket for Lancashire, caught W. G. Grace and then hit forty runs off the doctor's bowling. Both were outstanding games players.

In 1901 he married Margaret Rose Frances Voules. They had a son, Arthur Gordon Voules Hubback, born 11 May 1902 in Kuala Lumpur, and a daughter Yvonne Voules Hubback, born 24 October 1912 in Kuala Lumpur.

After the Boer War in South Africa (1899-1902) the Federated Malay States Volunteer Rifles was expanded and Arthur Benison Hubback became keenly involved. By 1910 he had been promoted to Major, and commanded the MSVR contingent to George V's coronation in 1911. He was promoted Lt. Col in the MSVR in 1912. With the war looming, he decided to move the family back to England and set up home in Thurlestone for his wife and children.

He joined the 19 Battalion of the London Territorial Force, 47th BEF Division in France, and by 1915 he was Lt Col commanding the 20th London Territorial. Promoted to Brigadier of 19 and 20 London Battalions. He became brigadier general of 2nd Infantry Brigade, 1st Division in 1916, and was awarded CMG on 2nd June "for services rendered in connection with military operations in the field". He became Brigadier General commanding of the 63rd Infantry Brigade, 37th Division B.E.F. in 1918. During the war he was mentioned in dispatches six times, and was awarded the Distinguished Service Order in 1920. Following the war he continued in the military, commanding the 5th London infantry brigade of the territorial army from 1920 to 1924.

Distinguished Service Order

His son, Arthur Gordon Voules Hubback, joined the Royal Navy in 1916 and attended Royal Naval College at Osborne and then Dartmouth, beginning a distinguished career in the Royal Navy in which he reached the rank of Vice Admiral. He was appointed a Companion of the Order of the Bath in 1953, and made a Knight Commander of the Order of the British Empire in 1957, and was appointed Fourth Sea Lord in 1958.

His daughter Yvonne Voules Hubback went to primary school in Thurlestone during the war and later attended Harrogate College, where she became Head girl of her House and Games Captain of the School. She was very good at tennis, playing in junior Wimbledon. She played her most exciting tennis match at Queens Club against Helen Willis, who went on to win Wimbledon in 1931.

**Vice Admiral
AGV Hubback**

Yvonne Voules Barbor (nee Hubback)

The family left Thurlestone in 1920. Arthur Benison continued in the army after the war. He commanded (from 1920 to 1924) the 5th London infantry brigade of the territorial army and then retired. He died at his home, 4 The Hollies, Broxbourne, Hertfordshire, on 8 May 1948, of heart failure.

Yvonne was happily married to a doctor for 54 years until his death in 1989. She then retired to Kingsdon, a little village in Somerset, and in October 2007 a large party was held in Kingsdon Village Hall to celebrate Yvonne's 95th birthday which was attended by her family from many far off countries. She died in 2010.

Inch, Arthur Henry (1883-1930)

Arthur Henry Inch was born at Winkleigh, Devon in the second quarter of 1883 and baptised in Winkleigh Parish church on 27 April 1884. He was the son of Henry Arthur Inch (1860-1921) a carpenter, and his wife Lucy Ford, who had married on 26 October 1882. Some time after the birth of their son they moved to Plymouth, and in 1890 were living at 26 Claremont Street, and Henry was working as a carpenter. In the 1891 census they have moved to larger premises in Oxford Place, and taken in two boarders.

Henry A & Arthur H Inch

By 1901 Henry had changed his occupation, and had taken over the licensed premises of the Prince Alfred Inn in East Stonehouse, next door to the Stonehouse Workhouse. Plymouth valuation records for 1910 show that he has moved to a beerhouse at 14 Buckwell Street. However, in the 1911 census the following year they have moved again and Henry is back working as a joiner from 2 Park Villas, East Stonehouse. Four years later Henry appears in the Electoral Register for 1915 running the Sloop Inn at Bantham. He was to continue there as mine host until his death on 15 May 1921 on the premises. His wife Lucy survived him only until 18 December 1926. Both are buried and have their headstone in Thurlestone churchyard.

Meantime, son Arthur had given up tailoring sometime after 1901 to engage in the licensed trade and 1911 finds him working as a barman at the Grand Hotel, Dawlish. In March 1914 the Banns were read at Thurlestone for Arthur Henry Inch of the parish of Holy Trinity, Plymouth, and Alice Louisa Underhill of Thurlestone parish. They were married on 25 March 1914 at Holy Trinity church, Plymouth. Their first son, James Ford Inch, was born 12 December 1914 and baptised at All Saints on 14 March 1915, when Arthur is living in Bantham and is a licensed victualler (presumably at the Sloop Inn with his parents), though he does not appear in the Electoral Register for that year.

His military service record has not survived, but we do know that he first joined the Devonshire Regiment as private 43548 before transferring to the Machine Gun Corps with the number 121082. He was absent on military service in 1918 and 1919. On demobilisation on 27 July 1919 he returned to the Sloop Inn, and was awarded the British War and Victory medals. On the death of his father in 1921 he took over the licence. His wife Alice Louisa gave birth to a second son Thomas Arthur Inch in December 1924, and a third son Francis Underhill Inch in the second quarter of 1926 but sadly did not survive to the end of that year and died in Plymouth Hospital on 23 December 1926. Arthur Henry continued to run the Sloop Inn until his death on 6 January 1930. Both Arthur and Alice Louisa are also buried and have their headstone in Thurlestone churchyard.

Their three sons prospered, and their grandchildren keep this Inch line flourishing.

The Ingram Family

The patriarch of the Ingram family was John William Ingram (1853-1940), born in South Milton on 28 July 1853, who became the village blacksmith and married a Thurlestone girl, Elizabeth Ann Jackman (1850-1887), in South Milton church in July 1875. They had seven children:

Frank Ingram (1877-1960)   Bessie Blanche Ingram (1879-
John Henry Ingram (1881-   Ethel Ingram (1882-1900)
Beatrice Annie (1883-1884)   Richard Jackman Ingram (1884-1887)
Rosetta Ingram (1885-1886)

After the death of his wife Elizabeth Ann Jackman in January 1887, John William married again to Eliza Ellen Heard (1865-1902) from Starcross before the end of the year, and they had four children:

Reginald Ingram (1889-1900)   Violet C Ingram (1890-
Courtenay Alphonso Ingram (1893-1976)   Daisy R Ingram (1895-

In 1898 John William moved his family and business from South Milton to West Buckland.

We are indebted to his youngest daughter, Daisy Rosetta, for a Memoir of Life at Buckland 1898-1908, which included the following account:

"In the year 1898 father brought his family from South Milton, his native home, to West Buckland. Here he worked at his trade as the village blacksmith and set up his forge at the site of the old Buckland farm that was destroyed by fire, or so we were told. We were eight children to the family - Frank, Blanche, Henry and Ethel by a former marriage of my father, and Violet , Reginald, Courtenay, and myself. The cruel hand of death struck our home and three of our family - my Mother, Ethel, and Reginald - were laid to rest in Thurlestone Church yard within three years.

After Mother's death my sister Blanche kept house and cared for us. I was seven years old at the time of Mother's death. Time is a great healer, and with Blanche's loving care and cheerful disposition our home once again became a happy one.

Father was as honest as the day and fair to all people, asking very little pay for the heavy hard work done over the blazing forge. The whirr of the bellows and the ring of the anvil as the big sledge and smaller hammers came down upon it are sounds I shall never forget.

In the Spring of 1905 father courted Mary Brinkworth, a spinster in her 40th year and engaged as cook in the home of the Lord of the manor, Squire Brunskill. A cause for repairs to the stove at the Brunskill bungalow at Thurlestone situated   in the field directly opposite the church brought about father's and Mary's acquaintance.

At this knowledge a cloud of gloom lowered upon our home and caused we children sad concern. Before their marriage father brought Mary to visit at our home. It was on a Sunday afternoon and we children on arriving home from Sunday School met Mary for the first time. We were very unhappy. Courtenay sat on the back steps and wept big tears and I not to be outdone sat beside him and wept too. In the meantime Blanche and Violet busied themselves with preparing the tea. Blanche behaved very stiffly. She had seen the hand writing on the wall and went to live in the

Henry Clark home at Bantham. Violet with father and with Blanche's good advice carried on with the housekeeping.

On the 18th May that year father brought to our home his third wife. From then on the atmosphere within the walls changed. Mary, with no conception of family life and no love of children, and domineering, set up a rigid routine to which we were unaccustomed, and we became as strangers in our own home. Courtenay being a boy spent much of his time outdoors and whiled away hours in the shop with father, making miniature tools, etc. I as a girl was forced to spend much time in the house and I longed for a return of the happy days of years past. My love for my father kept me obedient to Mary, and so time passed until I left home to be on my own and to earn my own living.

We shall ne'er see the like again of anything written in these memoirs, and when my generation has passed away all will be forgotten and told no more."

After the death of his second wife Eliza Ellen in November 1902 William John married for a third time, to Mary Ann Brinkworth (1866-) on 16 May 1905 at Buckland Tout Saints.

Daisy Ingram emigrated to Montreal, Canada, in 1916 aboard the Canadian Pacific Railway Atlantic Steamship liner "Sicilian".

Ingram, Courtenay Alphonso (1892-1976)

Courtenay Alphonso Ingram, born in South Milton 19 May 1892, was the youngest son of John William Ingram and his second wife Eliza Ellen Heard (1866-1902). He was just six years old when the family moved to West Buckland in 1898, and he appears in the 1901 census aged 8 years, and would have been a scholar attending the local school in Thurlestone.

After leaving school he worked as an apprentice for his father, learning to be a blacksmith, and in the 1911 census is still living at the family home in West Buckland. However, he decided that his future did not include staying in West Buckland, or England, and in March 1913 he sailed for Halifax, Nova Scotia, aboard the "Hyperion". By 1914, when the war broke out, he had moved to Quebec, and quickly presented himself for military service at Canadian Forces Base Val Cartier, set up as a military training camp as part of the mobilization of the Canadian Expeditionary Force, attesting on 23/09/1914.

His army personnel records show that he joined the Royal Canadian Horse Artillery and his unit sailed for Europe on 3 October 1914. He served in France from the 18th July 1915 with the rank of corporal (shoeing smith) and the regimental number 6036. No details are available of where he served in France, but he came through the war unscathed. On 4 July 1918 he was admitted to Canadian Field Ambulance with influenza and again in September of that year with turgescent rhinitis. He was eventually demobilised on 31/5/1919, giving his address as Grove Farm, Coronation, Alberta. Throughout his service he sent $10 per month back to his father in England.

He married Lucy Louisa Davis at Union Bay, British Columbia on 30 January 1926. She died in Victoria, BC, Canada in 1969, and Courtenay Alphonso survived her by seven years and died in Ladysmith, BC, on 30 October 1976.

Ingram, Frank (1878-)

Frank Ingram was the eldest son of John William Ingram and Elizabeth Ann Jackman. He was born on 25 Jan 1878 at Dodbrooke, Kingsbridge. Frank initially followed in his father's footsteps, and appears in the 1891 census as a 14 year old blacksmith.

HMS Hood

However, he decided to switch professions at the earliest opportunity, and enlisted in the Royal Navy at Devonport on 26 Jan 1896 on his eighteenth birthday for 12 years service, and was given the service number 172679. He became a very proficient seaman, rising through the ranks from Boy to OS, ABS, LS, and to PO 1st class by 1903. In the 1901 census he was aboard the battleship HMS Hood in Grand Harbour, Valletta, Malta.

After completing his 12 years he rejoined immediately in 1908, and in 1911 was a Petty Officer serving on HMS Temeraire, which was part of the first battleship squadron, Home Fleet, stationed at Portland. He then served as CPO on HMS Forth during the first half of the war. This was a Mersey class cruiser converted to a submarine depot ship, which served with the 10th and 9th submarine flotillas during the war. Frank then served at depot ships until his demobilisation on 24 August 1919. He was awarded the British Victory and War medals.

He married Edith Phyllis Pepperell (1878-) daughter of James Pepperell and Mary Luckham, at Kingsbridge in 1903. After completing his service in the Royal Navy Frank retired to Bantham, and in 1939 he and Edith were living at No. 1 The Watch, with Frank working as a jobbing gardener. Brother John Henry and wife Jessie were living at No. 3 The Watch.

Ingram, John Henry (1881-1970)

John Henry Ingram was the second son of John William Ingram (1854-1940), Blacksmith, and Elizabeth Ann Jackman (1850-1887), born in South Milton on 14 December 1880. Like his brother Frank, he learned the arts of the blacksmith from his father, and also left home to enlist for twelve years in the Royal Navy at Devonport, but not until he was in his 21st year, on 28 February 1901. He served as a naval blacksmith on a variety of ships and at shore stations during his twelve years, and on completion in 1913 he immediately re-enlisted.

From March 1914 to August 1918 he served aboard HMS Duke of Edinburgh. She was stationed in the Mediterranean when the First World War began and took part in the pursuit of the German battle-cruiser SMS Goeben and light cruiser SMS Breslau. After the German ships reached Ottoman waters, the ship was sent to the Red Sea in mid-August to protect troop convoys arriving from India. HMS Duke of Edinburgh was transferred to the Grand Fleet in December 1914 and participated in the Battle of Jutland in May 1916. She was not damaged during the battle and was the only ship of her squadron to survive. She was eventually transferred to the Atlantic Ocean in August 1917 for convoy escort duties.

Wartime postcard of HMS Duke of Edinburgh

After the war, John Henry was seconded to the Royal Canadian Navy with HMS Aurora. On 25 March 1920, the Canadian government accepted a British offer of one light cruiser and two destroyers to replace the two decrepit cruisers then owned by Canada. In 1920 HMS Aurora was re-activated to refit her for transfer to the Royal Canadian Navy. The Royal Canadian Navy commissioned her on 1 November 1920. She sailed shortly afterward from the UK for Halifax, Nova Scotia, arriving on 21 December with two ex-Royal Navy destroyers that had also been transferred. In August 1921, drastic budget cuts resulted in the decommissioning of Aurora. She was immediately paid off, and in 1922 she was disarmed. John Henry then reverted to the Royal Navy and completed his service on 27 February 1923, retiring on his Naval pension with his three war medals.

He married Jessie Adams Pepperell from Thurlestone at Devonport in 1904, a year after his brother Frank had married her sister Edith. John Henry and Jessie had a son Reginald Henry born in 29 April 1909. He enlisted in the Royal Navy as a Boy seaman on 1 October 1925, aged sixteen, and signed on for 12 years from 29 April 1927. He served on HMS Hood from 27 August 1927 until 28 June 1928, when having been promoted AB, he bought himself out of the service for the sum of £48. John Henry and Jessie settled in Bantham on retirement, together with brother Frank and his wife. In 1939 they lived at 3 The Watch, Bantham. John Henry died at Bromley in 1970 aged 89.

Jackman, Robert Henry (1875-1962)

Robert Henry Jackman was born 24 April 1875, and baptised 13 June 1875 at All Saints, the son of Roger (labourer) and Elizabeth Ann Pearce of Buckland. In 1891 he worked as a farm servant for Albert Stidston at Court Park Barton. Robert married Bessie Matilda Hicks in 1900 in Plympton, and was living in Bowhay Cottages, Eggbuckland, in 1901 working as a gardener. His son Robert Henry was born at Eggbuckland in 1900, and a second son Albert was born in 1902.

In 1911 the family were still living in Bowhay Cottages at Crownhill/Eggbuckland. On 3rd May 1915 he attended the wedding of Albert Edmund Ellis at Thurlestone, and signed as a witness. Perhaps the volunteering enthusiasm of the Ellis brothers persuaded him to sign on also, for although his military papers are not available, his name appears on the medal roll index of the 22nd Battalion (Welsh & Wessex) Rifle Brigade immediately before that of Benjamin William Jeffery, and their service numbers are consecutive.

"The 22nd were formed on the 29/10/15. It completed its training in Halton Camp East. The Battalion sailed from England on 3/1/16 in the "Olympic" transhipped at Mudros and sailed for Alexandria. They then entrained for Cairo, where they were stationed in the Citadel, performing garrison duty.

The Russians at this time were hard pressed in the Caucasus and, as the Gallipoli Peninsula was being now evacuated, it was necessary to draw off the Turkish reserves by the threat of a landing at Alexandretta. For this purpose Liuet.-Col. H. Needham, a Staff Officer at G.H.Q., Egypt, was directed to proceed with a battalion of infantry to Famagusta in Cyprus and there to make such preparations as might make it appear that the establishment of an advanced base for a large army was being undertaken.

The 22nd Battalion was the battalion detailed for this duty, and left Cairo on 22 April 1916, for Alexandria. There they embarked, eight hundred and forty-seven strong, in two ships with all due secrecy and all boats swung outboard in case of submarines which "were as common as sharks are in those parts." However, Famagusta was reached without incident, and after two or three days in camp there, half the Battalion was detailed to lay out a very large imaginary camp, clearing the ground, marking out the sites, and constructing regimental crests with stones. The remainder was moved very frequently from one place to another all round the island, selecting sites for camps, aerodromes, strong points and so forth, as well as finding patrols at likely landing places. "I am afraid," writes Colonel Needham, "that the Battalion, who were completely ignorant of their object in life, must have considered us beyond the pale of sanity, as we managed to draw fifty to sixty thousand Turks from the interior down to Alexandretta, where they worked like beavers digging every form of known entrenchment for several months to no purpose."

After six weeks in Cyprus, the Battalion again embarked, this time for Lemnos; they were stationed at Mudros till November 1916. But on November 1916 the Battalion was relieved at Mudros by the 3rd Royal Marine Battalion, and sailed in the "Royal George" for Salonika, arriving on 26 November. After a few days in camp the Battalion entrained for the Doiran front. Such a war was evidently a new and unpleasant experience. They arrived at Tanes, and marched to Vergetor, where they pitched their camp in a sea of mud. The Battalion worked daily on trenches and wire from 8.30am to 4.30pm, with an hour for lunch and one Sunday off every fortnight. On 4 March 1917 work stopped. The Battalion concentrated at Gramatna and began training. After eight days training at Kirkus they moved via Snevce and Aracli to a bivouac at Sokolovo, suffering their first two casualties (two Riflemen wounded) from enemy air bombing at Arcali.

On 23 August they relieved the 6th Bn. Leicestershire Regiment of the 10th Division on the right of their old positions, and spent the next eight months holding various sectors in this area, with periods in brigade reserve at Turbes. The second winter, though far from pleasant, was far easier to endure than the first, for though the rain was no less, duckboards and good roads had lightened the labours of those at the front and at the back alike.

The Brigade moved further west in March and relieved the 2nd Bn. Cheshire Regiment at Todorovo, near their original sector. Much work on trenches was required after the winter. on 24 September a move forward to the winter line was suddenly ordered. news came that on 20 September the Convention had been signed with Bulgaria.

The 228th Brigade was disbanded on 2 October and the Battalion, six hundred and ninety-nine strong, sent by train via Saragul to Akindzali, where they worked, near their old front line, on the reconstruction of the railway.

By 17 December they had reached the base at Lembek, and were suffering from the influenza epidemic. Demobilization was soon complete, and on 29 January 1919 the details were transferred to the 2nd Garrison Battalion of the King's Regiment."

(From a contributor to the Great War Forum website - 22 Battn Rifle brigade)

The Medal Roll document confirms that he served simultaneously with BW Jeffery from 18 Jan 1916 in Egypt (area 2), and then in Macedonia in the Balkans (area 2) from 26 November 1916 to 17 September 1918. We know that Jeffery suffered from rheumatism and malaria, but with no service papers available for Jackman it is not known how his health stood up - though he did survive to be awarded the British War and Victory medals.

After the war Robert Henry went back to being a gardener. Twenty years later, in the 1939 census Robert and Bessie were living at Little Bonnaford, Tavistock, and Robert was still working as a professional gardener. Bessie died two years later, but Robert Henry survived until 18 November 1962 when he died at Crownhill aged 87.

James, Augustine Edmund Lee (1874-1964)

Augustine Edmund Lee James was born at Watford, Hertfordshire, on 27 September 1874, and christened 25 October that year at the parish church of St Mary's, Watford, where his father, the Rev Richard Lee James, as well as serving as a chaplain to the Herts Yeomanry was the vicar for sixty years from 1855 to 1915.

The vicar and his wife Alice Thorold Parkinson raised a large family - nine boys (one of whom died in infancy) and three girls - born between 1856 and 1879. One brother, Reginald (1870-1966) followed his father into the church after graduating MA from Clare College, Cambridge in 1902, and became Canon of St Albans in 1933. Another brother, Basil Humphrey (1868-1936) emigrated to Canada. The youngest brother, Algernon Meyrick Alban (1879-1951) became a doctor, and served in the Great War as a Captain in the RAMC in Egypt (1917-19). All the other five brothers chose a career in the armed forces, and all served in the Great War.

Lt. Colonel Richard Donne Lee James (1858-1940) joined the Northumberland Fusiliers, but then transferred to the Militia Engineer Submarine Miners (Royal Engineers) at Plymouth, where he rose to be Major and Honorary Lt. Colonel. Retired to Chyanhall, Gulval, Cornwall.

Brigadier-General Cyril Henry Leigh James (1861-1946) trained at RMC Sandhurst. He was commissioned into the Duke of Cornwall's Light Infantry in September 1882, but two months later transferred to the Northumberland Fusiliers. He saw active service in South Africa, later commanding the 1st Battalion of his regiment (1905-9). In June 1911 he became GOC Warwickshire Infantry Brigade. He played an important part in the brigade's peacetime training and in its preparation for war, and commanded the unit during its first year on the Western Front, April 1915-May 1916. In June 1916 he was given command of 177th Brigade, accompanied the brigade to France in March 1917 and led it in the battles of the Menin Road Ridge, Polygon Wood and Cambrai. He was awarded CB (1916) and CMG (1918).

Captain Arthur Parkinson James (1864-1951) trained at Britannia Naval College, and rose from Midshipman (1880) to sub-Lt (1884) to Lt (1888) to Commander (1899) serving latterly on HMS Hood. He was Captain of HMS Bellerophon in 1904, when he retired with the rank of Captain. He was recalled to be Senior Officer in charge Auxiliary Patrol Area XIX, and Senior Naval Officer, Killybegs (1915-1918).

Captain Athelstane Spencer Beebee James (1872-1961) enlisted in the 18th Queen Mary's Own Hussars in 1894, and served in India (1895-8) and South Africa (1898-1902). He was gazetted Lieutenant in the 3rd Battalion South Wales Borderers in October 1914, and served in France from November 1914, subsequently promoted to Captain in the 2/30 Punjabis, and the 19th London Regiment.

Captain Augustine Edmund Lee James (1874-1964) also chose a military career, and was commissioned 2nd Lieutenant in the 4th Battalion, South Wales Borderers, on 9th April 1892.

He married Ella Maxton Browne, from Dublin, on the Isle of Wight, in 1910, and the couple set up home at Aunemouth, where they appear in the Electoral registers for 1911, 1912, 1913, and 1914 in Thurlestone. Their daughter Josephine was born 26 November 1913. Augustine would been mobilised at the outbreak of war, and left with his battalion in the BEF contingent which arrived in France on 22 August 1914. The family moved from Thurlestone in 1915, and their son Edmund David James was born in West Derby, Liverpool in 1918.

After the war they returned to Devon and lived at Combe Raleigh, Honiton from the 1920s to 1939, before moving to Penally Abbey, Pembrokeshire, where they were in 1944. They continued to live in Pembrokeshire until Augustine's death at Tenby on 7 May 1964.

Their son, Edmund David James, followed his father into the South Wales Borderers, reaching the rank of Captain. He was then attached to HQ, 4th Parachute Brigade, Army Air Corps, with the number 85626. Edmund jumped into Arnhem with the 4th Parachute Brigade on 17 September 1944. After an initial success, the paratroopers came under heavy fire from the German defenders of the town, which included an SS Panzer Division which British intelligence had not known of. Heavy fighting ensued, under desperate circumstances, with the paratroopers totally surrounded by Germans, with vastly superior firepower and numbers of men. On the third day, 4th Parachute Brigade led an attempt to break through the German lines north of Oosterbeek, but were held up, with heavy losses. On 20 September 1944, the fourth day of a planned two day defence, Edmund was killed during a gallant attempt to reach Oosterbeek to reinforce the beleaguered force which was holding the bridge, under the command of Colonel Frost. Edmund was 26 years old, and is buried in grave 6 D 19 at Arnhem Oosterbeek War Cemetery, Netherlands.

Quite a remarkable contribution to the defence of the realm by the descendants of the Vicar of Watford.

Footnote: Another James played an important role in WW2. This was Australian actor Meyrick Edward Clifton James, who impersonated Field Marshal Montgomery in 1944, to mislead the Nazis about our invasion plans. The episode was made into a film "I was Monty's Double" in 1958 starring James himself in the title role. The appearance of the name Meyrick in both families may suggest they could be distantly connected.

Jeffery, Benjamin William (1888-1977)

Benjamin William Jeffery was born at West Buckland on 25 August 1888, and baptised at All Saints, Thurlestone on 14 October, the only son of Benjamin Robert Jeffrey (Labourer of West Buckland) and Clara Hill. He worked as a labourer and gardener from his parent's home until 1909 when he married Sarah Jane Hosking (b.1887 Plympton but banns say "of this parish" and marriage cert says a domestic servant living at Aunemouth) on the 29ᵗʰ July 1909. Daughter Their daughter Olive Louise was born at East Buckland and baptised 7 August 1910 at All Saints, Thurlestone, after which they moved to South Milton (the 1911 census shows them living in 2 rooms at Horswell House) where he was working as a gardener.

Benjamin decided to volunteer soon after war was declared, and attested on 5 Dec 1914 at Plymouth as a private in the 5ᵗʰ Battalion Devonshire Regt. After basic training he was transferred on 29 May 1915 to war service in the 22ⁿᵈ (Wessex & Welsh) Battalion, the Rifle Brigade, with the regimental no. 204840. His fellow gardener Robert Henry Jackman joined the battalion about the same time and his regimental number was 204840.
Their war service will have followed a similar course within the battalion, and is detailed on the pages for Robert Henry Jackman. Benjamin served 4yrs 183 days (Egypt 18 Jan 1916 to 3 Dec 1916 , Salonika Dec 1916 to 11 Nov 1918). He suffered from rheumatism (June 1916) and malaria (Christmas 1917) and was treated in Mudros Hospital. He was promoted Lance Corporal and then full Corporal in 1918, but appears to have needed further hospital treatment (possibly connected with the flu epidemic) and was examined in Karahassis on 29 Mar 1919. He was eventually demobbed on 5 June 1919 and returned to East Buckland. Awarded British War Medal and Victory medal and shown as Acting Sgt on the Rifle Brigade Regimental Roll.

Sarah and Olive had probably moved back to live with Benjamin's parents in East Buckland in 1914 after Benjamin joined up. The family appears in the Electoral roll there in 1918 through to 1921. Benjamin of course was absent on military service until 1919. After returning to England, Benjamin resumed his former occupation as a gardener at South Milton, and they settled at Horswell Cottages where they continued to live for many years, appearing there in the 1939 census. Daughter Olive Louise was no longer with them by then, as she had married carpenter and joiner Clifford W N Goddard in the summer of 1938, and in the 1939 census they were living at "Horswell", Victoria Road, Fleet, in Hampshire.

Sarah Jane died in 1951. Benjamin may have subsequently gone to live with his daughter in Hampshire, for it was there that he died in September 1977 aged 89, a remarkable survival for someone whose health had been undermined by his illnesses during the war in the Balkans.

Jeffery, William Henry (1879-1963)

William Henry Jeffery was born at East Buckland on 12 January 1879 and baptised at All Saints church on 16 February, the son of John Thomas Jeffery (gardener) and Elizabeth Jane Lavers who had been married at All Saints on 2 April 1874. William Henry was their second child, the first having been a daughter, Mary, born 1875.

After leaving school William Henry spent time working on a farm and learned to handle horses. This led him to seek employment using these skills, and the 1901 census finds him in Tormoham, Torquay, and a boarder at the home of William Dale, carriage proprietor of 17 Wellswood Place, where he is described as a horseman. It was probably in Torquay that he met his future wife, Eva Dyer, as she was employed as a cook/domestic at the home of a Mr Bergsman, a Provident Society superintendent living as Seabury,Tormoham. William Henry married Eva Dyer at All Saints on 26 April 1905 when his occupation was given as driver. The witness at the wedding was Benjamin Jeffery.

William & Eva's
wedding 1905

The Hotel coachman

William joined the Grose family working as a coachman at the Thurlestone hotel. One of his duties was to drive the coach up to South Brent station where he would pick up the guests and bring them back to the hotel. The old coaches used for this remained in Thurlestone until at least the early 1970s and were stored in the back of the old farm buildings. These were seen by William's great grandson Keith when playing in the barns as a young boy. William spent a good part of his working life at the hotel and was joined at the hotel by his son Leonard when he was eighteen. Their home was at Park Cottage, East Buckland, and the 1911 census shows William Henry with wife Eva and their three sons Wilfred Charles (b. 29 April 1907), Leonard Henry (b. 23 February 1910) and Wallace Leslie (b. 23 May 1911).

At Park Cottage c.1915

When he was required for war service William Henry attested on 9 October 1916 giving his occupation as coachman. Though expressing a preference for the Army Service Corps, he was assigned with service no. 125745 as a gunner in Royal Garrison Artillery. He trained at Prees Heath depot and was posted to 330 Siege Battery on 20 Jan 1917. The battery served in France from September 1917-1919. After the armistice he accepted to stay on with a pay increase of 6d per day, and was granted leave to the UK from France in January1919. He was admitted to hospital in France on 4/2/1919, and then invalided

Gunner W H Jeffery

back to England on 22/2/1919 and admitted as sick to the Lord Derby War Hospital at Warrington, and demobilised and discharged from that hospital on 5 March 1919. However the nature of his wounds or sickness is not recorded. He was awarded the British War and Victory medals, and should have been entitled to the Silver War Badge, though he did not receive it.

In later years William went to work on the golf course at Thurlestone. During this time he helped to build all the walls around the 12th, 13th and 14th fairways with some Welsh miners. In the 1939 census the family had moved to 3 Jubilee Cottage, Thurlestone, and William was recorded as a groundsman at the golf club. With Willam and Eva was their son Wallace Leslie (carpenter). Their son Leonard Henry was two doors away at 1 Jubilee Cottages (recorded as a chauffeur at the Hotel), with wife Caroline. Son Wilfred Charles (mason) was also living nearby at Dorville (next to Vine Cottage) with wife Doris.

After Eva died in Nov 1954 William lived on his own for a while before selling 3 Jubilee cottages to his grandson Gordon Jeffery where he lived with June Jeffery (nee Barons). This was later the birth place of his great grandchildren Keith★ and Janice Jeffery who lived there until 1976. Following the sale of Jubilee cottage William went to live in Trethurle cottage with his son Leonard and daughter in law Carrie just three doors up the street. Apparently, whilst at the golf course, he was crafty or fortunate enough to join a pension scheme only 12 months before leaving for £3 p.a. which later paid him £3 per week for 19 years from the age of 65 to his death at 84. William remained healthy up until the end when he is said to have taken his daily walk up to the post office. He commented that the walk up the hill had been hard that day. On the way down the hill he dropped down dead. First on the scene was his grand daughter Angela.

Corporal Jeffery and family

★ I am indebted to Keith Jeffery for much of this information and all the pictures.

Jenkins, Francis (1877-1927)

Francis Jenkins was born at Clanacombe Manor, Thurlestone in June 1877 and baptised at All Saints on 5 July 1877 by the Rev Peregrine Ilbert. He was the only son of Henry Lionel Jenkins of Clanacombe, and joined an elder sister Mary Emily, who had been born in January 1975. The family were looked after by a household of six - Head nurse, under nurse, and governess to look after the children, as well as a Head Cook, parlour maid, and kitchen maid. Francis came from a family with a strong military tradition on both sides. His uncle was Major General Francis Jenkins, KCB, Commissioner of Assam for many years, and ADC to Queen Victoria, while his maternal grandfather, Charles William Short, had been a Coldstream Guards cornet at Waterloo and gone on to be Colonel of the regiment and a military historian.

Francis went from Harrow to Sandhurst Royal Military College, and joined the Coldstream Guards as a 2nd Lieut in 1896, promoted to Lt in 1898, and served in South Africa 1899-1902 (Queen's Medal, 5 clasps, and King's medal). Promoted Capt in 1903, he served with the West African Frontier Forces 1903-1911 including the Kano Sokoto campaign Nigeria (medal and clasp), and was Staff Officer WAFF at the Colonial Office 1911-1916, being promoted Major in 1913. He married the actress, Gaiety Girl, and famous beauty Margaret Campbell Fraser in 1914, and they had two daughters - Margaret (b.1916) and Elizabeth Anne (b.1918).

His father had acquired the neighbouring property Burnt House as a future home for Francis, but he had little opportunity to live there as his military and diplomatic career took him overseas for the last ten years of his life.

From 1916-1919 he returned to Nigeria as Lt Col of the Nigeria Regiment and Commandant WAFF, and was made CMG in the 1918 New Years Honours List before retiring as a half-pay Lt Col on 3 June 1919. Three weeks later Downing Street announced "The King had been pleased to give directions for the appointment of Lieutenant-Colonel Francis Jenkins CMG to be Colonial Secretary of the Island of Barbados." In 1920 the French president made him an Officer of the Legion d'Honneur. In 1921 he was appointed Secretary, and later Governor-General of the Southern Provinces of Nigeria, where he died on 8 November 1927 following an operation. A memorial service was held at Thurlestone Parish church on 13 November, conducted by the rector, Canon Stuart Majendie, and attended by a large number of parishioners.

Daughter Mary Emily Jenkins married Ashton Gilbert Radcliffe on 9 August 1894 in London, and they lived at East Grinstead in Sussex, where he was Headmaster of a private school. They spent many holidays at Clanacombe and became involved in local activities.

Daughter Elizabeth Anne followed a career as an examiner in ballet for the Royal Society of Dance before retiring to live at Clanacombe Manor, where she was well-known in the parish until her death in 2009.

The Johns Family

While Rev Coope would no doubt have welcomed the addition to his flock when they arrived in Thurlestone in 1915, the Johns family had for at least three generations been a South Milton family. The 1901 census reveals them at 2 Clarence Place as:

Joseph Henry Johns, b.1859, horseman on a farm
Susan Stone Johns (nee Gillard), b. 1859 at Goveton, housewife
John William Henry Johns, b.1884, horseman on a farm
Alphaeus Harold Johns, b.1885, horseman on a farm
Gideon Thomas Johns, b.1886, no given occupation
Alonzo James Johns, b. 1889, no given occupation

The first connection with Thurlestone appears in the 1915 Electoral Register for the parish, in which Joseph Henry Johns is listed as number 150, and has property in both South Milton and Thurlestone (successive). As there were no electoral registers for the years 1916 or 1917, the next record is for 1918. This register shows that most of the family have also now moved from South Milton to Thurlestone, and lists father John Joseph and wife Susan: son John William (absent on military service) and wife Ethel Mary: and son Gideon Thomas and wife Elizabeth Ellen.

Son Alonzo James had married Mabel Burton at Monkton Farleigh in Wiltshire in April 1908. He served in the war as a private in the ASC number DM2 (mechanical Transport Learner) with the regimental number 170737, and appears to have been based at a depot in the UK. He was awarded the British War and Victory medals. But he cannot be counted among Thurlestonians. Newspaper reports show that he took on the licence of the Ring of Bells Inn at Hilperton Marsh in 1928 while working for Messrs Ushers of Trowbridge. He died on 4 April 1951 while living at 65 Newtown, Trowbridge, Wiltshire.

Son Alphaeus Harold had married Ellen Froude Lidstone from Goveton on 18 June 1913 at Charleton. Their daughter Doreen F was born 19 July 1914. They lived in South Milton. No military service records could be found for Alphaeus Harold Johns.

Rev Coope lists both the other two brothers at Thurlestone as serving in the war.

Gideon Thomas Johns, (1886-1950)

Gideon Thomas Johns, a jobbing gardener, had married Elizabeth Ellen Luscombe in June 1909 and had set up home at Sutton, South Milton, but had moved to Thurlestone by 1918, and was not shown as absent on military service. It is possible that he served earlier in the war and was discharged before 1918, but no military service records could be found, nor does his name appear in the records for those awarded the Silver War Badge.

In the 1939 Registration he was living at 2 Sea View Gardens in Thurlestone, and he died at Plymouth in 1950. Also included on the Register is his wife and son R Maurice Johns born 4 Jan 1917.

John William Henry Johns, (1884-1936)

The eldest son, John William Henry Johns, was also a jobbing gardener. He enlisted into the Royal Garrison Artillery (No 125746) on October 9, 1916, along with William Henry Jeffery (125745), and trained at Prees Heath, and served with 330 Siege Battery in France from 20 Jan 1917 with him. Gunner Johns was discharged on June 21, 1919, when suffering from Tuberculosis of the lung (classed as 100% disability), and received the Silver War Badge (B235262) as well as the British War Medal and the Victory Medal. He was awarded a pension of £1 7s 6d a week with a review after nine months. His address in his discharge papers was The Cottage, Thurlestone. John William Henry married Mary Ethel Jose in Plymouth just before Christmas 1917 and they settled in Thurlestone. He died in February 1936 and is buried in the churchyard at South Milton.

Masters, John Alfred Owen (1893-1955)

John Alfred Owen Masters

John Alfred Owen Masters (known as Owen) was born on 14 September 1893 at West Buckland, Thurlestone, Devon, and baptised at All Saints on 15 October, the youngest son of Robert Gillard Masters (1860-1904), a farm labourer, and Ida Ford (1864-1898), who were married at All Saints on 7 November 1885.

He enlisted initially in the 7th Battalion of the Devonshire Regiment with the rank of private and the regimental number 290337, but was soon transferred to the 1/4th Battalion of the Devonshire Regiment. His role was a Battalion Cyclist, as a member of the Cycle Corps. With few field telephones, and no radios, cyclists were essential for conveying messages during battle.

The 1/4th Battalion Devonshire Regiment were formed in August 1914 in Exeter. Part of the Devon & Cornwall Brigade, Wessex Division. On 9 October 1914, they sailed for India, landing at Karachi on 11 November 1914, and came under orders of 3rd (Lahore) Divisional Area at Ferozepore. February 1915 saw the regiment moved to the independent 42nd Brigade of the Indian Army. They remained there until they were sent to Mesopotamia early in 1916.

They arrived on 28th February and landed at Basra with the independent 41st Indian brigade and moved up the Tigris to join the 14th Indian Division at Sheikh Saad a month later. Although shelled by the Turks, their most dangerous enemy was disease caused by the climate. In the summer of 1916, no fewer than 400 men were admitted to hospital. On 5 May 1916 the Regiment was transferred to 37th Brigade part of the 14th (Indian) Division.

On 3rd February 1917 the 1/4th Devons and 1/9th Gurkhas led a dazzlingly successful attack on the Hai Salient in the Turkish line south of Kut. Victory came at a price: of 15 officers and 403 men who attacked, only 5 officers and 186 men emerged unscathed. The survivors of the 1/4th spent the rest of the war in Amara and Baquba (north of Baghdad) building roads, guarding prisoners and administering refugee camps. At some point during his service, Owen was promoted to Lance Corporal and then to full Corporal. Having lost 80 officers and men killed in action, they were reduced to a cadre in March 1919 and returned home in August. In their single, gallant action they had won two battle honours for the Devon Regiment: Kut El Amara 1917 and Mesopotamia 1916-18.

Owen was always proud of his service in the 1/4 Battalion of the Devonshire Regiment, and the experience of active service in Mesopotamia which he called 'Messpot'! He felt that the actions of our soldiers in that part of the world were not given the recognition they deserved for their role in WW1. He was awarded the British War and Victory medals.

After the war he returned to Thurlestone, and in 1927 married Harriet Turner. From 1930 to 1946 Owen and Hetty ran The Sloop Inn at Bantham, together with Frank Walton. Their godson was Owen G F Masters, born in 1937, the son of Henry James Masters and Ivy Joan Turner, and named after him. I am particularly grateful to Owen, who has generously contributed much of the content and illustrations for these articles on his uncles, and been extremely supportive of the project.

Moore, Francis George (1887-1951)

Francis George Moore

Francis George Moore was born 11 January 1887 in Bantham, and baptised in All Saints on 27 February, the youngest son of George Henry Moore (1844-1925) and Elizabeth Ann Dolton (18-1889) and younger brother of John Thomas Moore (1881-1916). The family lived in the cottage next door but one to the Sloop Inn.

After leaving school Francis George was taken on as an apprentice blacksmith with John William Ingram, serving his 5 years apprenticeship from 1900 to 1906. He then enlisted on 10 May 1907 at Kingsbridge as a sapper in the Royal Engineers, service number 16521 and served three years before joining the reserves in 1910. In 1911 he was working as a jobbing gardener in Haslemere, Surrey, and boarding with a Garfield and Mary Hale at 8 Underhill Road.

As a trained reservist, he was mobilised on the outbreak of war on 5 August 1914 and went to France with the BEF. He was promoted to Lance Corporal on 14 April 1915 and on 1 May 1915 he was awarded the Croix de Guerre (reported in the London Gazette). This award was only instituted on 8 April 1915 to recognise acts of bravery in the face of the enemy, and Francis George Moore was one of the first recipients. On 21 December 1916 he was commended for gallantry and distinguished service in the field and Mentioned in Dispatches (London Gazette of 16 May 1917). In 1918 he spent two weeks in No 6 General Hospital before rejoining his unit on 13 December 1918. He was appointed acting Sergeant educational instructor on 13 January 1919 before embarking for the UK on 31 May 1919. He was also awarded the 1914-15 Star, the British War, and Victory medals.

After returning home from the war he married Amy Rosina A Williams, a Plymouth girl, in Kingsbridge in December 1919. Their daughter Eileen Frances Moore was born on 20th January 1921, and married Leonard George Tucker in Kingsbridge in 1946.

In 1939 Francis George lived at 56 Church Street, Kingsbridge, still working as a blacksmith. He died in March 1951 aged 64 years.

Croix-de-Guerre

Moore, George Frederick (1891-1956)

George Frederick Moore was born at Thurlestone on 1 June 1890, and baptised at All Saints on 10 August. He was the second son of Nathaniel Moore (1859-1932), boot-repairer, and his wife Emma Wood (1858-1918), who lived in Thurlestone at Church Cottages next door to the Ellis family. In 1901 they had James Coombes, the golf professional at Thurlestone Golf Club, as a boarder. After finishing school George worked as a farm labourer, and in 1911 the census shows he is still working on farms.

When the war came, George was an early volunteer though unfortunately his war service records have not survived. However, his medal roll and index card tell us that he attested for the Devonshire Regiment and served with the 8th Battalion as Private with the regimental number 10617. The 8th Battalion was formed in August 1914, and received intensive training at various camps including Aldershot while awaiting orders for France. It eventually set off for France on 25 July 1915, closely followed by the 9th Battalion, which joined them at Calonne in August. These two battalions were involved in heavy fighting especially at the battle of Loos in September 1915, when the 8th had 19 officers and 620 men on their casualty list.

With his records lost, there is no evidence to indicate whether George Frederick was ever wounded, how badly, or how many times. But clearly he was extremely fortunate to survive when so many of his comrades were killed or wounded. His luck also stayed with him throughout the war, until his demobilisation on 4 April 1919. He was awarded the 1914-15 Star, the British War, and Victory medals.

On returning to Thurlestone he married Elizabeth Ethel Oldridge, a Dodbrooke girl, in September 1919. They set up home in Kingsbridge at 1 Wisteria Row, off Fore Street. Their daughter Elizabeth E J Moore was born in 1921. In 1939 George and his wife had moved to 77 Church Street, Kingsbridge, where he was working as a County Court Bailiff. George Frederick Moore died 15 June 1956 in South Hams Hospital.

Moore, John Henry (1881-1961)

John Henry Moore was born 25 March 1881 at Thurlestone, and baptised at All Saints church on 8 May 1881, the eldest son of Nathaniel Moore (1859-1932) and his wife Emma Wood (1858-1918). After leaving school he first appears in the 1901 census when he was working as a domestic groom at the home of Ashley Froude and family at Collapit Creek House, West Alvington.

In December 1906 he married Kate Blewett Roberts at Helston, Cornwall, and they set up home at 4 Hea Cottages, Hea Moor, Madron, Penzance, Cornwall, where their first child Nathaniel John Moore was born in 1910. He did not survive long, as his death at Madron is recorded in April 1912. A second son William Arthur Moore, was born 13 April 1913 in Penzance. John Henry was still working as a domestic coachman at this address.

We know that his younger brother Arthur Owen went down from Thurlestone to Penzance some time in 1917/18, presumably to visit John Henry, and that it was from Penzance that Arthur Owen attested for military service in 1917/1918 (date unknown, but as he was killed in action on 11 August 1918 his enlistment date must have been some six months earlier). Whether John Henry attested for military service in WW1 is unknown, as we have found no war records for him, but as Rev Coope has him listed he may well have known more than we do.

In 1920 John Henry and his wife and son William Arthur emigrated to USA on 25 June, arriving in New York on 2 July, with their destination stated as Lead City. They moved on to South Dakota, where they made their home at 107 McLennan Street, Lead City, Lawrence County, and it is here that they are recorded in the 1930 census. John Henry worked as a shipping clerk in a department store, but William with no occupation In the 1940 census they have moved to 516 Mcquillan Avenue, Lead City. Willam was now a salesman., and went on to have a successful business career.

John Henry lived on until 16 Nov 1961, when he was buried in West Lead Cemetery, and William had the monument shown below inscribed at the grave.

Moore, Osmond (1886-1973)

Osmond Moore was born on 26 January 1886 at South Milton, the son of Josiah and Celena Moore of Hingston's Farm. After leaving school he worked as a farm labourer, and in 1901 he was a carter at Shute Farm in South Milton for Joseph Polyblank. He had moved to Thurlestone before his marriage, as the Banns were read by Rev Coope at All Saints. His bride, Blanche Tucker, was a Chivelstone girl, and it was at St Sylvester's, Chivelstone that the wedding took place on 10 April 1907. It is the only church in Devon dedicated to St Sylvester, a 4th century Bishop of Milan and Pope from 312 to 335 AD.

After their wedding Osmond and Blanche lived in Thurlestone, where Osmond worked as a coachman at the Thurlestone Hotel. When the war came Osmond was required for military service, but unfortunately no war service records for him survive, except for his medal roll card. There are medal roll cards for two men with the name Osmond Moore, one in the Royal Guernsey Light Infantry, and one in the RASC, a private with the service number M2/181206, signifying an electrician. As there are no other details on the cards, it is not certain which one is the Thurlestone Osmond, but the likelihood is that, as a coachman, he would have been assigned to the RASC. There are no dates for his period of service, and no record of where he served. All we know is that he was awarded the British War and Victory medals.

Medal Roll Card

After surviving his war service Osmond returned to his job at the Thurlestone Hotel, which subsequently involved driving a range of motor vehicles as they steadily took over from horse-drawn carriages. He continued at the Hotel until his retirement. In the 1939 census he and Blanche were living at Prawle, and looking after her father.

Osmond died in 1973 in Plymouth at the age of 87.

Moore, Walter Norman (1894-1964)

Walter Norman Moore was born on 14 April 1894 at Bantham, the second son of George Henry Moore (1844-1925) and his second wife, the widow Keziah Perring (see Family History notes for casualty John Thomas Moore). After leaving school (and probably during his schooldays as well) Walter worked as a caddie at Thurlestone Golf club, and this is his given occupation in the 1911 census.

At the outbreak of war he must have been one of the earliest to volunteer, for although his war service records have not survived, his medal roll card indicates that he was serving in France from 11 July 1915. He had been assigned to the Army Service Corps at his attestation, with the rank of private and the service number SS/12075. The letters SS indicate Supply Special and meant that the man was specially enlisted for his trade: in other words, he came from civilian employment in a trade that was of direct value to work in the Supply section: he may have been a clerk, butcher or baker, for example. This would indicate that Walter had acquired some other skill in addition to that of carrying a bag of golf clubs. He was transferred to the mechanical transport section on 9 November 1917 and assigned the service number M/331548.

With no service record available we do not know how long Walter served in France or whether he also served in any other theatre of war, but we do know that he survived and returned to his parents' home in Bantham in the autumn of 1920 and appears in the electoral register for that year. He was awarded the 1915 Star, the British War and Victory medals.

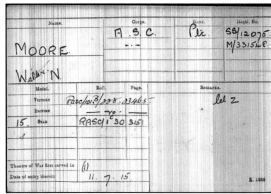

Medal Roll Card

The register for 1926 shows him now staying at the home of James Urban Moore and his wife Emma Matilda Burgoyne. In June of that year he married their daughter Pauline Moore. 1926 was also the year in which Commander Evans opened his Hexdown and Bigbury golf club, and Walter Norman seized the opportunity to take on the role of golf professional, greenkeeper, and general factotum at the club, with his wife Pauline acting as clubhouse steward. They lived in the little cottage known as Lincombe, adjacent to the seventh hole on the course, and continued to serve the club until Walter Norman's death on 18 October 1964 at Mount Gould hospital in Plymouth.

A Walter Moore memorial salver became one of the coveted prizes in the club's trophy list, awarded in the Bigbury Open competiton.

Morgan, William (1885-1974)

William Morgan was born at Churchstow on 7 February 1885, the son of Amos Morgan (1856-1923), a farmer, and Mary Ellen Distin (1859-1887). His mother died two years later in 1887 and Amos married again in 1890 to Louisa Lethbridge. When Amos and his new wife were expecting their first child young William was sent to stay with his grandparents, William Morgan, farmer and blacksmith, and his wife Jemima, the postmistress at West Alvington. He was still with them in 1901, when Jemima's younger sister Fanny had taken over the postmistress role, and Jemima was acting as housekeeper, her husband having died in 1894. Young William is not recorded in the census as having a specific occupation, but the letter L seems to indicate he was a casual labourer.

At all events, by 12 October 1909 he was sufficiently well established to marry Emma Elizabeth Norsworthy, born 1884 at Dittisham, at All Saints, Thurlestone.

Her parents had both died before she was eight years old, and she with her elder sister Mabel had gone to live with aunt /uncle William Hingston Pound, a grocer and carrier, and his wife Susan Shepherd Kendall in Thurlestone village. They were still living with them in 1911, when Pound was described as a shopkeeper (at home), and William Morgan was a carpenter.

It was also in 1911 that they had their first child, a daughter, Florence Ellen Mary, baptised at All Saints on 4 June. A second daughter, Elsie Kendall, followed in 1912, baptised on 16 September, and a third, Alice Mabel, was baptised 2 November 1913. Tragedy struck the following year when mother Emma Elizabeth died late in 1914, leaving William to cope with three baby daughters. Who looked after these children after their mother's death, and later while William was on military service, is not known, but the names of the witnesses at his wedding (see above) are sufficiently numerous to suggest that help and/or homes might not have been too hard for him to find for his young daughters.

William attested for military service with the army on 20 November 1915. At his medical it was recorded that he had both left and right inguinal hernias, and was classed grade three, and granted leave until 5 February 1918. On that date he re-attested and was transferred to the Inland Waterways and Docks branch of the Royal Engineers with the regimental number 332009 and posted to Bristol. On 18 February 1918 he was transferred to Portbury. The heavy manual work he had to do there aggravated his ruptures, and he was assessed on 29 December 1918 as up to 20% disability. He was demobilised on 29 January 1919, and returned to Thurlestone.

He married for a second time, to Elsie Pearl Bodman (b. 18 October 1893), later in 1919 and they settled in Thurlestone, where they appear in the Electoral registers through to 1939 at Sunny Ridge.

Daughter Florence married Leonard P Chave in 1926: daughter Elsie Kendall married William L Horn in 1937: but no record for a marriage of Alice Mabel Morgan could be located.

William died in Falmouth in 1974 aged 89 years.

Morris, George Marshall (1871-1932)

George Marshall Morris was born in Mussoorie, Bengal, India, on 22 August 1871, the eldest son of Colonel George Tomkyns Morris, Bengal Staff Corps, and Georgiana Boyes. His parents returned to the UK and in 1891 were living at 68 Chaucer Road, Bedford. George was educated at Bedford Grammar School, and matriculated in 1890 when he entered Edinburgh University medical school in October that year.

TO YACHTING MEN AND OTHERS.
OVERLOOKING SEA AND RIVER.

L OVELY DEVON (IN THE FINEST POSITION ON THE SOUTH COAST, Aune Cross and Higher Aunemouth ; ¼ mile of sea and 300ft. above same).—To be SOLD, this exceedingly choice PROPERTY, with up-to-date Residence, as above, HEATED THROUGHOUT and lighted by ACETYLENE GAS: 3 reception, billiard room, 7 or more bedrooms, bathroom ; lodge: cottage ; stabling and motor-house ; PRETTY GROUNDS, kitchen garden, orchard, paddock, and land, in all 54 ACRES ; also second House, with 2 reception, 5 bedrooms, bathroom ; stabling ; farmery. Property would be SOLD as a whole, or Residence, stabling, lodge, cottage, and about 5½ acres would be SOLD separately.—For SALE, privately, or by AUCTION, on May 24 next, by HARRODS (Ltd.), as above.

Advert in *The Bystander*, 30 March 1910

His forthcoming marriage to Grace Lilian Harcourt was announced in the Morning Post of 20 April 1905, (in which his name was prefixed by "Dr" although the UK Medical Register does not list him as having qualified) and actually took place in St Pauls, Ramsey, Minnesota, USA, on 23 July 1905. The couple returned to England from New York aboard the SS Minnehaha arriving London 21 August 1905. They continued to live at Aune Cross while Cecil Harcourt was at Dartmouth Royal Naval College, but then sought to rent it out. However, eventually it was put up for auction at Harrods and became the home of Wilfred Creswick's family from Sheffield.

After selling the Aune Cross house, they moved to Pennsylvania Park, Exeter, where the 1911 census records the household as containing:

Dr George Marshall Morris, private means (not medical practitioner)
Grace Lilian Morris, wife
Mabel Halliday Harcourt, stepdaughter
Katie Maud Violet Morris, sister
Margaret Ann Sanders, cook
Ellen Matilda Moore, parlourmaid
May Beatrice Moore, housemaid.

The two Moore sisters who had accompanied them from Aune Cross.

Medal Roll Index Card for Major George Marshall Morris

George became a regular Army officer in the 5th Northamptonshire Regiment, and served in France, being awarded the Star, and the British War and Victory medals, as well as (according to the above) the Silver War Badge.

In the 1920 Electoral register George and Grace were living at Hillingbury Lodge, Chandlers Ford, Hampshire. By 1924 they had moved to Thurlestone Lodge, Lee-on-Solent, Hants, and were there in 1929. By 1931 they had moved again, this time to 3 Fairthorne Mansions, Alverstoke, Hants. Tragedy struck the following year. George was involved in a driving accident on 27 April 1932 in which his front seat passenger was killed, and in which he, as the driver, was himself injured and died as a result in September, five months later.

"Mr. E. J. Bechervaise represented Major Marshall Morris, who was driving the car at the time of the accident. George Marshall Morris, retired Army officer, of Alverstoke, said he and three others left Old Portsmouth and proceeded return to Alverstoke by way of Fareham. It was raining at the time, and when he got to North End his car skidded on the tramlines and came into violent collision with a tram standard. The deceased man, who was sitting by the side of the witness was severely injured, and had to be lifted out of the car and was taken to hospital. The witness added that his speed at the time of the skid was about 30 miles hour, and his arm was severely injured as a result of the crash." (Portsmouth Evening News, 25 May 1932)

In 1939 Grace Lilian Harcourt was a widow, living at 33 Rivermead Court, Fulham, and had resumed the name of her first husband. She died 26 June 1960 when living at 13 Lower Street, Dartmouth.

Prettyjohn, Ernest Robert (1880-1964)

Ernest Robert Prettyjohn was born at Stokenham on 15 January 1880, the eldest son of Nathaniel Prettyjohn (1831-1915), an agricultural labourer, and Jane Jeffery (1832-1891). He was sent as a farm servant to live with farmer James Cole at nearby Kernborough at the age of eleven. He learned enough about handling horses to establish himself as a carter by 1901, when he was living as a boarder with a William Holmes in Dartmouth.

Ernest married Ethel Jane Beer (b. 20 July 1881) at All Saints, Thurlestone, on 30 September 1905 (interestingly, Ernest's occupation is given as "trapper" on the marriage certificate) and they went to live in West Buckland, where the 1911 census finds them with three children - Ernest W (5), Harold Nathaniel (4), and Florence May (2) - and Ernest working as a labourer. Ethel Jane was the daughter of William and Mary Beer, both originally from Bigbury, but who settled in Thurlestone in 1875 and were living at Clanacombe Cottage, where William worked as a gardener. Tracking Ernest in the Electoral registers for Thurlestone reveals that he was living in West Buckland in 1913, 1914, and 1915. With the gap in these records until 1918 he next appears as being absent on military service from his home at Clanacombe, where Ethel Jane is in residence. By 1919 he is back home again.

Unfortunately his military service records have been lost. The only surviving military information about him is that shown on his medal roll, and medal index card, which reveal that he served in the Royal Field Artillery as a gunner, and had the service numbers TF 661530, followed by 192249. The first number indicates a Territorial Unit, and this number was issued between 28 May and 16 September 1916. The second indicates a regular service unit, and would be the regimental number of the unit to which he was posted. His medal index card has a reference to 285 B, which may signify either Battery or Brigade, but no information about where he served, or when he was finally demobilised. He was awarded the British War and Victory medals.

From West Buckland Ernest and Jane moved with daughter Florence to 2 Sea View in Thurlestone, and later to 10 Seaview Terrace where he died on 14 July 1964. Son Ernest W married Lily Wilson in 1930 and died in December 1958.

Harold Nathaniel Prettyjohn was born 10 February 1907. In WW2 he was a Stoker First Class (service number 77333) on HMS Glorious, a converted aircraft carrier, when it was controversially sunk along with its two escort destroyers HMS Ardent and HMS Acasta, by the German battleships Scharnhorst and Gneisenau during operation Alphabet, the evacuation of British troops from Norway on 8 June 1940. Only some 40 men survived and the death toll of 1531 was the worst Royal Navy disaster of the war. The destroyer HMS Acasta fought to the last and succeeded in torpedoing the Scharnhorst, which was badly damaged and had to limp back to Germany for repairs. The HMS Glorious, Ardent, and Acasta Association (GLARAC), based in Plymouth, continues to organise appropriate annual gatherings and memorials to the events of 8th June 1940.

Florence May Prettyjohn, born 11 August and baptised at All Saints on 20 September 1908, married Frederick C Noyce in 1941 from her parents home at 2 Sea View, Thurlestone. She died in 1990 age 82 years.

Rendle, Alfred Thomas (1892-1961)

Alfred Thomas Rendle was born on 2 June 1892 and baptised at All Saints church, Plymouth on 22 July, the son of Alfred Rendle, a seaman, and his wife Sarah, living at 14 Camden Street, Plymouth. In the 1901 census he appears as an inmate at a foster home in Mount Gold St, Plymouth aged 8 years. What happened to his parents is unknown, but it is not surprising that on 2 June 1910, his eighteenth birthday, he presented himself at Devonport and signed on for twelve years in the Royal Navy.

HMS Earnest

Despite the problems he may have faced during his childhood and adolescence, his career in the Royal Navy was exemplary. He had a long and excellent record, with his character references never other than "Very Good", and his performance references invariably "Superior". He served as a Stoker, K7556, and gained regular promotion in this capacity right through to Petty Officer. During the war he served in destroyers of the seventh flotilla, principally in HMS Earnest, HMS Manley, and HMS Torrid.

Although having no previous family connections to Thurlestone, Alfred established one himself when in 1916 he married Eva Phyllis Foote, the daughter of Sidney Albert and Eliza Bartlett Foote of Whitley Cottage, Thurlestone. Eva had been born in Thurlestone and baptised at All Saints on 15 April 1894, and was working as a maid in the Thurlestone Hotel. They appear in the Electoral Register for 1918 as living in West Buckland, with Alfred absent on military service. Their daughter Muriel Kate Rendle was born 22 September 1919.

After the end of the war, Alfred spent 3 years (1922-5) with the Royal Australian Navy, followed by three years with the New Zealand Navy (1925-8) after which he retired having completed eighteen years service. He was awarded a Long Service and Good Conduct medal in 1925 to go with the Star, British War, and Victory medals from his wartime service.

In 1939 the family were living at 1 Lower Clanacombe, and Alfred was working as a gardener to supplement his Naval pension. Daughter Muriel Kate married Wallace Wallis in Kingsbridge in 1946 but moved away to live in Hertfordshire. Alfred died at Greenbank, Lower Clanacombe on 21 February 1961, and Eva Phyllis lived on there until 1974, when she died on 17 December.

Riley, M

Another one of Rev Coope's mystery men. There is no record of residence or family in Thurlestone, or in the 1911 census, or in the Electoral registers from 1913 - 1921. Similarly, no military records are traceable with a Thurlestone connection.

Robins, George Frederick (1894-1955)

The 1939 census shows George Frederick Robins living at 1 Sea View Terrace with his wife Emma Maud Ferris and a large family of children. It records his date of birth as Christmas Day, 25 December 1881. A search of the General Register Office Birth Indexes for 1881 and 1882 reveals only one George Frederick Robins with a birth registered after 25 December 1881 as having been born (or at least the birth registered) at Stourbridge, Worcestershire, in the December quarter of 1882. As registration was required within one month of birth, this is unlikely to be our man.

A stronger case appears to exist with an entry in the 1881 census at St Martin's, Worcester, taken on the night of 3 April 1881, for a George Robbins (aged 2 months), son of John Henry Robbins, a firemen/train driver for GWR, and Charlotte Perkins, a milliner. The birth was registered in the first quarter of 1881, making a birth date of 25 December 1880 feasible. Perhaps in 1939 George, or the recorder, got the year wrong. In 1891 the family is at 8 West Street, Stourbridge, and George is a scholar. By 1901 George has left home, and the family have moved to Wolverhampton.

South Milton church records show that George Frederick Robins and Emma Maud Ferris, both of this parish, had their banns read on 6, 13, and 20 July 1913, and their marriage was registered at Kingsbridge in the same quarter that year.

As with the majority of WW1 soldiers, the military service records for George Frederick Robins have not survived. However, there still some fragmentary records which tell us something about his service. The Medal Roll Cards of the Devonshire Regiment show a private George Frederick Robins, regimental number 15002, as having served in France from 17 March 1915. There is also a Medal Roll Index card which confirms that he was entitled to the 1914-15 Star as well as the British War and Victory medals, and that he continued serving until demobilised 21 March 1919. The Forces War Records website also have an entry which records his having been wounded on 8 August 1916 during the Battle of the Somme, and that he was entitled to wear a wound stripe.

After the war George and Emma settled in Thurlestone and raised a large family. Laura (b. 1919) married William A V Pugh in Kingsbridge in 1945; William J (b.1921); Freda M (b. 1924) married James C E Eva in Kingsbridge in 1945; Frederick G (b. 1925); Percival A (b. 1928) married Lara M Clark in 1928 at Kingsbridge; Iris J (b. 1930) married Robert R W Westgate in 1980 in Norfolk; Elsie M (b. 1932) married Douglas O Lane in 1970; Francis R (b. 1933) married Pamela Jennings in 1968 at Kingsbridge; Michael J (b.1942) married Ruth A Blake in 1966 at Kingsbridge.

The 1939 census shows the family living at 1 Sea View Terrace in Thurlestone. Wife Emma Maud died in 1954, and George had survived her by only one year when he passed away in 1955.

Robins, John Percival (1894-1935)

John Percival Robins was born in West Buckland early in 1894 and baptised at All Saints, Thurlestone on 4 March 1894, the son of George Robins, a carpenter, and Catherine Elizabeth Taylor. William Robins, John Percival's grandfather, a former seaman from Diptford, had married a Thurlestone girl and settled there around 1837.

After local school George worked from his parents' home as a farm labourer and a carter, until after the 1911 census. The electoral registers show him as living in East Buckland in 1913, 1914, and 1915. The 1918 electoral register shows him as absent on military service. Like many of his fellow soldiers in WW1, John Percival's service records have not survived. The only possible information relating to his military service is in a Medal Roll Index card, which indicates he could have been a driver in the Royal Engineers, service number 90236, and served in France from 27 August 1915, and thus entitled to the 1914-15 Star, British War and Victory medals.

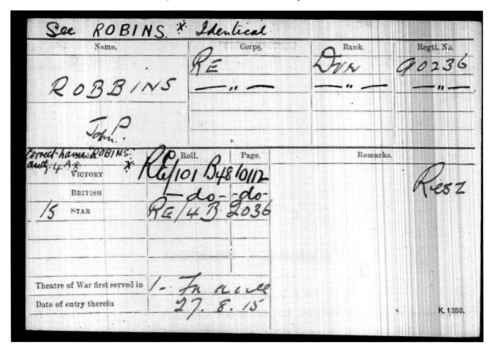

Spelling errors were not unknown in military records, but they do often complicate life for researchers! Unfortunately his demobilisation date is not recorded, but it is likely to have been early in 1919.

After the war, John Percival is recorded in the Thurlestone electoral registers as living in West Buckland through from 1919 to the 1930s, and probably until his death, which was registered in December 1935 at Kingsbridge. It would appear that he remained a bachelor throughout his life.

Rogers, James (1884-1956)

James Rogers was born at West Alvington on 5 January 1884. Seven years later the 1891 census shows that his father has died, and his mother Elizabeth Rogers (nee Hunniford) now a 50 year old widow, has daughter Sarah (16) and James (7) to support by working as a charwoman. As soon as he was able, James found work at the Devonport Naval dockyard and went into digs in Keyham Street, where he is found in the 1901 census.

When he first went to live in Thurlestone is unknown, but by 19 November 1905 when the banns were first read at All Saints for his marriage to Elixabeth Mary Bevell (b. 29 February 1884 - Leap Year's day), they were listed as "both of this parish". Three days after the third reading of the banns they were married in Thurlestone on 6 December 1905. James' father is named as John Rogers, labourer (but not deceased, though James' mother was described as a widow in 1891). James' occupation stated as mechanic.

In 1911 the young couple were living with Elizabeth's widowed mother Caroline Bevell in Thurlestone, where James worked as a mason/builder, and had started a family with the arrival of a daughter Doris Audrey, born in 1906. Doris went on to marry Wilfred C Jeffery in 1938.

With the outbreak of war in August 1914, James Rogers was one of the first to volunteer, and enlisted at Plymouth on 27 October 1914. He was assigned to the 22nd Battalion (Wessex & Welsh) The Rifle Brigade, and sent for training to Hatton Park Camp. By the end of 2015, however, there was serious concern about his mental well-being. He was admitted to hospital in Aylesbury for observation in November, and was evidently in the throes of a breakdown, exhibiting extreme anxiety, melancolia, and a persecution mania.

The understanding of mental health problems was not the RAMC's strong suit in 1915, but fortunately for James the hospital medical board fairly quickly decided to discharge him as no longer fit for war or military service, and he returned home to Thurlestone on 10 January 1916. It is not known how long it took for James to recover, but he was clearly able to resume his work as a mason some time later.

The family lived on in Thurlestone and made their home at Vine Cottage, Toyes Court, as recorded in the 1939 census. James died in 1956 and his wife Elizabeth Mary survived him by just two years.

Rogers, Richard Samuel (1891-1954)

Richard Samuel Rogers was born at Aveton Gifford on 9 November 1891, and baptised in Aveton Gifford church on 21 February 1892, the son of Richard Rogers, originally from Modbury but now a groom and gardener at Bridge End, and his wife Emily Jarvis, originally from Bigbury.. In 1901 their address is given as Heathfield Cottage, and Richard is attending the local school with his two sisters

In 1905 the family moved to Aune Cross cottage, in Thurlestone, where another son Albert Edward Rogers was born a year later. They are still there in the 1911 census, but son Richard Samuel has evidently taken advantage of the opportunity presented by the marriage of the widow Harcourt and George Marshall Morris to go with them to Thorne, Pennsylvania Park, Exeter, as the family chauffeur. He also found romance with the parlourmaid Ellen Matilda Moore, who had also accompanied the Marshalls to Exeter, and tied the knot with her at Kingsbridge in 1915.

They continued to live at Aune Cross cottage, and Richard now acted as chauffeur to the Creswick family. They appear on the electoral register from 1913 until after the war, when Richard is recorded as being absent on military service in 1918.

No detailed service records survive, but the Medal Roll Index cards have only one Richard Samuel Rogers, and he is recorded as having served in the Royal Engineers as a sapper, service number 121697, and landed in France on 28 September 1915 and served until demobilised on 14 December 1918. He was thus entitled to the 1914-15 Star, and the British War and Victory medals.

After the war Richard and Ellen continued to live at Aune Cross with the Creswick family up to the census of 1939, with Richard acting as chauffeur and gardener. It is understood that when the Creswicks left Thurlestone they left the cottage property to the Rogers who stayed on there. Richard Samuel died in 1954 aged 62, and sometime later Ellen Matilda moved to Poole in Dorset where she died in March 1980 aged 90 years.

Rundle, John Henry (1894-1969)

John Henry Rundle was born in East Portlemouth in 1894, the youngest child of Richard Rundle and Sophia Cranch, both originally of Malborough. Richard Rundle (b. 1843) had been a fisherman in his early days, but was working as an ag lab in Chivelstone in 1891, still a bachelor at the age of 48, and living with one of his relatives. Sophia Cranch, born in 1853, had first married William Henry Rowe, an agricultural labourer, in 1874 and they had five children between 1875 and 1889. In the 1891 census the family was living at East Portlemouth in one of the Holset cottages. William Henry died the following year at the age of 39, and two years later the widow Sophia (now 41) married Richard Rundle (53) at Kingsbridge in January 1894. Richard settled in with Sophia in East Portlemouth, continuing as an agricultural labourer, and their son John Henry was born towards the end of the year. In the 1901 census Richard and Sophia are living at Waterhead, East Portlemouth, with Sophia's youngest daughter Gertrude Rowe (12) and young John Henry (6).

In 1911 John Henry is still living at Waterhead, and is working as a farm hand for Charles Peter Giles, a farmer and coal merchant. His father Richard has died, and his mother Sophia is back at Holset working as a charwoman.

When the war came John Henry was an early volunteer. Although his service record has not survived, the Medal Roll Index card reveals that he served as a driver in the RASC, service number TI 3781, and was an early arrival in France on 15 January 1915. Unfortunately there is no record of his demobilisation date, but he clearly survived the war, and was awarded the 1915-15 Star, and the British War and Victory medals.
There is no record of the actual date when John Henry and his mother first made their home in Thurlestone, but the first appearance of their names in the electoral registers shows them living at Bantham in 1918, though John Henry is absent on military service.

Campaign :— **1914-15.**				(A) Where decoration was earned.		
				(B) Present situation.		
Name	Corps	Rank	Reg. No.	Roll on which included (if any)		
				MEDAL	ROLL	PAGE
(A) *RUNDLE*	*ASC*	*Dvr* TI *3781*		VICTORY	*RASC|101|B 3*	*2348*
(B) *John H.*	— " —	— " — — " —		BRITISH	— do —	—do—
				STAR	*RASC/12*	*89*
Action taken				*& 2*		
THEATRE OF WAR.	(1) *France*					
QUALIFYING DATE.	*15·1·15·*					

(6 34 46) W234—HP5590 500,000 4/19 HWV(P240)   K608   [OVER.

They were not resident in 1913, 1914, or 1915, but could have become resident sometime in 1916 or 1917 or 1918. John is back as a resident in 1919. Thereafter, both John Henry and his mother Sophia continue living at Bantham right through to 1929, the year of Sophia's death in March of that year.

After that date little or no information has been found about John Henry's residence, or occupation. A John Henry Rundle, with a birth date of 12 September 1894, died in Brent, Greater London, in September 1969. Nobody else of that name shares the same birthday, so this is almost certainly the right man. He would have been 75.

Sherriff, William Henry (1886-1944)

The Sherriff family in Thurlestone can be traced back to 1758. During the 1800s they were only outnumbered by the Moores in term of their appearance in the parish baptism, marriage, and burial registers. In 1891 there were twelve Sherriffs listed in the census, in three households; one of which was headed by James Sherriff (b. 1845) a carrier, and his wife Susan Treeby Lake (1846-1924), in East Buckland.

The youngest of their five children was William Henry Sherriff, born on 3 January 1886 and baptised at All Saints on 10 March that year. After completing his schooling, William went to work as an assistant baker and breadmaker with his elder brother John in Bantham. In 1911 John was still running his bakery business, but his address had become the Post Office, Bantham, and next door in The Cottage was his widowed mother Susan, together with William Henry, still acting as an assistant baker.

In the 1913, 1914 and 1915 electoral registers, William Henry is the occupier and tenant of Buckland Farm. Then in 1918 and 1919 William Henry is absent on military service. By good luck his military service records have survived, and so we can trace his wartime activities with some degree of accuracy.

He was not among the first to volunteer, but with conscription looming he attested at Newton Abbot on 10 November 1915. He was assigned to the Reserve, and was called again to complete his attestation at Plymouth on 20 March 1916. Here he was assigned to the Royal Garrison Artillery with the regimental number 65309 and posted to 205 Siege Battery. He spent the rest of the year in training at a number of different depots in the UK until a posting to the Middle East saw him embark on 18 December 1916 for Salonika, arriving eleven days later. He was stationed at a base depot in Palestine from 24/2/17 to 19/8/17.   He left Salonika on 29/8/17 and arrived in Alexandria on 5/9/17, where he was stationed until the end of the war. He was promoted to Bombardier (corporal) on 17 December 1918.

On 1 February 1919 he was selected for retention in the army of occupation, and promoted to acting sergeant three days later on 4 February 1919. After another seven months service he was posted to the demobilisation camp at Kantara. The   flu epidemic was rife at this time, and William Henry was admitted to the Kantara hospital on 14 September 1919. He appears to have spent ten weeks in the hospital before being discharged back to duty at Alexandria on 28 November 1919. His passage home was not delayed much longer and he embarked for England on 7 December 1919, where he was finally discharged on 20 December 1919. He was awarded the British War and Victory medals.

He remained a bachelor after the war and continued to live and work in Bantham until his death in 1944.

The Snowdon Family

The Snowdon family first made an appearance in the Thurlestone Parish Registers in 1815 with the birth of Alice Jarvis Snowdon, the daughter of John Snowdon, carpenter, and Agnes Jarvis, and the family expanded considerably, adding Elizabeth (1818), William (1821), Stephen (1823), George (1825), Thomas (1827), Henry (1829), Jane (1832), and Roger (1835). They lived somewhere in Aunemouth according to the 1841 census.

The branch of the family we have to follow for the participants in WW1 identified by Rev Coope is that of William (1821), who married a Dodbrooke girl, Jane Ford, in Stonehouse, Plymouth, in April 1849. Both the 1851 and 1861 censuses record that William was an agricultural labourer, though there is an entry in Merchant Navy records under his name between 1853 and 1857. They raised a family of five children between 1849 and 1860: Sarah (1849), Thomas (1852), William (1855), John (1858) and Elizabeth Ann (1860). And it is the branch of Thomas (1852) from which the four Snowdon veterans of WW1 spring.

Thomas Snowdon was a farm labourer like his father, and married Sarah Jane Wood from Malborough in July 1872. They lived in a cottage next door to the schoolhouse in Thurlestone, with their uncle Henry Snowdon (carpenter) on the other side. And here they raised their family of Kate (1873), John William (1874), Stephen (1876), Alice (1879-1882), Agnes Jane (1881), George H (1883), Ernest (1885), Lucy May (1887), and Tom (1889-1894). In 1897 the Connolly family arrived to become their neighbours in the schoolhouse. Thomas and Sarah Jane were still there in 1911 with unmarried daughter Kate and unmarried sons George Henry (farm labourer) and Ernest (gardener).

Old father William Snowdon finally passed away in July 1913 at the grand age of 92, underlining the fact that the Snowdons were made of sturdy stuff. And then there was war. But the younger generation of Snowdons (and friends) were more than ready to answer the call.

Snowdon, Ernest (1884-1968)

Ernest Snowdon

Ernest Snowdon was the fourth son of Thomas Snowdon and Sarah Jane Wood, born in Thurlestone on 27 September 1884. He briefly had a younger brother, Tom, who died aged 4 years of age, but otherwise he was the youngest of the four Snowdon boys who served in the war. His career followed the same path as his brother George Henry - local school, followed by work on the farm, and then in the 1911 census he has started work as a domestic gardener.

This may well have presented an opportunity for Ernest to get to know the girl he was to marry - Emily Augusta Broad, a Swansea girl who was working in service as a parlourmaid for the Ilberts at Rockhill. Their wedding took place at All Saints church in Thurlestone on 10 May 1911.

No.	When Married	Name and Surname	Age	Condition	Rank or Profession	Residence at the time of Marriage	Father's Name and Surname	Rank or Profession of Father
7	May 10th 1911	Ernest Snowdon	26	bachelor	gardener	Thurlestone	Thomas Snowden	Labourer
		Emily Augusta Broad	23	spinster	domestic servant	Thurlestone	Richard Broad	Gardener

19 11 . Marriage solemnized at the Parish Church in the Parish of Thurlestone in the County of Devon

Married in the Parish Church according to the Rites and Ceremonies of the Church of England by ——— or after Banns by me.

This Marriage was solemnized between us, { Ernest Snowdon / Emily Augusta Broad } in the Presence of us, { Fanny Louisa Powell / Albert Edwin Masters } Frank Cooper Rector.

Their son Albert Henry Snowdon was born on 19 January 1912, and the electoral registers for 1913, 1914, and 1915 show that Ernest was still resident in Thurlestone. By 1918 he was absent on military service.

Unfortunately his military service records have not survived, so we have no record of either the duration or location of his period of service. The medal rolls and index cards throw up two possibilities, one in the Royal Field Artillery (no. 223344, gunner) and one in the Royal Garrison Artillery (no. 181754, gunner), both of whom were awarded the British War and Victory medals. But that is as much as we know.

One piece of memorabilia which has survived is a postcard from Wendover which places Ernest's military service at 1915 at the latest. The date of 8 November 1915 quite possibly represents his first posting, while the quality of his handwriting pays tribute to the teaching skills of his schoolmistress Lucy Connolly. The fact that she lived next door may have had some bearing on his application.

Certainly the fine moustache of his army days lost nothing in returning to civilian life or in old age. And Ernest and Emily continued living in the old family home next door to the old schoolhouse. Ernest died in 1968, and Emily in 1970.

Snowdon, George Henry (1882-1953)

George Henry Snowdon was born 12 October 1882, the third son of Thomas Snowdon and Sarah Jane Wood. He is shown in the 1891 census as a scholar, and living with his parents next door to the Thurlestone village schoolhouse of Ada Gale, so he was clearly always early for his lessons! By 1901 his schooldays were over, and he was working as an agricultural labourer along with his father and younger brother Ernest. Nothing much changed over the next ten years, and the 1911 census finds George Henry still living at home with his parents, still single, and still working as a farm labourer.

Whether it was the looming prospect of war in 1914 (or a feeling that at 32 he had already been too long a bachelor) we will never know, but on 16 July 1914 George Henry married Annie Louisa Putt at her home village of Aveton Gifford. She had been working as a cook in domestic service in Paignton in 1911. Where they established their first home remains unknown, but it does not seem to have been in Thurlestone, for George Henry's name is absent from the Parish electoral register for 1913, 1914, and 1915. However, the next register taken, in 1918, does include George Henry and Anne, though George is noted as absent on military service. After the war they continued to live in Thurlestone and appear every year in the electoral registers until Anne's death in 1937. George Henry continued to live in Thurlestone, and worked for James Palmer of Buckland Park Farm for 26 years up to the suicide of his employer in March 1946. Seven year later the death of George Henry Snowdon was recorded as having taken place in Plymouth in 1953.

Although the electoral register for 1918 confirms that George Henry was away on military service, his military service records have not survived, and the only accessible information is to be derived from war medal records. As these do not record date or place of birth, all we can do is find the best match available. The medal roll of the Devonshire Regiment (Piece 0870), fortunately, provides a strong contender:

and is reinforced by the Devonshires Silver War badge roll, which also includes the dates of his enlistment and discharge.

From these we see that George Henry attested on 1 December 1915, and was assigned to the 8th Battalion of the Devonshire Regiment, and later transferred to the 2nd Battalion, before being discharged on 1 February 1919 having been seriously wounded and presumably still recovering in hospital until that date. Nevertheless, he would probably have considered himself lucky to have survived the war. The Keep Military Museum website (Home of the Regiments of Devon and Dorset) records the tragic statistics of the 8th and 9th Battalion casualties at the Battle of Loos, and their later heroics at Mansel Copse. "On the 4th July 1916 the Padre of the 8th Devons, Capt Crosse, buried 160 officers and men of both Battalions at Mansel Copse, erecting a plaque: The Devonshires held this trench. The Devonshires hold it still." In a final summary the website records "The two senior Service battalions (8th and 9th) fought side by side, won 18 battle honours for the Devonshire Regiment and together lost 1918 of their number killed in France, Belgium and Italy."

At some point in the reconstruction of the 8th Battalion, George Henry found himself transferred to the 2nd Battalion, and it is very likely that he would have taken part in the fighting recorded by the website.

"The German offensive on 21st March 1918 found the 2nd Devons in reserve. Rushed to Peronne, on the 24th and 25th they held off several German attacks, suffering 322 casualties before conducting a fighting withdrawal covered by their field gunners. On 27th May at Bois de Buttes their Brigade was overwhelmed by a huge German attack and, to buy time for the rest of the Corps, the 2nd Devons stood and fought. This action cost them 551 killed and missing. Among those killed was their Colonel. To recognise their courage the French awarded the Regiment the Croix de Guerre, whose ribbon all Devons wore on their sleeve.

In late October 1918 the rebuilt Battalion's last battles were near the River Scheldt. They were at Mons when the Armistice ended the war that had cost them nearly 1400 lives and earned them 11 battle honours."

Where and when George Henry sustained the wounds that led to his hospitalisation and eventual discharge will remain unknown. But he will have lost so many of his friends during these actions that his survival for more than three years was, if not miraculous, then certainly against the odds.

He was awarded the British War and Victory medals, and the Silver War badge (number 496186).

Note: In view of the fragmentary nature of the evidence, it is not conclusive proof that Private 26308 of the Devonshires was the George Henry Snowdon born in Thurlestone in 1882. But it does seem a very strong possibility.

Snowdon, John William (1874-1951)

John William Snowdon

John William Snowdon was born at Thurlestone on 14 September 1874, and baptised at All Saints on 16 January 1875, the eldest son of Thomas Snowdon and Sarah Jane Wood. Like many other young men of this period, as soon as his eighteenth birthday arrived he presented himself at Devonport and signed on for 12 years in the Royal Navy, being assigned the service number 155374.

His service in the Royal Navy saw him training at depot ships, rising quickly to ordinary and then able-bodied seaman, and spending three years with HMS Blonde from 1892-1895. He then joined the battleship HMS Collingwood and was promoted to Leading seaman during his time aboard. By 1899 he had reached the rank of Petty Officer. A spell of two years with HMS Thistle, a gunboat, took him across the Atlantic to Cape Verde, Barbados, Bermuda, New York, and Halifax, Nova Scotia, where she had a refit.

On 6 September 1904 he married Mary Jane Jeffery, daughter of John Thomas and Elizabeth Jane Jeffery at All Saints, Thurlestone. By 1911 three children had been added to the family: Ernest William (b. 11 June 1905), John Thomas (b. 1906), and Mary Evelyn Snowdon (b. 1909).

After completing his 12 years he signed on for further continuous service and spent time on the battleships HMS Hood and HMS Cumberland. In 1911 he was promoted to Chief Petty Officer and spent the war years as a CPO Instructor at home bases. He was finally demobilised on 23 April 1920 after 28 years continuous service.

In 1939 John William and Mary Jane were living at Belle Vue, West Buckland, close to Langman's Farm, with his children Ernest W (b. 11 July 1905) and Mary E (b. 13 September 1909) living with them. He was still there in 1951 when he was taken ill and moved to Freedom Fields Hospital, Plymouth, where he died on 21 April 1951 aged 77 years.

Snowdon, Stephen (1876-1943)

Stephen Snowdon was the second son of Thomas Snowdon and Sarah Jane Wood, born two years after John William, and baptised at All Saints on 17 September 1876. After attending the village school he was taken on by Farmer Sherriff at Buckland Farm as a Farm servant, and this is where he appears in the 1891 census. During the next decade he spent five years apprenticed to blacksmith James F Moore of Feoffe Cottages in South Milton, and then decided to ply his new trade further afield.

In 1901 the census shows him as a boarder at 5 Nashville Place, Hanwell, and working as a blacksmith and shoeing smith, but he has "adopted" a forename of John. Ten years later, in the 1911 census, he has acquired a wife, Mary Elizabeth Welch, and two children, Violet Agnes, born 9 July 1904, and Stephen Ernest, born 3 May 1905, and is living at 42 St Margaret's Road, Hanwell, and working as a Farrier (horse-shoeing), having moved from number 23 in the same road in the previous year. On the census form he returned to calling himself Stephen.

On 5th January 1915 Stephen signed up for the Army Service Corps at Woolwich (South London) for a term of 3 years minimum aged 38. He gave his trade as 'farrier' and was officially designated as a 'shoeing smith'. The enlistment document shows he had served a 5 year apprenticeship under a J.F. Moore in South Milton (Devon). When he signed up he again reverted to using the name John Snowden and continued to be listed under this name on later official documents and correspondence. He was transferred to the Army Veterinary Corps on 27 Jan 1915, with the no. SE 4359. Without any preliminary military training, he was shipped out from Southampton for France on 1 Feb 1915 and spent nine months in France before returning to UK. He was thus entitled to the 1914-15 Star, as well as the British War and Victory medals.

On 27th Jan 1916 was posted to the 'School of Farriery' Romsey, where he was promoted to the rank of 'Acting Farrier Sergeant' as an Instructor (though without additional pay). On 30th March 1917 he suffered injury to his left knee while shoeing a horse at 'Pitt Corner Camp' Winchester, and was admitted to the Military Hospital in Winchester for 28 days. On 9th March 1918 he was posted to the 'Veterinary Hospital' at Winchester, and on 26th March 1918 he was again admitted to hospital after injuries to his right ankle, not being discharged until 1st June 1918. He was finally demobilised on 21 March 1919.

Two more boys completed the family: Reginald A W (1918), and Eric A T (1924). In the 1930s Stephen and Mary, with daughter Violet, lived at 104 St Margaret's Road, Hanwell. Stephen finally married his wife of more than forty years on 19 June 1942 before his death on 21 April 1943 at Isleworth, London.

Stephen in retirement

Square, Francis Shath (1879-1948)

Francis Shath Square was born 20 May 1879, and baptised 29 June, the second son of Samuel Shath Square and his wife Bessie, at Farm Barton, Thurlestone. He would probably have gone to the primary school in Thurlestone, but not on to further education, and it may be surmised that he was not academically particularly well gifted. Nevertheless, it may also be surmised that he knew exactly what he wanted to become.

As we have already seen, many young men from rural areas took the opportunity as soon as their eighteenth birthday arrived to make their way to Devonport and sign on in the Royal Navy for 12 years. But this was not the future that Francis had planned for himself. It is not known what preliminary preparation preceded the event, but on 29 May 1897 (nine days after his eighteenth birthday) he presented himself for attestation at Windsor Cavalry barracks with a letter from a Major H Collins of the Royal Horse Guards, and duly signed on for twelve years in the Household Cavalry and was posted to the Blues and Royals (Royal Horse Guards) with the Regimental number 641.

After two years he had acquired an Army Certificate of Education (Class 2), and completed all his military and equestrian training, and on 29 November 1899 he took part in the South African campaign until November 1900 and was awarded the Queens South Africa medal with 5 clasps. He was also awarded the Coronation medal in 1911, presumably for taking part in the ceremonial processions. Although he came through the South African campaign apparently unscathed, his army medical record is littered with minor health problems arising from his activity with horses, usually sprains and contusions of the legs, an abscess, a leg ulcer, as well as tonsilitis, synovitis, and mumps.

A Trooper of the Blues

Thereafter, his career revolved around duty at either London or Windsor, with the exception of a brief spell of six months from June 1918 to January 1919 when he was transferred to the Guards Machine Gun Regiment. He was transferred back to the Household Cavalry prior to the termination of his military career on 11 Marc 1919, having completed 21 years and 314 days of pensionable service.

What he did as a civilian over the next fifteen years is unknown, but in 1937 he married Florence Louisa Isabella Markall with the wedding registered at Pancras, London. The 1939 census finds them living at 22 Emperor's Gate, Kensington, with Francis supplementing his pension (now increased to £80 per year) by acting as Head Porter for the building. Florence died in 1945 and Francis in 1948.

Square, Harold Shath (1873-1961)

"The Squares were one of the most prominent families in Thurlestone for at least 200 years up to about 1900. Some of their headstones, neatly aligned, may be seen on the narrow spit of cemetery in the far (north) side of the church, in a privileged position as near as possible to the altar." (Notable Residents of Old Thurlestone by Dr Neville Oswald in Village Voice, December 1995). He goes on to state that the last member of the family recorded in the parish registers was Miss Anne Jane Square, baptised on 14 January 1873. She was the daughter of Henry and Jane Square.

Our punctilious doctor, however, was for once in error. Later in the same year (1873), and even on the same page of the church baptism register, appears the entry on 7 September for Harold Shath Square, eldest son of Samuel Shath and Bessie Square of Farm Barton, a holding of 340 acres with eleven employed men in the 1881 census. By 1891 Harold has finished his schooling and is described in the census as "farmer's son". Before the turn of the century, however, all had changed.
Samuel Shath Square's tenancy had been terminated, the Thurlestone Golf Club had come into being, and the big farmhouse had been taken on by the Grose family and was being operated as a hotel.

With the family uprooted from the home he had known since childhood, Harold made the adventurous move of emigrating to Canada, and took passage on the SS Parisian of the Allen Line sailing from Liverpool on 5 August 1897 to Quebec. When the war came Harold attested on 7 October 1915 for the Canadian Expeditionary Force, and his attestation papers give some clue as to what he had been doing since his arrival in Canada. He gives his occupation as "farmer" (presumably his current occupation), but also records that he spent 12 years in the Royal Canadian Dragoons and the Royal Canadian Mounted Rifles. He also took a year off his age when attesting, possibly fearing that at 42 he might be considered too old.

Meritorious Service Medal

He was assigned to the Fort Garry Horse, as part of the Canadian Cavalry Brigade, 5th Cavalry Division, and served in France from 1916 to 1918, rising to the rank of Regimental Sergeant Major (476352) and being awarded the Meritorious Service Medal for gallantry in the field. The Fort Garry Horse sailed back to Canada after the war from Liverpool, arriving Halifax, Nova Scotia on 23 May 1919. Harold gave his address as 438 Balmoral St, Winnipeg. However, before leaving England, Harold found time to marry a London girl, Annie Bell, at Lewisham (1919 Q2 1d, 2459), before returning to Canada. Having settled up his affairs in Canada, he returned to UK aboard the SS Corsican in 1922. He rejoined his wife in Lewisham, where she

Fort Garry Horse Cap badge

was an assistant school mistress with the LCC, and opened a tobacconist and confectionery retail business at 23 Fordmill Road, Lewisham which he ran up to at least 1942.

The last record for Harold Shath Square is that of his death, which took place in Newton Abbot hospital, to which he had been admitted from Seaway Home, Torquay, on 10 July 1961 at the age of 88.

DUPLICATE.
x Records.

Awarded the "Meritorious Service Medal."

Corps __Fort Garry Horse. Can :__

Regimental Number __476352.__

Surname __SQUARE.__

Christian Name __Harold Hath Shath__ x

Rank __RSM. W.O.1.__ x

Date of Gazette __Peace Gazette.__

Registered Paper __0137/5618__ Schedule Number } __256902.__

W7208/RP2272 20.000 11/18 (X1034e) W. & Co. K841

Medal Roll Index Card

Steere, **James** (1887-1971)

James Steere was born on 16 November 1887 at 26 Island Street, Salcombe, the seventh of the eight children of Francis Steere (1848-1900) and Rosina Sibley (1853-1897). He was just 3 years old at the 1891 census, and by 1901 both his parents had died, and he had been taken in by uncle/aunt William and Sarah Murch who ran a farm at Higher Batson, Salcombe. He began work there as a farm labourer, but by 1911 had transferred himself to Thurlestone where he stayed with another uncle, Roger Saunders the thatcher, who had married his aunt Mary Anne Horn in 1877. The role of an agricultural labourer seemed to hold few prospects, and so a fortnight after his eighteenth birthday he presented himself at Devonport on 4 December 1905 and signed on for 12 years in the Royal Navy with the service number 309309 and a career as a stoker ahead of him.

He saw service on a wide range of ships, and progressed from Stoker II to Stoker I (1907) and then to Leading Stoker (1913). He spent the first three years of the war aboard HMS Warrior, an armoured cruiser, which was stationed in the Mediterranean when the First World War began and participated in the pursuit of the German battle-cruiser SMS Goeben and light cruiser SMS Breslau. From August to November 1914 she was ordered to Suez to defend the Suez Canal against any Turkish attack, before joining the Grand Fleet in December 1914 and being assigned to the 1st cruiser squadron.

HMS Warrior

At the Battle of Jutland on 31 May 1916, the 1st Cruiser Squadron was in front of the Grand Fleet, on the right hand side. HMS Warrior was closing to engage the light cruiser Weisbaden when she came under fire from the German battle-cruiser Derfflinger and four other battleships. She was hit by at least fifteen 11-inch shells and six 6-inch shells. HMS Warrior was heavily damaged by the German shells, which caused large fires and heavy flooding, although the engine room crew - of whom only three survived - kept the engines running for long enough to allow her to withdraw to the west. She was taken in tow by the seaplane tender HMS Engadine who took off her surviving crew of 743. She was abandoned in a rising sea at 8.25 am on 1 June when her upper deck was only 4 feet above the water, and subsequently foundered.

James was one of the fortunate survivors, and was promoted to Stoker Petty Officer, and later to Chief Stoker. After the war he married Evelyn Moore, daughter of Nathaniel Moore and Emma Wood of Bantham, in 1920 and continued living in Thurlestone, though his period of full time service in the Royal Navy was extended to 4 December 1927, making a total of 22 years continuous service.

In the 1939 census James and Emma are living at West Down in Bantham, and they probably continued living there until James' death in 1971. Emma survived him by three years, and passed away in Exeter in 1974.

Stidston, Arthur Edward (1899-1976)

The Stidston family were established in the South Hams as far back as the 17th Century, and indeed probably further. There may have been Stidstons in Thurlestone at earlier dates, but the first record of the arrival of the current family can be found in the 1880s, when Albert Edward Stidston (1863-1938) took on the tenancy of Court Barton Farm with his two younger sisters, Katie and Edith. They appear there in the census of 1891.

In 1894 when the Parish Council came into being under the Local Government Act, Albert Edward was among the original list of Councillors, and was appointed the first Secretary to the Council. He became Chairman of the Parish Council in 1913 and later served on Kingsbridge Rural District Council. In April 1896 he married Minnie Treneman, an Ermington girl, and they had four children: Una (1897-1988), Florence Marjorie (1898-1988), Arthur Edward (1899-1976), and Eric Treneman (1905-1999).

After finishing school Arthur Edward began to work on the farm at Court Barton. He was a big strong lad, and would have been a very useful asset to his father. When he reached the age of 18 in 1917 he would have been liable for conscription into the armed services, although his father might have been able to make a strong case that he was already doing essential work on the farm. Arthur may have wrestled with these divided loyalties for a while, but six months later he set off for Exeter and enlisted in the Army on 14 May 1918. He was immediately assigned to the 2nd Battalion of the Royal Guernsey Light Infantry as a private, service number 3660. After initial training at Fort George in Guernsey he was posted to 9th Platoon of "C" Company of the 1st Battalion of the Royal Guernsey Light Infantry.

One of his service record documents indicates that he was posted from Guernsey to the British Expeditionary Force (France) on 31 October 1918. A month later came the Armistice, and his father Albert Edward soon afterwards wrote to the Employment Exchange in Plymouth, which then passed the letter through channels to the Guernsey Light Infantry.

However, on the 5th February 1919 Arthur Edward had been admitted to Wharncliffe War Hospital, Sheffield, as a casualty, though the nature and extent of his injuries is not recorded in any of his military service records. He spent nine months there recovering.

On 13 October 1919 he was released from hospital and granted 28 days leave before being demobilised on 10 November 1919. It is clear that the injuries he received were serious enough to keep him in hospital for nine months, though he appears to have made a complete recovery and his claim for

a pension was turned down by the authorities. As the injuries were incurred after the end of hostilities, they were either the result of an accident or a severe dose of the Spanish flu - from which he would have been lucky to recover.
He was awarded the British War and Victory medals.

Arthur Edward may have returned to helping his father on the farm for a while, but he subsequently started on a new career as an electrical engineer. Court Barton farm was taken on by his younger brother, Eric Treneman, whose son Geoffrey still runs the farm today. Arthur made his home at Land Thatch with his mother Minnie, married Mary Evelyn Osborne in 1946, and died in 1976.

Woods, Frederick George (1868-1949)

The coastguard Frederick George Woods, who appears in the 1911 census for Thurlestone living at a Coastguard cottage in Bantham with his wife and daughter, was actually born with the surname Wood.

His birth certificate shows that he was born on 12 December 1868, the daughter of Isabella Russell of the House of Industry, Alverstoke, Hampshire, but no father's name is recorded. Frederick George was her first child, and she had three more by 1880, when she married their father George Wood, a Marine in the Royal Navy, in Alverstoke in the second quarter of that year. A fifth child, Isabella Minnie Wood, was born in 1881 when they were living at 3 Nelson Passage, Alverstoke. Sadly, father George died in 1883, and mother Isabella in 1886. The family of children then split up.

By 1888 Frederick George was twenty and working as a labourer. He took himself off to Portsmouth on 4 July that year and signed on in the Royal Navy for twelve years. His record card shows two anomalies. First, his name is recorded as Woods, not Wood. Secondly, his birthdate is given as 12 November 1868.

The two youngest daughters were taken into the Portsea Island Union Workhouse, where they appear in the 1891 census, aged 10 and 12. Second son William emigrated to North America in 1894 and married in Ontario in 1895. Eldest daughter Bessie also emigrated to Canada and was married in 1900.

Meanwhile, Frederick George had been issued the naval service number 146242 and had begun a long career as a stoker. After initial training he served on a variety of ships, but perhaps the most interesting one was HMS Inflexible, in which he served from 1890 to 1893 in the Mediterranean Fleet, and again from 1894 to 1896. Launched in 1876, HMS Inflexible was full of design innovations. She had a beam of 75 ft and a length of 320 ft, the smallest ever ratio of length to breadth in a metal first-class warship. Her main armament was four 16 inch muzzle loading guns weighing 81 tons each. She also had two bow-mounted underwater torpedo tubes,

HMS Inflexible

the first ship to have them, and she was also the first Royal Navy ship to be completely lit by electricity.

Frederick George Woods

A detailed account of the ship can be found in Wikipedia. For stoker Woods there were two boiler rooms, each containing two 17 ft and two 9 ft boilers, and gangs of stokers were continuously bringing coal from the bunkers to feed the fires.

Five years into his service Frederick George married a local Alverstoke girl, Georgina Rhoda Agnes Titheridge, a childhood sweetheart and in 1881 the girl next door, on 28 December 1893 in the Baptist Tabernacle at Alverstoke, Hants. They had three daughters and a baby girl who did not survive. The eldest daughter was Emily Florence Woods (1894-1961), the second Violet Minnie Woods (1897-1985) and the third Vera Evelyn Woods (1908-1973). None of the girls married.

After completing fourteen years as a stoker, Frederick George transferred to the Southern Coastguard in 1902 and spent a further seventeen years as a Leading Boatman, before retiring in 1919. He moved from Bantham to Weymouth after the war, and lived there with his wife and two daughters. His wife died in 1939, but Frederick George soldiered on for another decade, despite being bombed out of his home at 31 Franchise Street, before his death at 4 Norwich Road, Weymouth on 14 December 1949, just two days after his 81st birthday.

I am indebted to Donald J Woods, of West Linn, Oregon, USA, a great nephew of Frederick George Woods, for invaluable information on the family background, and these photographs. The one of Frederick holding a photograph was taken in Sidney, Australia, while serving on HMS Walleroo or HMS Katoomba which were part of the the Auxiliary Squadron of the Australia Station in 1897/8, and shows his stoker's propellor badge (right sleeve) and two sea service chevrons (left sleeve). The photo is of his wife Rhoda holding baby Emily Florence.

Mr & Mrs F G Woods

A Tribute to Nick Hide

Nick Hide was the second volunteer to step forward for the 2014 project, and finally Elaine Hanmer-Grant joined us to complete our research quartet. Nick's mother, Jean Hide, lived in Thurlestone at The Cottage, next door to Broad's Dairy and the Post Office for many years.

An experienced family history researcher, Nick lived in Hampstead in North London, which turned out to be real bonus for the project, as he was more than willing to make numerous journeys to various sources of information in the capital, particularly the National Archives at Kew, and so being able to turn up many invaluable pieces of information not available elsewhere.

Although Nick's personal remit in the project was just six of the twelve WW2 names on our War Memorial, he soon became involved in searching the London Record Offices for data on all the twenty four names under review, all at own expense, and thus became an invaluable asset for the other members of the Project team.

His grandfather, Captain Ernest George William Davidson RN, was not born in Thurlestone, never lived there, and was drowned at sea in WW1, so his name does not appear on the War Memorial. His widow Winifrede had a stone cross in his memory placed in the Thurlestone churchyard and linking his name with the SS Otranto.

The following article is Nick's own account of the loss of the Otranto and his grandfather's role in this tragic episode.

Chapter 5

Captain EGW Davidson and the Otranto

compiled by Nick Hide

Captain Ernest George William Davidson and the Otranto

By Nick Hide

It is quite rare for a person to have two separate memorials, but Captain E.G.W. Davidson was such a man, with a memorial in Thurlestone Churchyard in Devon, and his actual grave is on Islay, Scotland. It was his widow Winifred who made her home in Thurlestone in the 1930s having earlier bought The Cottage, in the centre of the village, in the 1920s with a sitting tenant . This subsequently became family home of her daughter Jean and the Hide family until Jean's death in 2009. Captain Davidson never knew Thurlestone as far as I can ascertain, but he was stationed at Devonport during part of his RN career. My mother Jean Davidson was born there.

The Davidson grave in Thurlestone Churchyard

Ernest George William Davidson was born in 1874 at Rangoon, what was then British Burma. His father was a senior Colonial Police Officer in Burma who had served for a brief period in the 60th Rifles on a purchased commission in the 1860s. The Davidson family were descendants of one of the junior lines of the extensive Davidson of Tulloch family, the chiefly family of the Clan Davidson. This Davidson family can be traced back to Cromarty, on the east coast of Scotland in the 1650s. Later they became very successful London West India Merchants and major landowners in Scotland. They purchased Tulloch Castle, Dingwall in 1760 from their cousins the Bayne family who found themselves in difficult financial circumstances. By the time EGWD was born, this mercantile heritage and great wealth had virtually all gone, but the family still had an extraordinary status. EGWD's uncle was Sir Arthur Davidson, who served as a very distinguished Royal Equerry from 1891-1922; initially as part of the team serving Queen Victoria; later he was a key member of Edward VII's team, and then that of his widow, Queen Alexandra right up until the day he died.

E.G.W. Davidson as a RN Midshipman

It is understood that EGWD never wanted to join the RN but had no choice, joining as cadet as a 14 year old in 1889. He served in many ships throughout his naval career, including one of the RN river gunships which patrolled the river Yangtse in China. This is where he met his future wife, Winifred Lamond. Later he commanded destroyers, cruisers and battleships. On 3rd September 1916 he took command of the Otranto.

Oranto in happier times, pre 1914

**E.G.W. Davidson & Winifred Lamond on their wedding day
at the British Consulate, Hanglow, China in 1903**

Loss of the Otranto

The Otranto was an unlucky ship from the day she launched, or rather wasn't. It took two goes to get her down the slipway at Belfast's Workman Clark shipyard, once on the 23rd March 1909 and then successfully on 27th March, being finally delivered to her owners, the Orient Steam navigation Company, in June of that year.

Although she was intended for the London – Australia run as a passenger and mail carrier, she spent the summer of 1909 cruising in Northern European waters and finally left London on her maiden voyage to Australia on 1 October 1909. Here she had some success and was back in England in time to take part in the King George V's Coronation Naval Review on 26th June 1911.

One week after Great Britain declared war on Germany in August 1914 the Otranto was requisitioned by the Admiralty for conversion to an auxiliary cruiser, having six 4.6 in (120mm) guns fitted. She was sent to the South Atlantic to join Rear Admiral Sir Christopher Cradock's West Indies squadron. It was this squadron that was subsequently diverted to the South-East Pacific to intercept the German Far East squadron under Vice Admiral Maximilian von Spee, which was attempting to make for Germany after the loss of its base in Tsingtao, China, to a joint Japanese-British force. It was HMS Otranto which spotted the German squadron on 1st November 1914 off the Chilean coast.

The subsequent battle, known as the Battle of Coronel, was a victory for the German squadron, but HMS Otranto managed to escape along with the light cruiser HMS Glasgow. Following the battle, HMS Otranto was ordered to the Falkland Islands to act as a guard ship, but returned to the England in March 1915 after her ex-Merchant Navy crew threatened to mutiny. By May 1915, HMS Otranto was in the Pacific patrolling the West Coast of America. She continued this task until recalled back to Britain, when she became an armed troopship employed in ferrying American soldiers across the North Atlantic to the Western Front in Europe.

E.G.W. Davidson wearing the uniform of a Commander RN

Only six weeks before the Armistice and the end of the Great War, the HMS Otranto was leading convoy HX50, bound for Glasgow and Liverpool, bringing with it 20,000 U.S servicemen and commanded by Captain Ernest George William Davidson who was also in charge of the convoy.

One of the soldiers wrote "Our trip was uneventful until the night of the 1st October when we collided with a French fishing schooner. We did not suffer any damages, but the schooner was sent to the bottom. There was no loss of life, as we picked up all of the crew, of thirty-six French sailors. We were delayed four or five hours."

On 5th October 1917, the American escort ships handed over to two British warships (HMS Mounsey and HMS Minos) off the west coast of Ireland and the convoy began the final leg between the North East coast of Ireland and the Western Isles of Scotland. By now the convoy was experiencing a major Atlantic gate in the deteriorating visibility.

Oranto becomes a wartime troopship

It was then that disaster struck. On 6th October 1918 the Otranto collided with HMS Kashmir, another liner which had been converted to a troopship. The subsequent court of enquiry, found that land was sighted so close to the ships that they needed to take immediate action, but because of the very high wave height and flying spray they were unable to visually signal their different intentions. HMS Otranto thought it had seen Ireland and turned sharply to port, while HMS Kashmir correctly thought the land was Islay and turned sharply to starboard – with the result that they collided. HMS Kashmir was damaged but made it safely back to port. However, the HMS Otranto was badly holed on the port side forward, and in the heavy swell, began to list. Captain Davidson, nursed the ship towards Islay, but the water soon swamped the engine room, and so with Islay so near, there was nothing for it but to anchor and hope for the best.

Captain Davidson in his cabin

Help came in the form of the destroyer HMS Mounsey, commanded by Lt Craven. He circled the stricken liner while Captain Davidson ordered many of the men to strip off their heavy clothes and be ready to jump as HMS Mounsey crept in towards them. The American soldiers lined the boat deck waiting patiently for rescue, and as the destroyer came near enough, they jumped for their lives. With huge waves sweeping over the foundering ship, many fell between the two ships and were washed away, but many more made it to safety. Four times HMS Mounsey came in, and altogether rescued almost six hundred men. By then the HMS Otranto had dragged her anchors and was starting to drift towards the rocks. HMS Mounsey, in danger of swamping herself with her huge cargo of troops, left for Belfast. There was nothing more she could do. When the Mounsey arrived in Belfast, many of the survivors were hospitalised there, until eventual transfer to England. It is not thought that any of the surviving American troops saw action on the Western Front, as the war ended soon afterwards following the signing of the Armistice on 11th November 1918.

The troopship, Kashmir

The HMS Otranto was now in a very bad way. She had grounded on the shore near Machir Bay, and with the heavy seas pounding her continually against the rocks, the ship eventually started to break up, and soon sank with the loss of 431 lives (351 American troops and 80 British crew members). Captain Davidson perished with his ship. During the following days, bodies were washed up all over Machir Bay, including that of Captain E.G.W. Davidson. This was perhaps one of the worst maritime disasters of the First World War.

Footnote:
Captain Davidson's widow Winnie sadly died as a result another accident of wartime. In February 1944, she was knocked down on the Fore Street, Kingsbridge by a boy cyclist who lost control of his bicycle on the hill. The boy was an evacuee from Worcester Park, South West London.

The grave of Captain E.G.W Davidson on the island of Islay, in the Hebrides.

Captain E.G.W. Davidson

Chart showing the location of the wreck of the Otranto off the coast of Islay

ARGYLLSHIRE CONSTABULARY.

SUBJECT OF
CORRESPONDENCE.   *Bowmore* Station,
                          2nd day of *November* 191*8*

Received from Sergeant Malcolm MacNiell Bowmore Islay, the aftermentioned property found on the body of Captain G. W. Davidson of H.M. Troopship "Otranto" washed ashore at Machrie Bay, Kilchoman Islay:—
1 Pair Binocular Glasses; 1 Wristlet Watch; 1 Gold ring; 1 Silver Cigarette Case; 1 Tobacco pipe

The official record of the finding and identification of Captain Davidson's body

Appendix

Appendix 1

MR. BRUNSKILL'S BANKRUPTCY—SETTLEMENT ANTICIPATED.
Re WILLIAM FAWCETT BRUNSKILL, gentleman, Torquay. Mr.
Halse (London) appeared for the trustee ; Mr. Swann (Bristol)
for the West of England Bank and some of the Kingsbridge
creditors ; Mr. Elliot Square (Kingsbridge), for the bankrupt.

Mr. HALSE said he did not to-day propose to examine the
bankrupt, as Mr. Whinney, the trustee, had personally examined
him as to every tittle of property he had been able to trace.
They had every reason to be satisfied with the exceedingly can-
did manner in which Mr. Brunskill had met all inquiries
addressed to him. Subject to anything that might be said on
behalf of outside creditors, he did not think it would be necessary to trouble his Honor again. There were investigations in
progress as to several mortgage securities which had been
executed by Mr. Brunskill. Witnesses were being examined
before the London Court, and therefore he would not apply to
have the case closed now, but ask his Honor to adjourn it
generally, so that if any further examination was considered
necessary before his Honor a special day might be fixed here.

Mr. SWANN agreed with this course, but he applied for an
order directing bankrupt to furnish a cash account to the
trustee from the 1st June, 1870, to the present time. The
reason he asked for it—and he thought his Honor would con-
sider it a proper application—was that since 1st June, 1870, and
prior to his bankruptcy, bankrupt had raised £1,100 by mort-
gages on his estates, and in addition he was in receipt of an
income from the estates of £5,000 to £6,000 a year.

Mr. SQUARE—Only £500 a year up to last year.

Mr. SWANN said that was immaterial, for at all events he had
had the £11,000, and therefore they wanted a cash account showing what had become of this money.

His HONOR said the only question was whether Mr. Swann
was perfectly assured that the bankrupt was not just as
ignorant as he was himself, looking at the enormous amount of
debts he had incurred and the income he had squandered. One
debt was £5,000 for jewellery, he believed.

Mr. SWANN said that was correct.

His HONOR said nothing but extreme inexperience could lead
any person of common sense to incur a debt of this description
unless he had £500,000 a year instead of £5,000. He doubted if
bankrupt could give a proper account.

Mr. SWANN said an inaccurate account was better than none.

His HONOR said if Mr. Swann had had as much experience as
he had he would know that not one tradesman out of a hundred
—and respectable tradesmen—could furnish a cash account—
therefore it was very doubtful if a person in bankrupt's position
could. And if accounts were not accurate they could not be
worth anything. It was an almost insane way in which this
young man had gone on since he had had the opportunity. He
could not see the utility of granting the order applied for, but
was afraid it would simply make matters more dilatory and
put traders to greater expense.

Mr. SWANN did not see that it would put the estate to any
expense.

Mr. HALSE said it was not for the trustee to put any difficulty in the way of outside creditors. The reason he had not applied for such an account was that the trustee had had Mr. Brunskill's bank book, and this showed how very much of the money had gone. Any account bankrupt could furnish would only be a transcript of his bank book.

His HONOR said whatever bankrupt paid by cheque would be shown, but it was idle to suppose that a young man at Cambridge who had foolishly spent his money as bankrupt had done, could give a cash account of the moneys he had paid out of pocket. To order the account would be giving trouble for no purpose.

Mr. SWANN—It's only trouble to the bankrupt.

His HONOR—But a bankrupt is not an animal to be worried to death for nothing.

Mr. SWANN said the bankrupt had not been worried to death in this case.

Mr. SQUARE said he objected to the application because it was impossible for the bankrupt to give the account asked for. He had given up all his accounts and papers, and his bank-book was the only account he could give. He did not think any benefit would accrue to the estate if it was ordered to be furnished.

His HONOR ordered the application to stand over.

Mr. HALSE said before the March Court he hoped he should be in a position to state that a scheme had been submitted to the creditors for the general arrangement of Mr. Brunskill's affairs under the 28th section. He did not think they would have occasion to trouble his Honor again if he would give a general adjournment, as this would be more convenient than if a particular day were stated, and the expense of advertizing would be immaterial.

His HONOR said he would adjourn it *sine die*.

Mr. HALSE said he thought it right to state that the bankrupt had never been in receipt of more than £500 a year. Until 26th of February he did not come into possession of his property, and therefore up to that time he could only have the £500 a year allowed him under his father's will. When he came into his property he had so far anticipated his income that since then he had only had £500.

His HONOR said everybody who lived in the neighbourhood knew the way in which this silly young man had been going on.

Exeter County Court, Wednesday 22 January 1873, before Judge Fortescue, reported in the Western Times, Exeter, Friday 24 January 1873.

Appendix 2

THURLESTONE, SOUTH DEVON.
Within ½ Mile of Kingsbridge, and facing
Bigbury Bay.

RENDELL & SAWDYE have received instructions to offer for SALE by AUC-
TION, at the Thurlestone Hotel, in Thurlestone,
on THURSDAY, August 29, 1918, at 3 p.m. the
undermentioned Valuable FREEHOLD PRO-
PERTIES, in the following or such other Lots
as may be arranged:—

Lot 1.—The Compact Farm, called "DID-
WELL," in the Parish of South Milton and
about half-mile from the Village, and comprising a comfortable Farmhouse, suitable
Buildings, and 45a. 1r. 16p. of productive
Land, in the occupation of Mr. Greek as a
yearly Lady-day tenant at a rental of £60.

Lot 2.—The most Productive, Compact, and
High-Class Farm, known as "COURT PARKS,"
situate close to Thurlestone Village, compris-
ing a modern Farmhouse, comparatively new
Model Farm Buildings, and about 207a. 2r.
of most Productive Land, in the occupation of
Mr. A. E. Stidston and others as yearly
Michaelmas tenants.

Lot 3.—A very Productive Farm at East
Buckland, Thurlestone, known as "LANG-
MANE," consisting of Farmhouse, Buildings,
Cottage, and about 114a. 2r. 35p., in the occu-
pation of Mr. S. J. Broad, junr., and others
as yearly Michaelmas tenants.

Lot 4.—A Small Holding, formerly "BUCK-
LAND MILL," comprising comfortable Farmhouse, Buildings, and about 14a. 2r. 29p., and
now in the occupation of Mr. Albert Moore
and Mr. S. J. Broad, junr., and Two Planta-
tions which are in hand.

Lot 5.—A Dwelling-house, Market Garden,
Field and Premises at East Buckland containing altogether 6a. 2r. 29p., in the occupation of Mr J. Morgan and Mr. S. J. Broad,
junr.

Lot 6.—A Small Pasture Field adjoining Lot
5, called "LITTLE FIELD," with the Garden
and pure waste, also the 4-Stall Stable, Harness Room, and large Covered Traphouse, and
occupied by Mr. S. J. Broad, junr., and containing about 2r. 36p.

Lot 7.—The Land, Premises, Tennis Courts,
and Buildings as now occupied by the
Thurlestone Golf Club, and comprising the
Links, and extending to about 30 Acres, besides
a great extent of Cliff. This Lot possesses un-
rivalled building sites.

Lot 8.—The Thurlestone Hotel, with the
Grounds and Premises, now occupied by Mrs.
Gross. This is a fully-licensed hotel, with
excellent accommodation, and is a most popular resort during the summer months.

Lot 9.—The well-built Residence, known as
"THE BUNGALOW," situate in one of the
most charming positions in Thurlestone, and
occupying altogether 2r. 29p., at present Let
on lease expiring at Lady-day, 1924, at the
annual rent of £50.

Lot 10.—Two Cottages, with Gardens and
Premises, at the head of the Village, occupied by Messrs. S. Moore and W. Hocking, and
others.

Lot 11.—Two Cottages, with Outhouses and
Gardens, adjoining Lot 10, and occupied by
Messrs. Tone and Pound, and others.

Plans, with Particulars and Conditions of
Sale, can be obtained of the Auctioneers at
their Offices, Newton Abbot, Totnes, and Ash-
burton; at the Thurlestone Hotel, Thurlestone;
the Links Hotel, South Milton; the Sloop Inn,
Bantham; or of

Messrs. HAROLD MICHELMORE & CO.,
Solicitors, Newton Abbot.
July 15th, 1918.

Devon & Exeter Gazette, 9 Aug 1918

A Tribute to Michael Day

When I put out a call in 2014 for volunteers to help research into the names on the War Memorial of those who lost their lives in the Great War it was Michael Day who was the first to step forward. He subsequently proved a tower of strength to the project, not only in his research into six of the twelve names, but also helping with the design and presentation of the Thurlestone at War Exhibition in the Parish Hall, particularly in the creation of a diorama of English and German trenches with No Man's Land in between. This was populated with model troops, machine-gun posts, horse artillery, etc., and proved a great attraction - especially with youngsters.

Of the six names that Michael researched he developed a keen interest in both the Inchbalds and the Ilberts. As a result of contacting the Inchbald School of Design he was able see and have a loan of "Jack" Inchbalds photographic album and save a copy for the Thurlestone Archive. He also turned up the fascinating biography 'Jack of all Trades' by Guy Inchbald, grandson of Peter Elliot Inchbald.

It was the Ilbert family, however, and their home at Bowringsleigh which really caught his imagination. The outcome of his further researches into this family was developed into a presentation for the Local History Group of the Kingsbridge Estuary U3A, in May 2015.

Sadly, Michael passed away on 10th February 2016. His researches into the Ilbert family are reproduced here, by kind permission of his widow Vivienne, as a tribute to the work that he did to further our knowledge of some of the families who lived in the parish and who played a part in its development through the 20th century.

Chapter 6

The Ilbert Family

compiled by Michael Day

The Ilbert Family

My interest in the Ilbert family began last year when I was researching some of the names of the men who had died in the First World War and who were remembered on the Thurlestone war memorial. One name was Geoffrey Arthur Ilbert, who, in fact, never lived in Thurlestone, but was killed in action on 28th February 1917 and is descended from this family through his great-grandfather Courtenay Ilbert (1780-1816). This led me to research the Ilbert family history so that I could understand the various relationships and the context with the Ilberts of Bowringsleigh.

My research will take us from West Alvington, via Thurlestone and South Milton to Canada, France, India, Australia and New Zealand as well as big game hunting in the Sudan, to the Houses of Parliament and attending Court at Buckingham Palace.

The name of ILBERT occurs in Domesday Book, as holding land in the county of Dorset, although it is reputed that the Ilberts came over to England with William the Conqueror and initially settled in the North of England. Prior to the 17th century, the family were wool merchants settled at Rill, in the parish of Buckfastleigh, in Devon. The Ilbert heraldic shield can be seen from the line drawing and the description in "A Genealogical and Heraldic History of the Commoners of Great Britain and Ireland, enjoying Territorial Possessions or High Official Rank but Uninvested with Heritable Honours" by John Burke, published in London in four volumes. Volume four published in 1838 records the Ilbert lineage to that date and their heraldic shield is described as;

ILBERT (R.L., H. Coll.). Or, two chevronels engrailed vert between three roses gules, seeded and barbed proper which roughly translated means gold background (Or) two shaped V chevrons green (vert) between three roses red (gules).

The Ilbert Crest

Nulla Rosa Sine Spinis

Mantling - vert and or. Crest — Upon a wreath of the colours, a cock pheasant argent, combed and wattled gules, holding in the beak a red rose slipped proper and standing on a mount vert.
Mantling - green and gold crest a silver or white cock pheasant (argent) combed and wattled red standing on a green mount.
Motto — "Nulla rosa sine spinis." "No Rose without thorns"; or "Every rose has its thorn" – meaning – to enjoy any beautiful or pleasant thing, you must endure something difficult or painful; or Every apparent desirable situation has its share of trouble or difficulty – Oxford English Dictionary.

The Ilbert family in the South Hams can be traced back over 400 years. They settled in a modest grey Elizabethan manor house, Bowringsleigh, just west of West Alvington. The family prospered mainly by three generations of judicious marriages that raised their wealth, status, nobility and forged aristocratic associations – even a royal connection to a descendant of William the Conqueror.

Bowringsleigh, once called Leigh, was originally built in 1303. The Bowrings were here by 1332 but the male line died out in the late 15th century. An early resident was Robert BOWRING, born in 1473 son of a distinguished Devon lawyer Thomas Bowring. Robert followed his father to the Middle Temple, where he became a barrister and was a justice of the peace in Devon.

He succeeded to his inheritance in 1504 and died on 3 May 1514. By his will, made on the day of his death, he made provision for his wife and left £40 each to his brother Ralph Bowring and his sister Alice Pyke. His daughter survived him by less than four years, dying on 13 Jan. 1518, and the inheritance passed to his brother Ralph, who died the following year in 1519.

"A Chronographical Description or Survey of the County of Devon" written in 1811 states that Bowringsleigh passed from an unknown Webber when it was acquired by Wiliam Gilbert in 1543. The Gilbert's were responsible for creating the beautiful interior of Bowringsleigh that can still be seen today. However it transpires that Webber and Gilbert were one and the same family – Webber alias Gilbert and Gilbert alias Webber of West Alvington is an example of alias names unique to Devon and they are recorded as such in official records. Nowadays we usually think of an alias as a false name, a device used by criminals to disguise their true identity. However this is a reversal of the original purpose of aliases which was to emphasize and make absolutely clear a distinct individual identity.

Returning to the Gilberts' and as late as the 15th century the Gilberts' were in possession of a greater part of West Alvington the parish adjoining Holwell in South Milton known to have been in that family then for at least 500 years. The surname of the ancient family of Gilbert is known to have flourished in Devon before the time of Edward the Confessor. There is also another resident of Bowringsleigh that conflicts with the record in Magna Britannia and is described in "The History of Parliament" and seems the most reliable account for the ownership of Bowringsleigh during the 17th century.

The resident was John Hale (1614-1691) and he was baptised on 19 March 1614, the first son of John Hale, a grocer, of Soper Lane, London and Harmer Green, Welwyn, Hertfordshire by Elizabeth, the daughter of Humphrey Browne of Essex. On 26 October 1637 he married Anne, one of three daughters of Robert Halswell of Goathurst, Somerset and co heir of Bowringsleigh. Robert Halswell had married Grace Webber at West Alvington on 23rd November 1612 the daughter of Nicholas Webber alias Gilbert. Robert Halswell died at West Alvington in March 1626 predeceasing his father Sir Nicholas Halswell.

John Hale held several Offices as Receiver of tithes, Devon and Cornwall. 1655; JP for Devon 1656-65, 1667-70, 1673-6, Commissioner for assessment 1657 and January 1660-1680; Militia 1659 - March 1660; Major of militia horse April 1660; Commissioner for inquiry into Newfoundland Government 1667.

By his marriage John Hale obtained not only an estate in Devon through his wife's inheritance, but a valuable political connection with Sir John Northcote, who married his wife's cousin. A parliamentarian officer in the Civil War he became the first of the family to enter Parliament. He was re-elected to the Convention for Dartmouth, 15 miles from his home. An inactive Member, he was named to only eight committees as 'Major Hale' and made no recorded speeches.

His wife Anne had succeeded to only one-third of the Bowringsleigh estate, but in 1658 John Hale bought another third for £1,350, and in 1675 John Speccot I, the son of the other co heir Paul Speccot, whose first wife Grace was Anne's sister, agreed to divide the remainder. John Hale died in September 1691, leaving the estate burdened with debts, and his surviving son, who had a large family and debts of his own, was obliged to sell out.

Magna Britannia was published in 1822 and the entry in the volume on Devonshire for West Allington or West Alvington states; "The Barton of Bowrings-leigh, which had been the property and residence of the ancient family of Bowring, passed, with its heiress, to the Pikes, by whom it was sold to Webber alias Gilbert. William Ilbert, Esq. purchased it off the Gilberts, in the reign of William III., and it is now the property and residence of his descendant, the Rev. Roope Ilbert."

"A Chronographical Description or Survey of the County of Devon" written in 1811 states that Bowringsleigh was purchased in 1695 during the reign of William III by William Ilbert of Rill, in the parish of Buckfastleigh since when it has continued in the family and is now the property of Rev Roope Ilbert the descendant of the purchaser.

All we can say for certain is that William Ilbert bought Bowringsleigh in 1695 where the family remained until the death of Miss Margery Ilbert in 1984 although it is still owned by relatives. The family thrived by trading in wool, England's chief commodity of the period. The Ilberts were joint Lords of the Manor with the nearby Bastard family. In the 17th century the estate of Bowringsleigh was some 1,200 acres.

The present house is the most important in the South Hams but not on a scale of the principal Devon houses such as Saltram House, Powderham Castle and Ugbrooke House. Bowringsleigh is set in a park on a well-treed valley side hidden from view from adjacent lanes. The mansion still retains traces of its medieval origins but is substantially an Elizabethan and Jacobean house in date built with slate-stone supplied by its own quarries.

Bowringsleigh is described in Nikolaus Pevsner's Buildings of England, written in the 1940's, with the Devon volume published in 1952 in two sections – North Devon and South Devon. He remains the pre-eminent art historian and authority on historic buildings and his description of Bowringsleigh is worthy of note.

Bowringsleigh as seen from the East

"An estate of the Bowring family until the early 16th century acquired by William Gilbert in 1543 and by William Ilbert in 1695. The present baronial appearance with its castellated four storey tower to the right of the tudor frontage of the mansion is the result of Richard Coad's restoration of 1868-1873 for William Roope Ilbert after the east wing had been damaged by fire in 1843 and the house let as a farmhouse. South front with three storey porch, two storeys of regularly disposed mullion and transom four light windows (all renewed), battlements, gables and dormers (all added 1873).

The sturdy tower is a restrained version of a more ambitious project embellished only by a polygonal turret on the west side and some galleried windows for the chapel on the ground floor, one dec, one perp. Inside much remains of Gilberts remodelling of the late 16th to early 17th century. Hall to the left of the porch with attractive 16th century plaster ceiling with single-rib intersecting pattern and central pendant. Fireplace in the back wall with flattened ogee arch; overmantel modified from a four poster bed.

The outstanding feature is the magnificent screen, a very accomplished classical piece of the 17th century with six Corinthian columns, a rich cornice, doors with fretted panels in strapwork with ebony inlay. Beyond the hall, the dining room, with an entertaining late 17th century ceiling depicting war with contemporary horsemen, guns, cannons, and victories. Despite the rustic detail their arrangement around a central octagon displays an awareness of the new court style of the Restoration (cf Bovey House). Bolection moulded double doors to the study beyond.

On the other side of the screens passage, entered by a stone doorway the library refitted in the restoration (it had a ceiling devoted to Peace, destroyed in 1843). Beyond this in the 19th century tower, the galleried chapel with a much restored screen brought from South Huish, arranged in two tiers. On the upper tier five damaged painted panels with figures. Ceiling with bosses.

Behind the tower facing east, a large late 19th century neo Tudor drawing room with two-bay windows and a quatre foil patterned ceiling, and a later billiard room. 19th century main staircase beyond the screens passage. The service rooms were largely rebuilt in the late 19th century on old foundations.The house gives the appearance of being very large, but in fact its generous width is a deception. The frontage is considerable and built in such a way all the rooms open into each other along the whole front. At the rear is a courtyard surrounded entirely by kitchens, servants' hall, and dairy.

William Roope Ilbert the younger inherited the estate after his father died in 1862. He added the great tower in a 15th century style and the house was extended eastwards to include a new drawing room and billiard room. At the same time the existing roof was made steeper to create accommodation in the attic storey. The ground floor of the tower contains the chapel which may date from the early Bowring days and has a richly coloured chancel rood screen from South Huish church rescued when that church fell into ruin in the middle of the 19th century and purchased in 1870 by William Roope Ilbert for the sum of twenty guineas".

Richard Coad (13 February 1825 – 1 November 1900) was a 19th-century Cornish architect born in Liskeard, Cornwall on 13 February 1825. He was articled to Henry Rice of Liskeard and subsequently worked as assistant to Sir George Gilbert Scott from 1847 to 1864. He was clerk of works on the Albert Memorial in London, and worked under Sir George Gilbert Scott's supervision on improvements to Lanhydrock House near Bodmin in 1857. He returned to Liskeard in 1864 to open his own independent practice,and opened a London office in 1868. When the building at Lanhydrock was severely damaged by fire in 1881, Coad returned to the site to rebuild the house to accommodate the 2nd Baron Robartes's large family.

Richard Coad was also architect on the building of Galmpton Church in 1866/67 to replace the old church at South Huish which may explain how the rood screen came to be installed at Bowringsleigh. William Roope Ilbert spent his later life not only modernising and improving the house but also the restoration and enhancement of gardens and woodland and enlarging the estate. Todd Gray in his "Garden History of Devon" states that the records of the Ilbert gardens, including Horswell House are among the most detailed to survive in Devon. His father, William Roope Ilbert the elder, was elected as a member of the Royal Agricultural Society of London in 1842 and for the most part resided at Horswell House, South Milton, the ancestral home of the Roope family and there are no records that confirm he ever lived at Bowringsleigh.

In 1831 Bowringsleigh was advertised "to be let for a term of seven years either furnished or unfurnished. It was described as the residence of William Roope Ilbert with good stables, Coach House and Offices attached and has very productive gardens and an orchard. The premises are situate one mile from Kingsbridge and three miles from the sea. The Taker can also be accommodated with about 15 acres of land, for the same term, if required".

Following the death of William Roope Ilbert in 1902 the estate passed to his sisters and in turn to their nephew, the son of his only married sister who had married the Rev Alfred Earle, later suffragan Bishop of Marlborough and Dean of Exeter. The nephew, Colonel Francis Ilbert (who had changed his name by Royal Assent) was a professional soldier with little money, but any inclination to maintain, let alone improve the house or estate was lost when his only son was killed in the Sudan in 1933. This resulted in the paying of massive Death Duties, and necessitated the disposal of a large portion of the estate at a time when agricultural land was virtually unsaleable. Chattels, and a large proportion of the family silver collection also had to be sold at this time. In 1959 Col Ilbert died, leaving his only daughter Miss Margery Ilbert to attempt to keep the place going, but by the time of her death in 1984, the house was in a sad state, with the buildings and garden almost derelict.

Michael Manisty is the current owner and his late father was Miss Ilbert's first cousin and he inherited the house and the remaining estate when she died. Since then he and his wife have been bringing the estate back to life. The house had had little

attention between the end of the 19th century and 1984 with only rudimentary electricity and plumbing. What central heating there was had been removed in the First World War to make munitions. The Manistys undertook a thorough restoration programme, which involved a completely new roof, elimination of dry rot, death watch beetle and other structural problems. New plumbing, electricity and central heating were installed as well as additional bathrooms and a modern kitchen. Complete redecoration has already been undertaken twice in the last twenty years. Although the gardens were kept in reasonable shape until the 1920's, gradually it slipped into dereliction. The glasshouses and orangery as well as walls, paths, and some terracing became completely overgrown and in some cases actually collapsed. By 1984 most of the original shape of the garden had disappeared and was submerged by fallen trees, brambles and undergrowth. At this point the decision was made to clear the overgrown areas and remove dead, dying and diseased trees. During this process some original features which had not been seen for decades were uncovered. However, in terms of planting, what is seen today is almost all the result of efforts made since Miss Ilbert's death. This includes an arboretum planted to celebrate the Millennium in an area of a lime wood that was lost in the great storm of 1989.

The lineage of the Devon Ilbert family is recorded in "A Genealogical and Heraldic History of the Commoners of Great Britain and Ireland, enjoying Territorial Possessions or High Official Rank but Uninvested with Heritable Honours" by John Burke, published in London in four volumes. In 1838 when volume 4 of Burkes Peerage was published the estates of Bowringslea and Horswell were owned by William Roope Ilbert, who had inherited from his uncle in 1826. His younger brother was the Reverend Peregrine Arthur Ilbert, born and baptised in Quebec in 1810 who was Rector of All Saints Church, Thurlestone from 1839 to 1894.

But to begin at the beginning, the first recorded Ilbert in Burkes Peerage was WILLIAM Elbert, left two sons, WILLIAM, his heir, and John, who was married to Susan Sumpter, and left an only child, John, who died young.

The elder son, WILLIAM ILBERT, m. in 1605, Alice Hanaford, and had two boys and five girls; William, who died before his father.; PETER, who inherited; Elizabeth; Ann, m. to James Bovey, of Buckfastleigh; Margaret, m. to Samuel Mitchelmore; Maria; Johanna, and Alice. The second son, PETER ILBERT, born in 1616, married Katherine, daughter of Henry Dotin, esq. of Slapton in 1646, and died in 1691, leaving three sons, of whom the eldest (the only one who married),

WILLIAM ILBERT married Mary, daughter of Henry Luscombe, esq. of Rattery, in 1668 and died in 1679, leaving, a son and successor,

WILLIAM ILBERT was a major of the Devon militia, commanded by Sir Francis Drake and it was he who purchased Bowringsleigh in 1695. He first married Jane Osborne, of Crebar, in Devonshire, by whom he had a son, WILLIAM, his heir, and a daughter, Jane. He wedded, secondly, in 1719, Catherine, daughter of Jonathan Elford, esq. of Bickham, but by her had no issue.

Major Ilbert was succeeded by his son, WILLIAM ILBERT, Esq. of Bowringsleigh, in Devon (1700-1751) was the first Ilbert to live there all his life. He married on January 29th 1735, Bridget, the fourth daughter of Sir William Courtenay, of Powderham Castle – the 4th Earl of Devon - by the Lady Anne Bertie, his wife. She was the daughter of James, first Earl of Abingdon and a Lady of the Bedchamber to Queen Anne during the whole of her reign between 1702 and 1714. They had five sons and seven daughters. Part of Bridget's dowry was the property known as Snapes Manor at Batson near Salcombe of which more shortly.

This marriage to one of the richest, most powerful and respected Devon families established the Ilberts into Devon society if not the aristocracy. William and Bridget had eight children;

1. Catherine the first born in 1738 married Roger Prideaux, esq.of Kingsbridge.
2. WILLIAM (1739-1785), his heir,
3. William-Elford (1739-1792), a twin with William, colonel of the South Devon militia. Land Tax records show that William Elford Ilbert was occupier of Snapes Manor in 1780, having acquired the reversion after 1777. It seems likely that William Elford inherited Snapes Manor on the death of his father in 1751 but could not take possession until the termination of a leasehold tenancy – the property having previously been let to seven generations of Weymouths by the Courtenays of Powderham, the Earls of Devon, who had acquired the property in 1340 and held it until the marriage of their daughter Bridget Courtenay in 1735. Weymouths were still recorded as living at and farming the property in 1747-1751 but unfortunately the next 29 years of Land Tax Assessments have been lost. William Elford Ilbert lived there as owner occupier until his death in 1792 when the property passed to Peter Ilbert, his nephew, son of his elder twin brother William who had died in 1785, and by 1841 to William Roope Ilbert when the estate was let as a tenanted farm.

The acquisition of the 12th century property by Colonel William Elford Ilbert prompted the partial remodelling of the house in Georgian style in 1784. In common with other houses in rural Devon, modification of the house rather than complete replacement was planned with a three storey residential block occupying the site of the parlour and hall of the earlier cross passage house, at its south east end. This had two principal rooms at ground floor level, a dining room and with drawing room for after dinner drinks.

The staircase is exceptionally grand, rising through three storeys with semi-circular curved landing handrails creating a most unusual repeat pattern when viewed from above and below. If viewed in isolation from the older block to the west, the exterior of the new house stands as a particularly fine Georgian block with variable window sizes to emphasise its vertical scale and the slate hung upper floors with their dentil cornices at first floor and eaves level making a striking effect. The ground floor was deliberately left unclad with slate ashlar voussoired windows and a flat top door hood on carved timber brackets (the triangular pediment is a modern addition).

Snape Manor, Batson, on the Salcombe estuary

Intriguingly, perhaps unfortunately, the older house to the west side makes the addition look lopsided and faintly ridiculous. It is such arrangements that make Devon's rural houses so unusual and fascinating. The work of reconstruction seems to have taken place over two seasons, spring to autumn 1783-84, probably with interior fitting during 1785. During the late 19th century Snapes Manor was renamed Ilbertstowe

until about 1966 when it reverted to its original name. The house was sold to the National Trust around 1990 and has been described as the most beautiful house on the Salcombe estuary. In 2010, Snapes Manor with 5.6 acres of exquisite grounds was purchased for £3.825 million pounds.
The remaining children of William and Bridget were

4. Henry, born in 1740, died in 1741.
5. Peregrine, twin with Henry, died also in 1741.
6. Hugh, born in 1743, died in 1748.
7. Bridget-Anne born in 1745, married William Birdwood,M.D. of Totnes.
8. Jane, born 1747, married J.G. Pearse, Esq. of South Molton.

Their eldest son, WILLIAM ILBERT (1739-1785), was born at Bowringsleigh, succeeded his father in 1751, and served the office of Sheriff for Devonshire in 1768. He married in 1761, Frances, daughter and sole heiress of William Roope, Esq. of Horswell House, South Milton, Devon, and they had eleven children;

1. William-Roope, R.N. born in 1762, drowned in Torbay, 1781.
2, ROOPE, born in 1763, heir to his father and succeeded in 1785 at the age of 22, when just starting as a student at Pembroke College Oxford, BA 1789 In 1798 he was appointed rector of Stockleigh Pomeroy and Cheriton Bishop, Devon, and died at Bowringsleigh on May 8 1823.
3. Peregrine, born in 1764 a scholar of Christ Church Oxford, BA 1786; fellow of Balliol College Oxford, MA 1793; In holy orders - Prependary of Exeter 1798; Archdeacon of Barnstaple in 1799, and rector of Farringdon, in Devon. Died in 1805 and buried in West Alvington churchyard.
4. PETER, born 1765 and successor to his brother Roope in 1823 but died 2 years later in 1825, Captain in the North Devon Militia, and lived at Horswell House.
5. Frances Roope Ilbert (November 1766- December 1766) Lived about 10 days.
6. Bridget-Mary, born in 1769, married Francis Cross, esq. of Great Duryard, in the county of Devon, died in 1834.
7. Frances, born in 1771 married James Somerville Fownes of Dinder House, in Somersetshire, died in 1824.
8. Willoughby, born in 1773 and served in the East India Company's naval service; died in 1795 and buried in West Alvington churchyard.
9. Sophia-Maria born 1778, married Robert John Harrison, Esq. of Caer Howel, in the county of Montgomery, died in 1836.
10. Courtenay, Captain Royal Artillery, born in 1780, and in 1804, married Anne, daughter of Geoffrey Taylor of Sevenoaks, in Kent. He died at Valenciennes France in 1816, leaving two surviving sons: William Roope born on 15th April 1805 at Woolwich, Kent and successor to his uncle Peter Ilbert in 1825, and Peregrine-Arthur, born 18th April, 1810 in Quebec, Canada.
11. Augusta born in 1783 died at Haverfordwest in 1848.

So in summary William Ilbert (1700-1751) who married Bridget Courtenay in 1735 had already inherited Bowringsleigh upon his father's death in 1726. Their first son William(1739-1785) inherited from his father in 1751 aged 12, and married Frances Roope ten years later in 1761 adding the wealth of the Roope family and Horswell House in South Milton to the estate. William died aged 46 in 1785 but his eldest son William-Roope had already predeceased him in 1781, and the Bowringsleigh and Horswell estates were inherited by the younger son Roope at the age of 22 in 1785 and who died unmarried in 1823.

Back row: Helen Ilbert, Willoughby Ilbert, Owen Ilbert, gap for Lewis Ilbert, Donald Ilbert. Seated are Arthur Ilbert, Ann - Peregrine's widow, Courtenay Ilbert and Marian Ilbert

Rev. Roope Ilbert preached the first sermon in the rebuilt chapel at Salcombe on Sunday 23 January 1803. He has been described as learned and zealous in his work in the diocese. The estate then passed to his younger brother Peter, also unmarried who died two years later in 1825. Peter was a Captain in the North Devon Militia and resided at Horswell House for most of his life and had also inherited Snapes Manor. Peter renamed the house Ilbertstow. On his death the Bowringsleigh and Horswell inheritance passed to his nephew, William-Roope Ilbert, the eldest son of Courtenay Ilbert, as all five of Peter's brothers had predeceased him.

We will pick up the story of the Ilberts with Courtenay Ilbert who seems to have been the first member of the family to marry or make his career outside Devonshire. He was commissioned into the Royal Horse Artillery, based at Woolwich, Kent and married Ann Taylor from Sevenoaks, whom he had met at a military Ball, on June 12th 1804. Service in the Army took Courtenay, with his wife and their baby son William Roope Ilbert born on April 25th 1805 to Canada to fight the French where a second son Courtenay was born in August 1808 but died ten weeks later. A third son Peregrine Arthur Ilbert(1810-1894) was born in Quebec on April 18 1810.

The family transferred to Spain and then France where Captain Courtenay served in the Battle of Waterloo in 1815 but then died at Valenciennes in Northern France the following year from fever when he was on his way home to England. Widow Ann Ilbert returned to England with her sons William Roope Ilbert and Peregrine Arthur Ilbert. In 1841 Ann was living at Quay House, Kingsbridge, at the head of the estuary, with Peregrine, his wife Rose and her parents. Quay House had been built by Lieutenant Colonel William Elford Ilbert in 1789.

The subsequent history of the Ilbert family around Kingsbridge Devon effectively follows the fortunes of these two brothers.

William Roope Ilbert inherited Bowringsleigh in 1825 from his uncle Peter Ilbert(1765-1825) and we will return to him later. In the same year Peregrine Arthur Ilbert, his younger brother went to Trinity College Cambridge, gained a BA in 1832 and an MA in 1835. He took Holy Orders and was first appointed curate at All Saints Church, South Milton before he became Rector of Thurlestone in 1839 where he served for 55 years until 1894 "for and among his parishioners" as the memorial tablet in All Saints Church records, restoring the church, farming his glebe of 35 acres, improving cottages, founding the village school in 1842, keeping drink and dissent at bay and turning by degrees into the local patriarch.

The School wasn't at first universally welcomed by the locals; one farmer was quoted as saying at the time, "When they had no education we had the pick of them to work for us on the farms; now the best of them, boys and girls, go away and better themselves, and we have to take what is left". The school thrived, however, and in the late nineteenth century moved from a small thatched building near the church into a building on the present site.

The Reverend Peregrine Arthur Ilbert not only opened the eyes of his family to a world that existed beyond the county boundary but also Thurlestone itself, which until that time had been a primitive and remote village, existing in no small part on wrecking and smuggling. Until the Rector put a clock on the church tower there

The Memorial to Reverend Peregrine Ilbert at All Saints Church, Thurlestone

was no timepiece in the village. Peregrine Arthur Ilbert married Rose Ann Owen in 1840 at Tiverton, Devon and brought her back to Thurlestone where they raised eight children, six boys and two girls, all born in Thurlestone and baptised in All Saints Church and brought up in the Rectory on Main Street. They were:

1. Courtenay Peregrine (1841-1924) m. Jessie Bradley (5 daughters)
2. Arthur (1843-1899) m. Beatrice Alice Porter (2 children)
3. Marian Lucy (1844-1938) m. Robert Campbell (3 children)
4. Owen (1846-1896) m. Mary Elizabeth Elder (4 children)
5. Willoughby (1848-1928) did not marry
6. Donald (1850-1941) did not marry
7. Helen (1854-1934) did not marry
8. Lewis George (1856-1940) m. Ann Barrack (1 daughter)

Enterprise and Education were taken for granted in the Rectory not only from their parents but also Peregrine's mother Ann "who had seen the world" and one of her nieces, Lucy Taylor, who helped with the children's education. Lucy's family background included the radical Lord Stanhope who was her grandfather and William Pitt the younger her great uncle and the family's benefactor. Thanks to her "the ghost of Pitt floated over the Rectory schoolroom, leaving in her little pupils' minds the conviction that they had a real and

Courtenay Ilbert

intimate connection with the great world of public affairs, "joining Charlemagne and Canadian wolves in the family mythology from their grandmother". Courtenay remembered all his life tales of his grandmother travelling across Spain and France with her two little boys ahead of Wellington's army.

And how the children prospered!

The eldest child, Courtenay Peregrine Ilbert (1841-1924) was educated at Marlborough School and won several scholarships whilst at Balliol College Oxford, graduated with first class honours and was elected a Fellow of Balliol in 1864 and as President of the Oxford Union Society in 1865. A glittering career as a lawyer and in parliamentary service followed. He was called to the bar (Lincoln's Inn) in 1869 and joined the Parliamentary Counsel Office, the department for drafting parliamentary bills. Between 1882 and 1886 he was the legal advisor of the Council of Governor-General of India and lived there with his wife and four young daughters. Shortly after his appointment came a difficult time in Anglo-Indian relations with a Bill proposed in 1883 by Viceroy Ripon that sought to abolish racial prejudice from the Indian Penal Code. Earlier in 1873, the British government by an Act had proclaimed that in criminal matters no Indian judge could try a European accused. This discrimination between the Indians and the Europeans appeared to be inhuman and unjust to the liberal Viceroy Lord Ripon. Under Lord Ripon's instruction, Courtenay Ilbert, The Law Member of the Council, introduced a Bill which sought to abolish the discrimination between the Indians and the Europeans by allowing Indian judges and magistrates the jurisdiction to try British offenders in criminal cases at the District level as a compromise between two previously suggested bills and it became forever known as "The Ilbert Bill".

The Bill proved divisive in England and although various reports conflict - it was supported by the Gladstone administration back in London but The Times tried to stir up opposition to the Bill and there was a vigorous and united opposition to the Bill. However the British public was generally supportive in their opposition to racial discrimination. The Europeans living in India regarded it as a humiliation and the introduction of the Bill led to intense opposition in Britain as well as India (by the British residents) culminating in violent protests that ultimately played on racial tensions and led to its withdrawal before it was reintroduced in 1884 and enacted in a severely compromised state. The bitter controversy deepened antagonism between the British and Indians and was a prelude to the formation of the Indian National Congress the following year.

Lord Ripon had to concede to the pressure of the European community and the new Act that was passed modifying the Ilbert Bill that virtually signified victory for the European community. The amended bill had the provisions that the Europeans could be tried by both European and Indian District Magistrates and Sessions Judges alike. However, a defendant would in all cases have the right to claim trial by a jury of which at least half the members must be European. Thus, this enactment held that European criminals would be heard only by the Indian Judges "helped by the European Judges".

The amended "Ilbert Bill" was passed on 25 January 1884, as the Criminal Procedure Code Amendment Act 1884 and it came into force on May 1, 1884. However the Ilbert Bill has acquired a special significance in the legal, constitutional and political history of British India, especially in Bengal on the ground that it quickened the processes of nationalism and anti-colonial mobilization. Despite the controversy over the "Ilbert Bill"– forever linked with his name – Courtenay Ilbert's career continued to go from strength to strength.

On his return to England he was appointed assistant parliamentary counsel to the Treasury in 1886 and parliamentary counsel in 1899. He was knighted in 1895 with the award of the Knight Commander of the Order of the Star of India. In 1908 he was made a Knight Commander and a Knight Grand Cross in 1911.

In February 1902 Sir Courtenay Peregrine Ilbert was appointed Clerk of the House of Commons, a position he held until 1921. He gave guidance on procedural issues arising from bills such as the Parliament Act and gained a reputation for providing legal expertise invaluable in the drafting of bills while remaining impartial to political divides caused by controversial legislation. Despite attaining high office in Parliament he remained a lawyer at heart, seeking the correct legality for political changes. His influence was considerable in the production and style of modern legislation.

He was also a prolific writer and lecturer and continued to follow events in India with keen interest and fondness for that country. Among his works were;

> Legislative Methods and Forms,
> The Government of India 1898 updated in 1916,
> Parliament; its history, construction and practice,
> Manual of Procedure in the Public Business of the House of Commons,
> The Mechanics of Law Making.

It was announced in the Western Times on the 18th March 1921 that "Sir Courtenay P Ilbert, the well-known Devonian, who is retiring from the clerkship of the House of Commons, is in his 80th year. He has occupied the seat in front of the (Speakers) chair during the reign of office of four Prime Ministers - Mr Balfour, Sir Henry Campbell-Bannerman, Mr Asquith and Mr Lloyd George." - and throughout World War 1. It was reported that "There was carried unanimously in the House of Commons yesterday a resolution moved by Mr Lloyd George, expressing its appreciation of the House of the manner in which Sir Courtenay Ilbert had discharged his important duties as Clerk for the House over a long period".

Sir Courtenay Ilbert died three years later at his Buckinghamshire home two months after the death of his wife. Tributes to his wisdom, kindliness and learning flowed in. From Thurlestone his sister Helen who had spent time with him in India helping to raise his daughters wrote "I owe nearly all the joy in my life to him and his brother Lewis. He was the very best of brothers and the most lovable man in the world".

Courtenay Peregrine Ilbert had married Jessie Bradley on June 27 1874 at Trinity Church, Paddington, London and they had five daughters:

1. Lettice Ilbert 1875-1956 married Herbert Fisher a tutor at New College, Oxford at Trinity Church, Paddington;
2. Olive Ilbert 1878- 1950 married Michael Heseltine, son of a Norfolk vicar at St Margaret's Church, Westminster;
3. Jessie Ilbert 1880-1946 married George Young (Sir George Young 4th Baronet) at St George's Church, Hanover Square;
4. Margaret (Moya) 1882-1952 married Arthur Cochrane (Sir Arthur William Steuart Cochrane) Officer-at-Arms to the Crown also at St George's Church, Hanover Square;
5. Joyce Ilbert 1890-1957 did not marry. Jessie Ilbert was presented to the Princess of Wales in 1900 by Lady Ilbert and it was reported in the London Standard thus:

"The Princess of Wales on behalf of her Majesty held the Second Dining Room of the season yesterday afternoon at Buckingham Palace. (Presentations to the Royal Highness in this Court are by the Queen's pleasure considered as equivalent to presentation to Her Majesty). Lady Ilbert, who was accompanied by two daughters,

The memorial to Courtenay Peregrine Ilbert in All Saints Church, Thurlestone

one a debutante, wore a train of golden olive green velvet lined with shrimp pink satin and finished with a flounce of old mechlin lace. Her gown in floral brocade was trimmed with some of the fine lace, and the delicate green velvet softened with pale pink chiffon. Miss Olive Ilbert's Empire gown in white crepe de chine had the corsage and the hem of the skirt embroidered with gold and white chenille and was finished with an azure green sash, muslin lined white mousseline, trimmed with soft frills edged with the soft green. Miss Jessie Ilbert's presentation dress was also of white crepe de chine, the Empire bodice being formed of lattice work in chiffon and snowdrops, similar trimmings appearing at the bottom of the skirt, and forming the sleeves. The train was of white broche, and she carried a bouquet of white snowdrops".

I think you could say the Ilberts had arrived in London Society.

The second son Arthur Ilbert (1843-1899) was a successful merchant living for some years in Shanghai, China. He married Beatrice Alice Porter at the Cathedral of the Holy Trinity Shanghai in 1886. They returned to England to live at Upwey near Weymouth, Dorset. They had two children;

Courtenay Adrian Ilbert (1888–1956) was born on 22 April 1888 and educated at Eton and Kings College, Cambridge. He won honours in mathematics and became a civil engineer, concentrating on railway projects in India. He also became a recognized authority on the subject of antiquarian horology and brought together the most important collection of watches ever achieved by a private collector and one of the greatest horological collections of the 20th century covering almost every aspect of the history and development of mechanical horology.

He began collecting clocks and watches whilst still at Eton and after retiring from his engineering career in the early 1930's devoted most of his life to his pursuit of horology with his most active period of collecting in the 1920s and 1930s. He was a Liveryman of the Worshipful Company of Clockmakers and a Fellow of the British Horological Institute; the Antiquarian Horological Society was founded in his drawing room at Stanley House, 10 Milner Place, London on the 1st October 1953.

Following his death in 1956, Ilbert's extensive library of books was bequeathed to the British Horological Institute and a longcase clock, made by Tompion for the Royal Observatory at Greenwich, was left to the National Maritime Museum. When Ilbert's estate was settled in 1958 his vast collection of clocks, prints and other related material was destined to be auctioned at Christies Auction House on 6th and 7th November 1958. There were approximately 2,300 watches and watch movements, 40 marine chronometers, 210 clocks, including the Drummond Robertson collection of Japanese clocks, and various prints, horological tools, watch papers and other items of horological interest.

Following protracted negotiations with the government of the time, a private donation of £60,000 by Gilbert Edgar CBE, chairman of the H. Samuel watch retailers and jewellers, and a public subscription organised by the Clockmakers' Company, the sale was cancelled and the entire Ilbert collection was finally purchased for the nation in December 1958 from the beneficiaries of the Ilbert Estate and the collection was acquired by the British Museum where it has received international acclaim ever since. The collection, now known as the Ilbert collection, includes the Earnshaw 509 chronometer, one of only two surviving from the voyage of the Beagle. Ilbert's watches were then acquired with further funds from Gilbert Edgar, public donations and government funds.

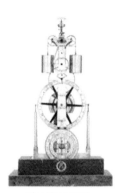

The Breguet Napoleon Clock

Some sixty years later his name is still much revered in horological circles and his authority has seldom been surpassed.

His collection was bequeathed to his nephew Michael Inchbald who shared Courtenay's house in Milner Street, whilst an architectural student. One of the clocks is an important timepiece known as the Breguet "Napoleon" Clock No 111 – Pendule a trois roues, with both Gregorian and Revolutionary annual calenders sold on 15 June 1795 to Breguet's London agent Louis Recordon. It is 23 inches high and was valued in 2014 at between £700,000 and one million pounds.

Arthur Ilbert's daughter Evelyn Rosemary Ilbert (1894-1958) married Geoffrey Herbert Elliot Inchbald the younger brother of John (Jack) Chantry Elliot Inchbald who died in World War 1 and is also remembered on the Thurlestone War Memorial. Michael Inchbald was Geoffrey's son.

Peregrine and Rose's first daughter Marian Lucy Ilbert (1844-1938), (bottom right in the photograph on page 166) was born in 1844 and married Robert Campbell, a Barrister and Advocate in 1867 at All Saints Thurlestone. They had three children and lived in Kensington before retiring to Bantham House in Bantham between 1901 and 1911 and where Marian lived until her death on December 16 1938, 26 years after her husband.

The next son Owen Ilbert (1846-1896) was educated at Marlborough School and was elected to a classical scholarship at Corpus Christi College Oxford in 1865 and graduated with first class classical honours in 1870 and his MA degree in 1872. He married Mary Elizabeth Elder in Rochford, Essex in 1875, and their first child a daughter, Rose Dorothy, was born on 27 November 1877 at Crowthorne, Berkshire, whilst he was teaching at Wellington College.

Owen Ilbert was then appointed assistant master at Tonbridge in Kent, where three more children, all boys, were born - Peregrine Edward (1878-1938), Owen Lewis (1880-1968) and the youngest Geoffrey Arthur Ilbert who was killed in action on 28th February 1917 and is remembered on the Thurlestone War Memorial. After holding assistant masterships at Wellington College, Clifton College, Christ's Hospital, and Tonbridge School, Owen Ilbert was appointed headmaster of Crediton School in Devonshire in 1884, and held that office until 1891. However his life was a series of tragedies.

Firstly his wife Mary died in 1888 in Crediton and then his own poor health compelled him to leave England. He sailed alone from Plymouth on December 12th 1891 bound for Auckland, New Zealand having been appointed as Chief Classical and English Master to Auckland College and grammar school because of his high scholarship and wide scholastic experience. On August 17 1893 his three orphaned sons aged 14, 13 and 10 joined him sailing from London bound for Wellington, New Zealand, but their father's health failed to improve and just over three years later Owen Ilbert died on 12th December 1896 and the school's obituary refers to "a master of exceptional talent and of the highest character".

The eldest child of Owen Ilbert and Mary, their only daughter, Rose Dorothy Ilbert remained in England and married George Gordon Coulton, a Cambridge academic and lecturer in religion at St John's College, Cambridge, at All Saints Church, Thurlestone on 19 July 1904. He was a lecturer at Cambridge, where they lived, and where she died on 29 March 1959. Their daughter, Mary Rose Coulton became better known under her pseudonym of Sarah Campion, a well-travelled teacher and author of several novels set in Australia where she finally resided before her death in 2002. Eldest son Peregrine Edward Ilbert remained in New Zealand where he worked as a farmer and fisherman, married Ida Mildred Wilson, and lived in Waikato, North Island, until his death in March 1938. Second son Owen Lewis Ilbert returned to UK and studied electrical engineering at Chelmsford before moving to Shanghai, where he married Gertrude Margaret Howard Moneypenny, a minister's daughter, on 24 September 1907. After retiring he lived in the USA and UK until his death in Surrey in 1968. Geoffrey Arthur Ilbert, the youngest son, went to Auckland Grammar School but had little inclination for an academic career. On January 1 1902 Geoffrey was a lieutenant in the Royal Marines Light Infantry and in May 1903 failed to qualify in Naval Gunnery on HMS Excellent. On June 4 1903 Geoffrey's name was removed from the list of those who had failed the Naval Gunnery course after a confidential report to his uncle, Sir Courtenay Peregrine Ilbert, The Clerk to the House of Commons.

After eighteen months with the RMLI, he joined the Royal Canadian Mounted Police and spent three years as a "Mountie". Returning to New Zealand, he decided to stay there and learn all about sheep farming, perhaps encouraged by his eldest brother. The records show that he worked as a farm labourer and storekeeper in Te Araroa, Bay of Plenty, between 1911 and 1914. At the time of enlistment on 13 November 1914 Geoffrey worked for Mr J Smith, a contractor, of Takapau, Hawkes Bay and he lived at Pilling's Boarding-house, Upper Hutt, New Zealand.

Geoffrey married Mate Kino Ariare on 20 November 1911 at the Auckland Registrar's Office, although this marriage appears to have been short-lived as Mate Kino remarried in 1915 and when he enlisted in November 1914 he declared himself to be single on his Attestation Form. Private Geoffrey Arthur Ilbert of the 1st Battalion, the New Zealand Expeditionary Force was killed in action 28th February 1917 on the western front. He is buried in the London Rifle Brigade Cemetery Comines-Warneton, Hainaut, Belgium, half a mile beyond the village of Ploegsteert, Belgium. His obituary in the Auckland Weekly News of 29th March 1917 read as follows:-

"Private Geoffrey Arthur Ilbert, killed in action in France on February 28, was an Auckland Grammar School boy, and the youngest son of the late Mr. Owen Ilbert, classical master of the school. He left New Zealand in January, 1915, and was attached to the Wellington Infantry Battalion. After a few months' service in Egypt he was transferred to the Army Service Corps. Afterwards he was transferred to the New Zealand Veterinary Corps, and remained with that unit till it was disbanded. At the time of his death he was acting as battalion stretcher-bearer in the Auckland Infantry. He was 33 years of age."

A Memorial Plaque in All Saints Thurlestone Church is inscribed:

"In Memory of Geoffrey Arthur Ilbert PRIVATE (acting stretcher bearer) 1st Auckland Infantry Batt (New Zealand) youngest son of Owen Ilbert, grandson of the Rev. P.A.Ilbert who gave his life for his fellow men 28th February 1917 and is buried at Ploegsteert in Flanders aged 33".

The Memorial to Geoffrey Ilbert at All Saints Church, Thurlestone

Of the remaining four children of Peregrine and Rose Ilbert: Willoughby Ilbert (1848-1928) was a pupil at Marlborough School and became a solicitor, practising first in Cornwall and Exeter and then in London. One bizarre event occurred involving Willoughby Ilbert at Penzance was reported in the Cornishman on April 26 1883 under the headline:

Strange Conduct of a Gentleman

"Mr Willoughby Ilbert, son of the Rev Ilbert of Thurlestone, near Kingsbridge and brother of Mr Ilbert, whose proposed changes in the laws of India have lately created so much interest, is a solicitor who has been for five or six years in the employ of Mr T Cornish of Penzance, and has had charge of the conveyancing part of the business. For some time Mr Ilbert has suffered from bodily illness and his mind has been occasionally affected; but not to such an extent as to interfere with the discharge of his professional duties. The chief peculiarity seems to be a kind of absentmindedness during which Mr Ilbert strolled into hotel and private houses, apparently in search of apartments or in quest for friends.

Special Annoyance at the Queens

This has happened so often at the Queens hotel and visitors quite strangers to Mr Ilbert became so annoyed – in some cases frightened – that Mr Hora had to ask him to forbear from calling at his house. About 9 o'clock on Wednesday evening a servant drew the attention of Mr Hora, the lessee of the Queens, to the fact that Mr Ilbert was in the billiard room and alone. Proceeding thither Mr Hora asked him what his business was and repeated his caution that his presence in the house was undesirable and that he must not stay there. Mr Ilbert argued that the room was a public one. The uninvited guest did not take the hint and Mr Hora said he must turn the billiard room lights down. Mr Hora again requested him to leave and put his hand on Mr Ilbert's left arm to guide him towards the front door. Directly as he did this Mr Ilbert raised his right arm, pointed a loaded six chambered revolver at and close to Mr Hora's breast and said "if you touch me I'll shoot you". Mr Hora refrained from further action and said "I shall certainly now send for a policeman and give you in charge". Mr Ilbert seemed to acquiesce. He replaced the revolver in his pocket and was moving towards the door but Mr Hora detained him, sent for a policeman and gave him into custody of PC Casley.

Willoughby Ilbert, Courtenay Ilbert and Lewis Ilbert pictured on the beach at Thurlestone

Mr Ilbert, when requested to do so, gave the pistol to the policeman. On being taken to the police station it was found that each of the six chambers of the revolver were loaded. He was locked up for the night. Mr Ilbert was charged with having on the 18th April in the borough of Penzance assaulted Mr Hora by pointing a loaded pistol at him and threatening to shoot him. The magistrate said he must deal with case as he would with any other and not be influenced by the position or profession of Mr Ilbert. Because the case was of considerable importance Mr Ilbert was remanded to appear in court the next day and was allowed to pass the night at the Western Hotel in the custody of PC Casley and on Friday morning his father arrived from South Devon.

On Friday morning (an extra issue of the Cornishman on Thursday afternoon having made known the unexpected occurrence throughout Penzance) the Town Hall was filled by persons anxious to hear the facts. Mr Ilbert pleaded not guilty to the charge of assault by pointing a loaded pistol and threatening to shoot Mr Hora.

In evidence Mr Hora stated that as soon as he saw the pistol he said "You infernal scoundrel". Asked if he really thought he was going to fire Mr Hora said "I cannot say what a man intended but I don't stand in fear of him. The pistol certainly touched my breast. I think he had a pipe in his left hand. My only object is that he shall not come to our hotel. I do not press the charge that he attempted to do me bodily harm."

The defence lawyer accepted that Mr Hora had given them an accurate and fair statement of what transpired and by it the bench saw that the charge was accurately laid (if charge at all) as one of common assault. It was not a charge of assault with intent to do any bodily harm, but merely an assault by pointing a pistol without (as Mr Hora has shown) any intention of firing it off. That there was no such intention was proved by the fact that it was impossible to fire it off in the way in which it was held,or by one hand, so that there really was, in law, no assault at all. The defence expressed Mr Ilbert's extreme regret for what had occurred but he explained Mr Ilbert had no intention to do any harm with his pistol, and it was quite impossible that he could do any harm because the pistol was of a peculiar kind, its trigger lying flat in the stock and not being raised by the hand that held the weapon.

Mr Hora had admitted that Mr Ilbert has a pistol in one hand and a pipe in the other and that having regard to the construction of the weapon it could not be discharged with one hand. Mr Hora said "All I want to be assured is that Mr Ilbert will not annoy the house or me by coming there. It was a very foolish act". Mr Ilbert's lawyer admitted that and added he was now able to state that Mr Ilbert had already made arrangements to leave Penzance within a few weeks and would give his word that so long as he remained he would not enter the Queens Hotel or cause any further annoyance to Mr Hora and that he was here to also to express Mr Ilbert's extreme regret for what had occurred and to tender to Mr Hora the most ample apology.

The Bench, which included the mayor, consulted for several minutes and on their return the mayor said "Willoughby Ilbert the charge against you resolves itself into one of common assault but that charge Mr Hora does not wish to press, if he can be protected from the annoyance of which he complains. We therefore refrain from dealing with this case in that respect. But we order you to enter into your own recognizance in £250 to be of good behaviour for 12 months and to find surety for a like amount and time. The pistol will be impounded." Mr Ilbert's father and defendant entered into the required sureties. The Rev Peregrine Ilbert was 73 years old at the time and Willoughby 35 years.

Two years later the Exeter and Plymouth Gazette on 29 May 1885 announced "The Lord Chancellor has appointed Mr Willoughby Ilbert of the firm Hirtzel and Ilbert, Solicitors, Exeter to be a commissioner to administer Oaths in the Supreme Court of Judicature of England."

Eighteen months later the partnership was dissolved by mutual consent. A Notice in the Exeter and Plymouth Gazette of 14 January 1887 stated; "Notice is hereby given that the partnership heretofore subsisting between us, the undersigned George Hirtzel and Willoughby Ilbert carrying on business as Solicitors at No 12 Bedford Circus, Exeter, and at Okehampton, in the county of Devon with the style or firm of Hirtzel and Ilbert has been dissolved by mutual consent as and from 31st December instant." And the witness to Willoughby Ilbert's signature was William Beer Solicitor of Kingsbridge. By 1901 Willoughby Ilbert was in practice as a solicitor at 12 South Square, Grays Inn, Holborn in London and did not return to live in Devon. He died on 27th April 1928 at 9 Upper Montague Street, Marylebone, London.

Donald Ilbert (1850-1941) did not leave Thurlestone and lived with his widowed mother at Rockhill Thurlestone in 1911. He was the last of the eight children to die and lived at The Old School House in Thurlestone at the time of his death. He attended Marlborough College, like his father, but did not achieve much distinction academically, attributed to a fall as a baby off the nursery table on to his head and had never been quite the same since. He was however selected by the Headmaster to meet Queen Victoria when she visited the school "because of his royal connections" – a small drop from John of Gaunt and Edward III came via his descent from the Courtenay's of Powderham Castle. He travelled the world as a young man, journeying across Canada and America, collecting a redskin outfit, useful for Fancy Dress dances, tried his hand as a cowboy and took part in the Gold Rush and lost most of his money to cardsharpers on board ship. He later reached Fiji. He had a heart of gold and was often referred to as "simple minded". He was accident prone, one of his fingers was missing and two cut off short.

Helen Ilbert (1854-1934) also spent most of her life in Thurlestone, apart from her time in India with her brother's family to help with looking after his children through various illnesses and nursing and comforting his wife, who was invalided with a serious injury to her knee suffered in a carriage accident. During her time in India her brother insisted she must see the main sights of Northern India.
After a visit to Sir Charles and Lady Aitcheson, who was Lieutenant-Governor of the

Punjab, Courtenay accompanied her in his private railway carriage to visit Sir Alfred Lyall, Lieutenant Governor of the North West Provinces, with whom he had business, combined with a rapid tour of Dehli, Agra, Muttra, Cawpore and Benares. The trip turned out to be an anti-climax for Helen after the visit to the Aitchesons where she had witnessed and been dazzled by carriages with gold and silver trappings; horses and elephants brilliant with gold clothing; jewels; acts of homage; trays of presents that might not be kept; fireworks, bands, and scarlet-clad soldiers. The central figure was a fourteen year old Maharaja, dressed in brilliant silk coat of shot maroon lined with blue, bright green nether garments, necklace of emeralds and pearls and turban of pale mauve.

At Benares Helen had the bizarre experience of being escorted by a recently retired member of the Legislative Council, "an old Rajah, and an opponent of Courtenay during the Ilbert Bill agitation" when it was only a short time since each had been burnt in effigy "the Rajah by the people of Benares because of his opposition to the Bill and Courtenay by the Europeans of Coorg for just the opposite reasons". After the India experience life in Thurlestone must have seemed very dull indeed. Helen lived at Rockhill, Thurlestone until her death in 1934.

Lewis George Ilbert (1856-1940) travelled abroad and became a tea planter in Assam before returning around 1900 to Dunstone, near Yealmpton in retirement. He married Ann Barrack and they had one daughter. Lewis is buried in All Saints Churchyard, Thurlestone. He also spent time with his brother Courtenay during his time in India. The Western Morning News of 1 March 1940 carried the following report;

Laid to Rest at Thurlestone
Late Mr Lewis G Ilbert

"In a corner of the windswept churchyard, looking out to sea, a member of one of the oldest Devon families was buried at Thurlestone yesterday. He was Mr Lewis George Ilbert, who died at Dunstone, Yealmpton, in his 84th year and who was interred in a grave lined with snowdrops, ferns and ivy. The Western Morning News has received the following appreciation of the late Mr Ilbert. The death of Lewis George Ilbert at Dunstone, Yealmpton, has brought sorrow to his family and a large circle of relations and friends. His personality was known by all for his singular charm, its kindness and noble courtesy. His fine and generous nature was devoid of all small-mindedness and self-seeking.

The tradition of the Ilberts goes far back into the web of England's history. Although they were never given to public affairs their lives stood for something in the neighbourhoods - charming, gifted, courteous and always kind. The late Lewis George Ilbert was a such example of that family tradition. He was the youngest son of the late Rev Peregrine Ilbert, rector of Thurlestone for 50 years.

He was born in Thurlestone on December 7 1857. In 1879 he went to Assam, to the Moran Tea Garden with which he spent 30 years of his life, from an assistant, then a manager and lastly for many years as a director of the company. He retired from this position a few years ago because of failing health. (The Moran Tea Company amalgamated with McLeod Russel India Ltd in 2008 to create the largest tea company in the world.) His work in Moran was distinguished by a consideration and understanding which has since proved of great value to the labour problem in Assam. He was a keen sportsman, a good shot, and a good polo player. He started two polo clubs in Assam.

In 1898 he married Ann, daughter of Rev John Barrack of Falkland, Fife and had one daughter Margaret Ann, wife of Lieutenant-Colonel Walter Fawcett. In the last war having been rejected on the grounds of health for service with the Indian troops, he conceived the idea of the Volunteer Corps of Veterans - the VTC - which was brought to fruition at Exeter. The Yealmpton unit was exceptional in its efficiency and strength under his supervision. After the war his advice was sought on reconstruction and he advocated the reafforestation of Dartmoor. He was indeed the true and parfait knight and handed on the tradition of the "gentlefolk" which his family have been for generations in the county of Devon.

Quite a remarkable standard of scholastic achievement and professional and business prowess and acumen for the family of a village rector and a farmer's daughter!

We left the Bowringsleigh estate in the hands of William-Roope Ilbert who had inherited the estate in 1825, at the age of 20, from his uncle Peter ten years after he returned to England from France with his widowed mother and younger brother Peregrine.

He married his first cousin Augusta Jane, daughter of James Somerville Frownes of Dinder House, Somerset, and Frances Ilbert, on 31st March 1830 in Old Church, St Pancras, Middlesex after being educated at Corpus Christi College, Cambridge.

William Roope Ilbert was High Sherriff of Devon in 1837 and the family of two sons and three daughters lived at Horswell House, South Milton, the seat of the Roopes inherited by the Ilberts in 1761 rather than at Bowringsleigh. Horswell House, surrounded by 18th-century parkland, was built between 1720 and 1740. There are stucco stone walls to the front range with a double hipped slate roof to the front and a gabled end to the rear wing. The house is a good example of an 18th-century double-pile house with a very unspoilt exterior, being symmetrical with five bays. It has two storeys with dormers and a shell-hooded porch. Its market value today is over £3 million pounds.

William Roope Ilbert died on June 30 1862 at Horswell House and was succeeded by his elder son William Roope Ilbert at the age of 29. He was educated at Oriel College, Oxford and was conferred with an MA on June 10 1858. He was unmarried and lived at Bowringsleigh with five servants and, as we have seen, was responsible for the remodelling by John Coad between 1868-1873.

William Roope Ilbert was a strong promotor and Director of the Kingsbridge Railway Company and in 1873 the company advertised a prospectus of a shares issue for £160000 with the directors listed including Thomas Woollcombe, chairman of the South Devon Railway; and Richard Bassett – a Director of the Great Western Railway.

William Roope Ilbert died on April 30 1902. His obituary in the Western Times of Friday 2 May 1902 reads;
"Mr William Roope Ilbert of Bowringsleigh, Kingsbridge died on Wednesday evening,

after a long illness. The deceased gentleman comes from a very ancient family, having settled in Bowringsleigh in the latter part of the 1500's. Mr Ilbert was born on April 2 1833. He was a barrister-at-law, JP for Devon, Duncombe Trustee for Kingsbridge, Governor of the grammar school, and was for many years Chairman of Salcombe Local Board before it transferred into an Urban Council.

The deceased gentleman never took a very active part in public affairs, and being reserved in manner was not often approached by the people. He was a large owner of property. The funeral takes place on Monday. It is understood the bulk of the property has been left to the son of the Bishop of Marlborough, Mrs Earle being a sister of Mr Ilbert."

The sister referred to was his elder sister Frances Anne Ilbert born in 1832 who married Alfred Earle in November 1866 at All Saints Church, West Alvington. Alfred Earle was the son of the distinguished surgeon, Henry Earle (1789-1838), who himself was the third son of a famous surgeon, Sir James Earle (1755-1817).

Alfred attended Eton College and Hertford College in Oxford, and he was ordained in 1858 and was a curate of St Edmund's Salisbury and then rector of Monkton Farleigh, Wiltshire before becoming vicar of West Alvington. From 1872 to 1888 he was the Archdeacon of Totnes. He was also Canon Residentiary of Exeter Cathedral (1865-88). In 1888 he was appointed by Queen Victoria Bishop of Marlborough, suffragan Bishop of West and North West London and Rector of St. Michael´s, Cornhill, London until 1900 when he became Dean of Exeter, and served there until his death in December 1918.

Frances and Alfred Earle had two sons; William Henry Earle born 1868 and Francis Alfred Earle born in 1869. Little can be traced of the elder son upon leaving school but Francis Alfred Earle was a Justice of the Peace in Devon and a Lieutenant-Colonel in the Royal Warwickshire Regiment who served in the Nile Expedition of 1898 and was present at the battles of Ondurman and Atbara. In the Great War he served on the staff of the 42nd Division at Gallipoli. He inherited Bowringsleigh in 1902 and in 1925 assumed by Royal Licence the surname and arms of Ilbert. He had married Margaret Henrietta Nugent Bankes, daughter of the late Henry Hyde Nugent Bankes, of Wraysbury, Bucks, on December 1st 1898 at Bellary, Madras, India and they had two children:

Timothy Earle Ilbert, Gentleman, born in Exeter in 1905 and died in 1933 in the Sudan; and Margery Frances Earle Ilbert born in 1908 and who died in 1984.

"A memorial service was held at West Alvington, near Kingsbridge, Devon, on Wednesday for Lieutenant Timothy Earle Ilbert, aged 28, who was killed by a buffalo near Mongalla, Sudan, on Sunday, whilst big game hunting. Lieutenant Ilbert was the only son of Lieutenant-Colonel Ilbert of Bowringsleigh, Kingsbridge, and was seconded from the 2nd Battalion Duke of Cornwall's Light Infantry to the Sudan Defence Force. Lieutenant Ilbert was very popular in the district and at Bodmin, where he was stationed for two years. His engagement to Miss Daphne Grace Cooke-Hurle, younger daughter of Major and Mrs T A Cooke-Hurle, of Holne, Devon, was announced in January of this year."

Margery Ilbert was the last surviving of the Ilbert family to reside at Bowringsleigh. She never married and died on March 12th 1984. Her death was announced in the Gazette of March 16th 1984 under the heading:

Death of Miss Ilbert means end of an era

"Miss Margery Frances Earle Ilbert – the last of a family which has been one of the major landowners in the South Hams for three centuries – died at her mansion home at the weekend. She died at her centuries old family home at Bowringsleigh, aged 75, after a two month long illness. A private family funeral will be held today at All Saints Church, West Alvington, and she will be buried alongside her father and mother in the parish churchyard.

Miss Ilbert is the last direct descendant in the Ilbert line. She never married and her only brother was killed in an accident in Africa in 1933. Miss Ilbert was born in Exeter where her grandfather was Dean of the city. She came to live at Bowringsleigh with her parents and elder brother. When her father Lt Col F A Ilbert died in 1959 she inherited the estate with the land at West Alvington and South Milton. Much of the land has been rented out to tenants but right up to her death Miss Ilbert remained personally involved with the farming of the land around the house and she kept her own herd of Guernsey cows.

Since coming to Bowringsleigh in the late 17th century the Ilbert family has always been heavily involved in the community. Following in family tradition, Miss Ilbert was deeply interested in church matters. She sat on the Exeter Diocesan Synod, the Exeter Diocesan Parsonage Board and since 1956 the Exeter Pastoral Committee. She was concerned in education and was a governor at both Kingsbridge School and West Alvington Primary School and the chairman of the foundation governors of the Grammar School. Kingsbridge School headmistress Miss Margaret Lorenz said "Miss Ilbert continued her family interest in the school and was a staunch supporter of all our ventures. She provided the impetus for the Westville pavilion modernisation and urged us all to see the original Foundation still carried out an appropriate responsibility. I found her tremendously supportive in every aspect of my task as head of the school. She attended functions, was interested in people, used her influence to support our activities and, above all, showed what dedicated service to the community means. Noone can replace her. All we can do is be grateful that we knew, worked with and shared laughter with such a wonderful person."

Her concern for young people extended to the Scouting Movement. She ran a Cub Scout pack at West Alvington from 1938 until 1974. The group met in a hut in the grounds of Bowringsleigh. They met throughout the war years. She held the position of assistant district commissioner for many years and for the last three years was president of South Hams District Scout Council. For her services to Scouting she received one of the highest awards in the movement.

She was also involved in many other aspects of the village community. Two years after her father died she stepped into his position as chairman of the parish council. This she has held ever since. She also took up his position as the representative for West Alvington on the rural district council until the local government reorganisation in 1974. She had only recently been re-elected as the vice president of the local Conservative Association. She was also involved in the establishment of West Alvington WI in 1956. She was the original treasurer and on her death was the vice-president. For the past eleven years,since it began, Miss Ilbert has been president of the South Hams Hospital League of Friends. Her father originally donated the land on which the hospital was built in the 1920's.

Of the many committees she was associated with one was the Cookworthy Museum Committee. On many occasions articles from Bowringsleigh have been exhibited at the museum. Miss Ilbert was also instrumental in establishing the nature reserve on the reed beds on her land at South Milton Ley. Through her the warden was able to trace the wildlife story back to the 19th century, by studying the number of wildfowl shot in the estate records!

Four hundred people packed All Saints Church, Malborough for a memorial service to Miss Margery Ilbert, held there rather than West Alvington Parish Church to allow more people to attend.

The story of the Ilberts is one of a family which contributed selflessly and no less effectively to the prosperity of Devon through succeeding generations and their endeavours and attentions to county and local affairs. They earned a considerable reputation over a wide area. Two members of the family served as High Sheriffs of the County, and many others served as soldiers and churchmen. There is no doubt that, for the most part, the Ilberts lived a life of privilege, wealth and status. However, through the contemporaneous accounts in newspaper obituaries and other publications they were well-liked and respected, gave service to the community and Kingsbridge would have been much the poorer without them.

Michael Day

About the Author:

Robin Macdonald was born in Birkenhead and graduated with a BA (Hons English) from Liverpool University before pursuing a career in commerce and management consultancy. Robin and his wife Pat settled in Thurlestone in 1977 and became deeply involved in community activities. Robin's passion for family history research led to a project to research the Thurlestone War Memorial, and an exhibition of the results was staged in the Parish Hall in 2014. The project was further developed to include all the Thurlestonians who had served in WW1, and whose lives and service records are now catalogued in this book.